Fleeing Baltimore: A ringside seat at the collapse of a city

Beau Monde Press

ISBN 978-0-9652344-3-6

Photos and graphics by Jeannette Belliveau

First edition

Publication: March 2026

Printed in the United States of America

Fleeing Baltimore

A front-row seat at the collapse of a city

By Jeannette Belliveau

How it was

I have lived in one house in Baltimore for nearly 45 years. It has changed in that time, as I have — but somehow it still remains the same. ... It is as much a part of me as my two hands.

— H.L. Mencken, 1926

How it's going now

A Redditor made a joke and said he doesn't understand the phrase "a robbery gone wrong" and asked, what's a "robbery gone right"? When all the parties leave satisfied?

— Family member of a Baltimore professional killed in a "robbery gone wrong"

Table of contents

Endorsements

It takes a lot to fall out of love with a city that can be as charming as Baltimore. This captivating book is a story of falling out of love, the result of heartbreaking criminality, incompetent politicians, and the sorrowful circumstances associated with many of the innocents killed in Baltimore over the past few decades.

If you love or have loved Baltimore, this is a must read.

— Anirban Basu, Sage Policy Group

Fleeing Baltimore reminded me how torn I am between my beloved city — with all its quirks — and needing to take a stand because of my son Tim's murder.

Shouldn't my stand be that I stay? It won't bring Tim back either way, but I'm really sad as I navigate my lifetime grief journey.

Fleeing Baltimore

This book helped me appreciate I'm not alone, with Belliveau's genuine account of what it's like to live here.

— Andy Moriconi,
father of homicide victim Tim Moriconi

Belliveau's book is a powerful and deeply human portrait of Baltimore's decline, focused on the lives of its most overlooked victims — "outliers," non-criminal residents caught in the city's violence. Her concept of tracking outliers adds a sobering and original lens to interpreting homicides and underscores how they should be recognized, and the crimes against them not tolerated.

She weaves her investigative focus on the city's outliers with Baltimore's political demise, cultural history and legendary local figures.

A hilarious chapter about her neighbor's Mega Millions win provides comic relief midway through the book.

It's an honest, engaging and unforgettable read.

— Tim Howard, former Baltimore resident

Acknowledgements

This book wouldn't exist were it not for a chance conversation about writing goals with whitewater rafter Marie Minder as we floated along Idaho's Salmon River in September 2024. Heartfelt thanks go to Marie as well for providing in-depth feedback on draft chapters.

Thank you so much to Janet Lottero for meticulous copy editing, friendship over the decades and suggesting a list of key figures.

Thanks to Denise H. Gibbon, Esq. for providing pre-publication legal review.

Quotations from *The Baltimore Sun* and *Baltimore Magazine* used with permission.

Excerpt from the poem "To My Killers" used with the permission of Shirley J. Brewer from *After Words* (Apprentice House, 2013).

A note on sources

This is a work of non-fiction providing historical information about the subjects discussed. The author has recreated events, relationships and conversations based on public records, news articles and broadcasts, and personal correspondence and interviews with involved parties, provided in the bibliography.

To maintain the privacy of some individuals, their names have been changed. Although the publisher and author have made every effort to ensure that the information was correct at press time, no express or implied warranties or guarantees are expressed or implied by their choice of content.

The publisher and author assume no responsibility for errors, inaccuracies, omission or any other inconsistencies, and shall not be held liable or responsible to any person or entity with respect to any incidental or consequential damages alleged to have been caused, directly or indirectly, by the information contained herein.

Key figures

Reese **Bowman.** 8-month-old smothered to death by daycare worker in 2017.

Carnell and Angela **Dawson**. Burned to death in 2002 in a firebombing along with their five children after reporting drug dealers.

Sebastian **Dvorak,** a popular bartender fatally shot in the stomach in Canton in 2017.

Bernadette "Bernie" **Gietka,** winner of record Mega-Millions lottery of $183 million in 2003.

Freddie **Gray,** a 25-year-old who died in police custody in 2015, sparking two days of riots.

Craig Kinlaw "Baby Boy" **Jones,** a 19-year-old drug dealer shot fatally in 2009

Joel **Lee,** a Korean student at Towson University, shot dead in a 1993 street robbery.

Kim **Leto,** a popular bartender in Canton, fatally shot in her home in 2014.

Molly **Macauley,** a space economic pioneer fatally stabbed while walking with her dogs in 2016.

Cheryl **McCormack,** a Door Dash driver and grandmother fatally shot in 2022 by two teens.

Barbara **Mikulski,** a former U.S. Senator mugged outside her door in Fells Point in 1995.

Timothy **Moriconi,** a 25-year-old contracts professional shot dead in a street robbery in Riverside in 2018.

Marilyn **Mosby** was Baltimore's state's attorney from 2015-23, with record homicides on her watch.

Martin **O'Malley,** Baltimore mayor from 1999 to 2007, had his agenda derailed by the Dawson firebombing.

Pava **LaPere,** a tech CEO killed on the roof of her apartment building in 2023, the most publicized case of all the "Outliers" — homicide victims with no criminal ties or domestic disputes.

Chesley **Patterson,** a Little Italy restaurateur killed in a robbery after work in 2022, two hours before Cheryl McCormack's murder.

Stephen **Pitcairn,** a Johns Hopkins Medical researcher killed in 2010 while talking to his mother on the phone.

Robert "Robbie" **Ponsi,** a waiter stabbed to death by a gang of youths in 2016 while riding his bike home.

Kevin **Plank** is CEO of Under Armour, a Baltimore-based sportswear company.

Aysha **Ring** was a high school educator whose neck was slashed in 2008.

Zach **Sowers** was a Johns Hopkins financial analyst attacked in 2007; he lingered with a brain injury in a coma for 10 months.

Alex **Wroblewsk**i III was a popular South Baltimore bartender shot fatally in a 2017 robbery.

Setting the stage

What if ...

... a child of the D.C. suburbs moved 45 miles to the northeast, to an urban oasis of quirky charm and architectural beauty, with real estate at bargain basement prices?

And what if, in this village within a city, turning any corner would bring her to some aspect of magic:

- a dusty marine-goods shop with a pair of real scarlet macaws, as well as ships' barrels, wheels, lines, compasses, sea chests, a diving helmet and exotic salvage?
- an Indonesian tall ship with gaudy, ornate woodwork in the harbor for a festival?
- a fruit vendor out of a 19th-century tintype, with cantaloupes and corn on a pony-drawn cart?
- a herd of elephants being unloaded for a downtown circus?
- and behind a nondescript grey-fronted rowhouse, at the rear of a hidden garden, a three-story treehouse, designed to look like a faux rowhouse itself?

If this newcomer wanted happiness and joy at the push of a button, she could visit an avant-garde museum with an immersive music and light show, accessed by lying on your back inside a model of the mouth of a medieval king. This was the joy of visiting the American Visionary Art Museum.

Or she could enter an undersea landscape of sea turtles, playful dolphins and sharks constantly on the move (the National Aquarium, of course) just a bike ride away. With another 10 minutes on her bike, she could view professional baseball, football or indoor soccer teams, or catch Tom Petty in one of his last concerts.

I'm that suburbanite. My waterfront wonderland, initially Tolkien's cozy Shire, morphed after dark into his bleak Mordor.

Baltimore's rough port roots always showed, with its Fells Point bar fights befitting sailors and stevedores. But something far more ominous than brawls on Broadway was manifested as the years wore on. I noticed and began tracking the tragic targeting of many of the city's most accomplished, spirited and attractive innocents, far removed from the drug trade's shadows and echoing too close to my rowhouse haven.

A good story requires a hero on a journey. The 75,000 residents who fled post-2002, after a tragedy the mayor called "Baltimore's Alamo," might not be heroes exactly, but each showed wisdom in leaving — each made a tough choice with the deep affection Baltimore can also engender.

It might seem like it's harder to stay in a criminal cesspit than it is to leave. But Baltimore is a paradox, especially to the artistically or creatively inclined who see its gold under the dross. The same crime that makes it close to unlivable also provides a real estate discount that acts as a magnet to bohemian, artistic types.

My 33-year story looks at the collision of wonderment and dismay I experienced and how a perfect storm broke Baltimore's spell. From my roof deck, I had a 360-degree eagle's-nest view, spotting migrating geese at eye level. The Blue Angels roared 100 feet overhead for days before airshows; once, A-10 Warthogs circled downtown in an unannounced war exercise, sparking panic.

Forty feet below my deck, life was both charming and alarming. A publisher friend, watching naked children play on Pratt Street below, asked, “Are you going to write about this, Jeannette?”

One night, I heard, then saw, six hefty female teens, screaming down a deserted Pratt Street under harsh lights — not cheerleading or rapping, but exuding anger and menace. My instincts screamed danger, a “gift of fear” absent in some transplants to the city who paid with their lives. I’d internalized Baltimore’s street code: stay vigilant, avoid trouble. My brick rowhouse, three stories plus a deck, felt safe, and skipping my dog’s late-night walk spared me likely harm.

Yale sociologist Elijah Anderson noted in “The Code of the Streets,” a 1994 article in *The Atlantic,* that inner-city girls were increasingly violent, forming groups to attack or rob. Pratt Street reflected this: In July 2016, two women maced a neighbor after asking the time, dragged her by her ponytail, stomped her and stole her iPhone.

About me

My career sheds light on my shift from urban journalist to rural resident. I started in the quiet corridors of government, clerking at the U.S. Department of Health, Education and Welfare, then the Food and Drug Administration, before finding my voice as a medical writer at the National Institutes of Health.

But the more demanding pace of the newsroom called: I became an education and features reporter in Montgomery County, Maryland, chasing local stories with a notebook in hand. Later, as a Business desk editor at the *Baltimore Sun*, I watched the city’s pulse through late-night deadlines in the Calvert Street newsroom. A demanding job followed as graphics editor for the *Washington Post’s* National, Investigative and Foreign desks, and I’ve copy-edited for publications from England to Alaska.

Fleeing Baltimore

For three and a half years, I lived near London, and traveled to six continents — everywhere but Antarctica. Mostly on my own dime, though a journalism fellowship took me to Hawaii, China, Japan and Borneo, where I took notes amid rainforests and neon cityscapes that grew into my first book. Back home, the journalism landscape crumbled as Craigslist gutted newspaper classifieds. In my career I've taken three buyouts, enjoying my moniker, "the buyout queen."

For four years, I remotely copy-edited and designed rural Alaska newspapers, emailing layouts under the glow of my rowhouse fluorescents, living on Alaska time and feeling a virtual part of moose hunts, salmon fleets and sled dog races.

My "talent stack," as Scott Adams might say, spans writing, editing, graphics, data analysis, web design — and hospitality. Renting rooms in my historic Baltimore rowhouse — a solidly built 19th-century gem on Ann Street — became my lifeline as journalism faltered, blossoming into a decades-long practice that paid the bills and filled the house with eclectic tenants. I taught myself web design, bartering sites for necessities: food from a taqueria, a dentist's filling, even therapist's sessions to untangle the stress of a city unraveling around me. Writing remained my core: I poured my travels into two books, *An Amateur's Guide to the Planet* and *Romance on the Road*, and a shorter work, *Eden Under Siege,* revisiting the first book's opening chapter with a heavier heart.

This is my story of navigating "what ifs." Baltimore, once a great American city where I'd chased stories and built a life, had morphed into a place that wore me down — a city that fumbled its essential task of protecting residents for far too long.

Cutting those deep ties after 33 years — half of my life — was a challenge but not a heartbreak, more a quiet relief as I packed up the last echoes of my rowhouse memories. I bid goodbye to the gritty streets of a metropolis for the uncertainty of yet another adventure: a 21st-century version

Setting the stage

of wagon-trainers finding peace and a home in the barely tamed lands of North Central Idaho.

Jeannette Belliveau
March 2026

Part I. The honeymoon

Fleeing Baltimore

Earliest impressions

The first Baltimoreans to captivate me were an unlikely duo: basketball icon Earl "the Pearl" Monroe and filmmaker John Waters.

I grew up in a competing universe to Baltimore's, that of the Maryland suburbs around Washington, D.C. Myself and my five younger siblings were raised in what my nuclear physicist father and homemaker mother called "the Little Green House," a humble suburban single-story home.

Around 1963, at age 9, I first glimpsed Baltimore when Dad drove us via Route 29, pre-Capital Beltway, through the farms of Howard County and then the two-story rowhomes clad in Formstone, a type of stucco facade, of a downtrodden neighborhood called Pigtown. Under cold, blue-gray streetlights, they evoked grim East German worker housing, though the winter streets were free of junkies.

At the Baltimore Arena (later renamed), we watched Earl "the Pearl" Monroe dazzle for the Baltimore Bullets. As a third-grade Catholic Youth Organization basketball player, I begged for the outing.

Aside from this uncommon adventure, we grew up D.C.-centric. Rockville was our home, and Washington, D.C., seven miles southeast, was our hub. Dad took us to movies such as *2001: A Space Odyssey* at Cleveland Park's Uptown Theater. We watched Fourth of July fireworks from the *Exorcist* steps in Georgetown, visited our dentist near the White House, and roamed D.C.'s free museums. As a teen without a license, I bussed to Wisconsin Avenue's hippie shops for Jimi Hendrix posters, protested the Vietnam War at American University, and caught comedians David Steinberg and Cheech and Chong, plus Jackson Browne, Patti Smith, Bob Marley and Van Morrison at venues like the Cellar Door, Constitution Hall and Lisner Auditorium.

D.C. had the edge, with the Merriweather Post Pavilion (1967) and the Kennedy Center (1971) sealing its cultural dominance. In every domain but one. I watched all the local and national teen dance parties, and the Baltimore programs — Buddy Deane (segregated racially) and then Kerby Scott (integrated), coming in fuzzy on our long-distance antenna, had the best dancers. Better than even *American Bandstand*, its big rival, still filmed in Philadelphia, *The Buddy Deane Show* would later inspire *Hairspray*.

My *Baltimore Sun* editor friend Helen told me that as a child, people would yell up and down her street, "colored on Buddy Deane!" once a month when the show had black teen dancers, and everyone would run indoors to watch.

Seeing 'Pink Flamingos'

In 1973, as a University of Maryland sophomore, I attended a *Pink Flamingos* screening at the Student Union, my only Baltimore tie beyond that Bullets game a decade earlier. John Waters, a lanky gay man with a pencil mustache, introduced his raw third film — far from *Hairspray's* later mainstream appeal — to a raucous, foot-stomping crowd. Baltimore reveled in bad taste, unlike D.C.'s wholesome blandness, making us College Park students appreciate our neighbor to the north.

As a 1970s fan of *National Lampoon* and P.J. O'Rourke, I was tickled with *Pink Flamingos'* premise — trailer trash vying for a tabloid's "filthiest person alive" title. Coincidentally, I'd later mirror its characters' escape to Boise, Idaho, the film's tongue-in-cheek antithesis to Baltimore's depravity.

At Martick's, a gay-friendly French restaurant on Mulberry Street, Waters met his early crew. Unique to Baltimore, its barricaded door guarded against crime; you were buzzed in for top-tier European cuisine. Martick's closed in 2008, its derelict site auctioned in 2021, leaving a legacy as the world's best food in the worst location.

A dangerous image

Baltimore's rough edges starred in *Homicide: Life on the Street,* and HBO's *The Wire, The Corner* and *We Own This City,* cementing its media image as a hotbed of corruption and danger, with *Hairspray* as a rare bright spot.

The "Charm City" nickname, inexplicable given crime statistics, emerged from a 1974 campaign by rah-rah Mayor William Donald Schaefer to lure tourists amid suburban flight and industrial decline. *Baltimore Magazine* recalled late-1960s slights from *Sports Illustrated*, dubbing the city "A Loser's Town." As a counter, ads featuring stripper Blaze Starr boasted: "Baltimore has more history and unspoiled charm tucked away in quiet corners than most American cities put in the spotlight." The campaign showcased crabs, rowhouses, Mencken and Babe Ruth.

Baltimore's charm wasn't Southern but a bold, Brooklyn-esque style — more sporty than D.C.'s polish, less violent than Philly, and warmer than Boston's aloofness. Its peak as a top U.S. city was centuries past, yet it retained a folksy core. A book called *When the Colts Belonged to Baltimore* recounts fans baking black-walnut cakes for Johnny Unitas' birthday, delivered at Memorial Stadium's player tunnel — a small-town warmth that charmed this D.C. transplant.

Moonlight illuminates the *Nighthawk*

After the Bullets' game with Earl Monroe, I did not return to Charm City until I interviewed at *The Baltimore Sun*. I passed the copy desk test and got a job offer.

My peripatetic life had included travels around the globe and a few years of living and working in England. Still, Baltimore represented a chasmic leap from my hometown of Rockville, a classic 1950s suburb with mixed white- and blue-collar neighborhoods. Rockville grew from 20,000 to 45,000 during my childhood and teen years. It was home from a few days after my birth in 1954 until my college graduation in 1976, and again in the mid-1980s.

The most famous name associated with it was that of F. Scott Fitzgerald, who was originally buried in Rockville Union Cemetery then reinterred in 1975 to our family's place of worship, St. Mary's Catholic Church. I took flowers to the first location and weeded the neglected, obscure site.

Armed with a sense of urgency to be settled before starting with *The Sun,* I had no idea where to start looking for an apartment. A newspaper friend had recommended the maritime district of Fells Point as colorful with its bars and restaurants. She did note with a laugh that while visiting, she had witnessed a stabbing. The laugh was indicative of the "walk on the wild side" appeal at the time of Baltimore to suburban visitors.

In January 1987, I moved to an apartment at Ann and Aliceanna streets, two blocks from the Fells Point waterfront, and started work. I could see the water taxi from the roof deck and run down to catch it when I didn't feel like walking the whole way to my job.

While only 45 minutes from Rockville, Fells Point stands a universe apart. Its bars weren't just Party Central for local colleges. History ran deep. Settled in 1726 and officially founded in 1763, the Point, with two arms pointing into the Northwest Branch of the Patapsco River like crab legs, lies southeast of downtown. Abolitionist Frederick Douglass was taught the alphabet and rudimentary reading skills by Sophia Auld, his owner's wife, in a house around South Durham and Aliceanna streets. Jazz singer Billie Holiday grew up a few blocks to the north.

In 1987, my life there was good. After a career at smaller newspapers, I was on my way to earning a much bigger salary at a unionized big-city daily. And my money would go far, given depressed real estate prices.

We editors would work on the copy desk until midnight or 1 a.m., and then decamp to John Steven Ltd., a waterfront bar two blocks from my apartment. The other editors had endless quirky stories about Baltimore, no surprise given the later success of the shows *Homicide* and *The Wire, which* mined the city's reality for plot lines.

Crab cakes, classical music, a good mix of patrons and a doorway-framed view of the *Nighthawk* schooner distinguished the John Steven pub. A small, silent man who appeared Greek would come in the door with a basket of roses and wordlessly hold them out for sale at each table. And you'd never know when Louis "the Hawk" Hawkins would arrive to tap dance, shim sham, Walk the Dog and pass the hat. "Hell yeah," he shouted in a Louis Armstrong rasp from under his porkpie hat.

For me, Fells Point fed a hunger for a more entertaining and exotic world than that of Rockville. It was a fascination shared by other "expatriates" from the D.C. suburbs, who were among Baltimore's biggest champions. One such emigre, Martin O'Malley, even became mayor of Baltimore and eventually governor of Maryland.

Butchers Hill and the crime discount

My first month at work, in January 1987, I was editing Metro stories, including the police blotter and crime articles. I had to proofread a disturbing account of four women who were raped in and around a laundromat in Butchers Hill. The dark side of this neighborhood to the northeast of Fells Point intruded on my heretofore magic realm.

The laundromat was 10 blocks from the apartment where I lived at the time. It was the first dent in armor of realizing that while Southeast Baltimore had much going for it, it wasn't the safest place. I rationalized somehow that Butchers Hill was just a bit more risky than Fells Point.

Crime stories like this had a profound, paradoxical and crass benefit. In Baltimore, you could buy the best house for your money of any Eastern seaboard city. The homicides, robberies, burglaries, rapes and carjackings depressed the price of the housing stock, which often had historical value and architectural character. Rowhomes offered huge potential if you wanted to renovate and live in a showpiece.

As an example, I had professional friends — not wealthy per se — in the Mount Vernon neighborhood who put together enough dough to buy the historic Tiffany Mansion. In any other urban Northeast setting, such a prize property would be out of reach for the non-wealthy.

Hailing from the more expensive D.C. area, at first I had no expectations as a single woman of being able to afford a home of my own. But it turned out that most of my single women colleagues at *The Sun* owned homes. In fact, some were building wealth by owning several, and had gotten into house flipping and acting as landlords.

The cheapest neighborhood in DC, is Baltimore.

— Popular saying

Gradually I opened my mind to the idea of buying a house. On my first day of searching, the fifth property my realtor and I visited was a historic row home on Ann Street, built in 1848, likely for a ship's captain given its high-ceilinged third floor.

The property listed for $125,000. It had a brick facade, ornate metal cornice, a roof deck, two fireplaces, a kitchen and dining area, and three sizable bedrooms, each with an en suite bathroom. Way more than I needed, but I'd loved the hardwood floors from the minute I stepped in the front door, and it was within my price range. It always seemed to impress visitors from D.C., where it would have been listed as a million-dollar baby.

Cheap real estate in Baltimore — median house prices are about two-thirds less than Washington, D.C. — offered prospective purchasers a significant "crime discount." The phenomenon has been documented in numerous studies by academic researchers and think tanks, who note that aggravated assault and robbery nearby particularly harm values. If you could live with disorder and personal risk, you got a lot of home for your money. The challenge was surviving to enjoy your personal palace.

So in 1990, I bought that Ann Street home near the intersection with Pratt Street, in Upper Fells Point. The neighborhood of about 4,000 people was listed in 2025 as 62 percent white, 17 percent Hispanic and 11 percent black.

I was now six blocks closer to Butchers Hill, a neighborhood still grappling with issues like mailbox and car bombings, including a notorious 1994 incident tied to a pair of teens feuding with a police officer's family. Over decades, Butchers Hill steadily gentrified, and since the 1980s, its annual house tour has showcased striking renovations. The area's larger townhomes, including historic mansions, outshine many of those in Upper Fells Point. As a strong community group took the reins, Butchers Hill stood out less as being a hot spot.

In many ways, my location was ideal. My rowhome was almost exactly halfway between downtown to the west and Patterson Park to the east. It was also the midpoint between Johns Hopkins Medicine to the north and the Fells Point waterfront to south.

To the immediate west, the Perkins Homes public housing project (now demolished) and a vast, rough area north of Johns Hopkins could bring tough characters through my intersection at any moment, possibly scoping out targets for robbery or casing homes for burglary. The opposite of a gated community, our area saw constant foot traffic. Several neighbors, frustrated by these "transients," fled to quiet Canton to the southeast.

My corner offered a snapshot of life in Baltimore. Scenes from my front steps:

- A lifeless-looking Hispanic man carried by four friends, one per limb, on a frigid Christmas Day.
- A block party buzzing with moon bounces and grilled food.
- An NFL star rumored to have been arrested on my steps for soliciting a prostitute.
- Hundreds of kids visiting for Halloween candy, and Latino Catholics re-enacting Christ's Calvary procession on Good Friday.
- A 60-something neighbor in her teen bridal gown and veil, remarrying her husband.

Rockville was never this vivid, vital or risky. Baltimore's microclimates were stark: My block's midpoint could be eerily calm, while my corner was hopping.

Lively streets

Around 1850, Fells Point earned fame as the birthplace of clipper ships racing tea from China and India to Britain and the U.S. By the 1980s, its lively waterfront bars drew crowds celebrating St. Patrick's Day and New Year's, packed with undergraduates from Towson and College Park.

In a 1994 *Washington Post* article, seven years after moving to Baltimore, I described a Fells Point walking tour for friends. Visitors could explore "a neighborhood dining scene that is gathering enormous force ... Or a harbor circuit that shows Baltimore at its best ... A tour of spots featured in famous movie scenes ... Or a Bargain-o-Rama sweep of dollar bins, used bookstores and warehouse liquidators."

Fells Point mixed the middle class and the downtrodden: "You may see trash pickers, be offered stolen cassettes, step over Colt 45 bottles and around unfortunates and streetwalkers." Prostitutes plagued my corner for years. A neighbor claimed New York Giants running back Dave Meggett was arrested for soliciting on my steps before I arrived, though 1990 news reports show he was likely arrested a few blocks south and eventually acquitted.

Unhealthy-looking addicts, offering sex to men who slowed their trucks on my corner, reportedly hid drugs in their socks to sell to their johns. Early Sunday mornings were prime, with men dropping families at church and rolling by. One afternoon, a female neighbor, walking her dog, sighed, "I'm old and heavy, and the men still drive up slowly and ask for a 'date.'"

Tolerating streetwalkers posed a risk to the law-abiding residents of knifings and drive-by shootings tied to the drug trade. I'd approach the ladies of the streets calmly, saying, "Do you want to deal with this by leaving now, or with the police, or with my neighbor and his gun?" This usually sent them sauntering east on Pratt.

Unlike D.C.'s polished marble or Annapolis's nautical gloss, Baltimore embraced its flaws. "Anyone can love a perfect place, loving Baltimore takes resilience," wrote author Laura Lippman. To me, those imperfections were its allure.

My *Post* article advised: "Be streetwise. And keep your ears open: This is the world capital of public domestic altercations." Two exchanges linger: a woman's Saturday night retort, floating to my roof deck, "Fuck me? Fuucck yoouuuu," and a neighbor's spicy morning shout from her Ann Street doorstep, in a thick East Baltimore accent, "You can suck my pussy, and I ain't douched in two days."

My article observed: "Where the literal minded will see lingering seediness and dereliction amidst the gentrification, others will recognize the vitality of one of America's most entertaining neighborhoods — the wellspring for the humanist and comic visions of Anne Tyler, Barry Levinson and John Waters."

Small details told big stories. Red-tile stars with silvery borders, embedded in sidewalks, marked old brothels. Jingling harness bells signaled a street arabber's pony cart, peddling produce turn-of-the-century style.

The most charming stop on my tour was Thames Street's China Sea Marine Trading Company, "Thames" pronounced locally to rhyme with "aims." The shop brimmed with provisioning barrels, antique steamship signs, life preservers, diving helmets, ships' wheels, and replicas.

Its macaws, Saigon and Singapore, shared the shop with Jack Nasty, a green parrot, who greeted visitors with a hearty "Hello!" When he died in 1992, the Wharf Rat bar hosted his wake with a 48-star U.S. flag and a *Baltimore Sun* feature. "Jack has dropped anchor for the last time," said proprietor Steve Bunker. "We'll all miss him." When Bunker left for Maine in 1999, it took a lot of wind out of Fells Point's sails.

When China Sea Marine thrived, it preserved the Point's anachronistic charm — at a delicate moment in time between its 1960s' decay and the glitzy future of Recreation Pier and Bond Street Wharf.

Merchant of moods

My friends and I often stopped by P.J.'s Place, a quirky card shop on Lancaster Street, where Jack Troutwein, a kind-eyed older man with a thick white beard, curated an eclectic collection.

Nearby, on Eastern Avenue, a blue neon sign glowed: "Sabina — Merchant to the Melancholy." The antique shop held statuettes of women with illuminated globes, salvaged from London's Palace Strand Hotel. Its cryptic name sometimes misled men to mistake it for a massage parlor.

Sabina, the crinkly-eyed proprietress, dressed in a Jazz Age tunic and turban. She showed off Deco telephones, late-19th-century music boxes, and mechanical birds once cherished by Germany's royal children.

Why "merchant to the melancholy"? "Res ipsa loquitur," she told me. "It speaks for itself." She cranked a music box, its jolly tune and winsome drumming prompting her to add, "We've had people come in here, so melancholy, so depressed, and leave here laughing."

Duda's Tavern, still thriving at the trapezoid corner of Bond and Thames, was run by Antoinette Duda Flury and her husband, John, who cooked in the back. A photo behind the bar captured Antoinette's parents, Walter and Pauline Duda, under a giant National Premium bottle cap, beside a calendar frozen on Jan. 14, 1943. Today, Duda's remains a cozy Baltimore gem, with its warm buttercup walls, dark wood, lively jukebox, extensive menu and 100 beers.

On the walking tour, I'd point out the green-doored rowhome in the 600 block of Ann Street, belonging to U.S. Sen. Barbara A. Mikulski. I'd spot her coming and going to Capitol Hill. After she saved Fells Point from an Interstate 95 spur in the 1960s, Maryland elected her to the Senate, where she commuted daily, never forgetting her roots despite working in a millionaires' circle.

The 4-foot-11 senator stepped out often, shopping bags in hand, buying tea from owner Deb at Fells Point Coffee in the Broadway Market.

An Orioles soundtrack

In summertime, rowhouses would sizzle, and the action moved out front to the sidewalk. Families ate steamed crabs off newspapers; children made chalk drawings or splashed in kiddie pools.

Residents perched in lawn chairs to view rowhouse fires, evictions or just the passing traffic. The near-constant auto accidents at Ann and Pratt would instantly summon forth blankets and cordless phones (in the days before mobiles) from the permanent audience.

As a turban-wearing neighbor noted as she watched an arrest near me, “It’s gonna always be something.”

In the 1940s, people still slept overnight in Patterson Park during hot summer nights. The practice was revived — just for single nights of camping — in 2019 and 2024 under police protection.

When the Orioles were playing, the balm of Jon Miller’s radio voice issued in all directions from windows, shops and stoops, echoing down the rowhouse canyons of Birdland in quadraphonic stereo. One vivid memory was of a grossly obese man, shirtless and in tight shorts, cradling a chihuahua in a low lawn chair. They listened together to the game on a tinny transistor radio in the 200 block of Ann. A scene straight from Federico Fellini or John Waters’ *Pink Flamingos,* he looked like actor Glenn Milstead, Divine *sans* drag.

Post-game, East Baltimoreans streamed home from Camden Yards, strolling four to eight abreast along Eastern Avenue.

On my walks, screen paintings on doors and basement windows stood out. They depicted rural farms, harbor boats or the Patterson Park Pagoda. Circa-1850 rowhouses boasted original stained-glass house numbers, like the stunning transom above my door.

Bricolage — window displays of statuary — showcased Elvis, the Virgin Mary (sometimes paired), penguin families, leprechauns or, during Desert Storm, mannequins in combat fatigues. Elderly Polish and Ukrainian residents, ever-vigilant behind their windows, upheld these traditions. I’d warn friends to smile quietly at the quirkier displays, avoiding loud comments near their creators.

As Fells Point grew upscale and original Polish families left or passed away, bricolage faded. Walking tours shifted to Durham Street’s striking murals, a half-block away, celebrating Billie Holiday’s childhood home.

Moonlight illuminates the *Nighthawk*

A working port

By the waterfront, I'd guide friends along cobblestoned Thames Street, past the *Nighthawk* clipper ship and Recreation Pier, a frequent backdrop in *Homicide*. Moran Towing tugboats — *Cape Romain, Patricia Moran, Judy Moran, Hawkins Point, Cedar Point* — berthed here, when they weren't nudging containerships at Seagirt or Dundalk terminals or barges down the bay.

"It's remarkable that Baltimore has its own voice, so close to Washington, Philadelphia and New York," a British academic remarked.

"You're so lucky to live here," concluded my friend Janet, a Tuscany-educated sophisticate, charmed by a ventriloquist outside Lexington Market.

Another friend, Sandra, eyed Fells Point's waterfront and referencing a big developer, noted, "Struever Brothers would've turned this into Old Town Alexandria" — a sanitized, faux-historical shell.

Just off the water on the Square, Jimmy's Restaurant was the breakfast spot. In the 1990s, waitresses greeted with "Hey hon," serving coffee, pancakes or waffles swiftly on red-checked tablecloths. Diners might sit beside tug crews, film teams or even Maryland's governor. In May 1993, Hillary Clinton visited, learning from Jimmy's tireless waitresses — most unable to afford health care — about grassroots concerns. Opened in 1946, Jimmy's sold to new owners in 2021 for $1 million.

At Brown's Wharf, we'd stroll the brick promenade, famed from *Sleepless in Seattle,* where Meg Ryan's character gazes across the water, pondering Tom Hanks' radio voice. Director Nora Ephron captured its magic. Even before the 1993 film, this was my spot to reflect, watching seagulls and freighters at Domino's raw sugar dock.

On July 4, 1994, my friend Jane visited to escape Arizona's heat, only to find Baltimore 10 degrees hotter. Seeking a Fort McHenry stamp for her national park collection, we took the harbor shuttle, passing the warehouse from *Avalon's* fire scene. Jane got her stamp, while I took in the view back toward land: downtown Baltimore's glass buildings, like Tiffany lamps, kept a human scale, less daunting than Chicago or Hong Kong. And Fells Point resembled an Irish fishing village with three-story bars in aqua, sage and weathered brick.

An urban village with ponies

Fells Point felt like an urban village, akin to a London borough, where residents rarely needed to leave. You could browse shops, spot feral cats near Shakespeare Street, enjoy a salsa concert at Broadway's foot or inhale the scent of the cinnamon raisin bread baked overnight at H&S Bakery.

On one walk, a piebald pony pulled a green-and-gold cart along Aliceanna Street, its harness bells jingling as an arabber — local slang for street hucksters — shouted, "strawww-berries." A 19th-century East Coast tradition, arabbing's survival marked Baltimore as a living relic. Remarkably, arabbers even delivered food during the 2020 Covid crisis.

Despite constant predictions of their demise, in 1988, a half-dozen of Baltimore's 42 licensed arabbers still groomed ponies mid-block on North Chester Street. Curious, I detoured to their stable. "Lawrence, just Lawrence," said a man giving his name. He brushed Champ, who leaned into the strokes, shedding a winter coat. Carts, produce boxes and Champ's stablemates — Buck, Lil, Georgia, Short and Duke — crowded a narrow strip between rowhouses leading to a neat stable.

"The average person who drives a horse, he looks out for him," Lawrence said. His cart of bananas, cucumbers, and greens earned $35–$40 daily (1988 dollars, ~$100 in 2025). "Supermarkets hurt us a lot," he added. "They run specials. But we do our best. It's not boring. Keeps you off the corner."

His nemesis, the city inspector, demanded better scales and water carried onboard. "You can get water at any filling station," Lawrence countered. "Anyone'll give you water. Carrying it, it gets dirty, warm, and splashes out." The inspector pressed for cleaner livery. As an animal lover, I worried about ponies trotting on hot asphalt. Champ's dull coat, despite Lawrence's brisk brushing, didn't dim their affection for each other.

If Champ's harness was retired, horse-drawn carts might vanish from the U.S., as Baltimore is likely their last stronghold. But as of 2025, they endure.

Walking to work

As a resident, I finally explored Baltimore's tourist gems: the National Aquarium, Edgar Allan Poe's house and grave, the Science Museum, the Museum of Industry and Baltimore's Washington Monument, standing at about one-third the height of its D.C. counterpart. Yet, over my 33 years in Baltimore, my heart belonged to the city's functional core, not its tourist spots. These were the places I lived, worked, shopped and relaxed, forming an east-west band: Patterson Park, the Canton and Fells Point waterfronts, the Inner Harbor and Midtown.

From 1987 onward, I was captivated by the city, as I enjoyed a immersive experience walking to work. Five afternoons a week, Wednesday through Sunday, I'd stroll two miles for an evening newspaper shift.

From my apartment at Ann and Aliceanna streets, my route traced the harbor to my copy editor job at the *Baltimore Sun* on North Calvert Street.

This was a more extensive route than my walking tour for friends around just Fells Point. My path wound west along Aliceanna Street, over footbridges linking the Inner Harbor's finger piers, then north on Guilford or Calvert streets. Walking was the way to experience it all. Shopkeepers, street musicians, tap dancers and vagabonds animated the route.

Walking map Fells Point to Midtown

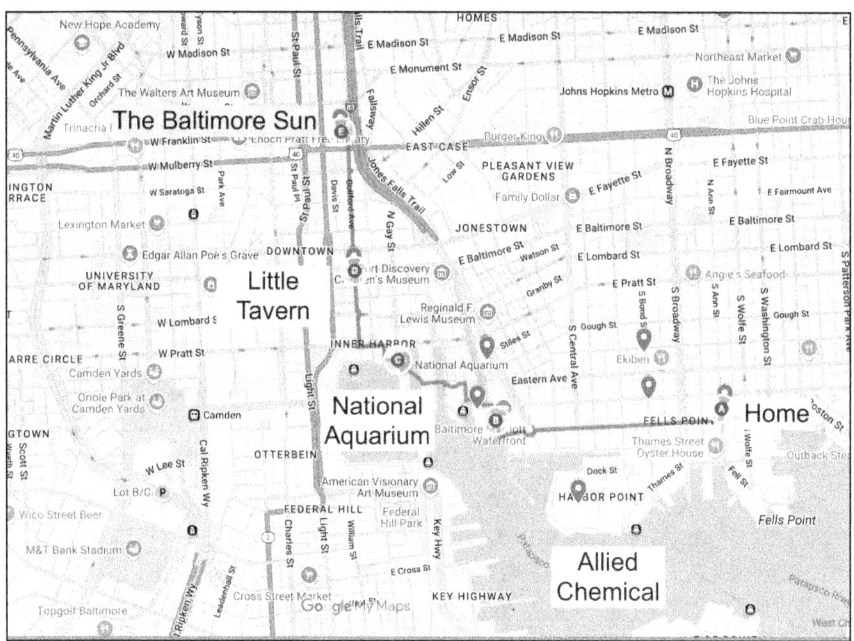

I might spot a sound check crew for a touring nostalgia act or a Dutch frigate gliding toward the Atlantic. At lunchtime, hungry men in worn clothes and thick beards lined up outside the Beans & Bread soup kitchen, evoking the Depression era. With historic warships like the USS Constellation at anchor and fruit vendors with pony carts, Baltimore offered vivid glimpses of the 18th, 19th and early 20th centuries.

Avoiding blandness

My route traversed a skyline of shipyard cranes and soybean conveyor belts. In an earlier era, the city had thrived on shipping, steel production, shipbuilding and textile weaving, and became a canning hub for oysters, tomatoes and corn.

Baltimore's blue-collar muscle was visible in the industrial waterfront and the hard-hatted men with mullets and sleeveless T shirts at intersections. This brawny identity was a draw to newcomers, distinguishing the city from the blandness of other American cities. Its warm friendliness and fierce neighborhood pride, paired with a relaxed acceptance of its place in the world, kept Baltimore free from the cutthroat rivalries of D.C. or Philadelphia, except during the occasional World Series. Charm City's humble funk and underdog spirit made it the affordable, unpretentious sister to Washington.

In my early days making this journey, what would become Harbor East was a flat, rubble-strewn stretch of blocks, where I once saw circus elephants being unloaded to stretch their legs in a fenced area. No one foresaw that this wasteland was to later replace the downtown, becoming a magnet for Manhattan financial firms, wary of centralized risk, who quietly moved in after 9/11.

While signs of Baltimore's decline were evident on this stretch of my walk, to a newbie like me, Charm City excelled in livability. Compared to Washington, D.C., it had cheaper housing and laid-back personalities. And perhaps its so-so economy allowed anachronisms to linger, when progress would have have swept them aside.

My walk traced west along Aliceanna Street, just inland from the water. It often started with a nod from Frank, perched on the stoop of Second Time Around, his antique shop unthinkable in a sterile mall. "Hi babe, running late?" he'd call, or occasionally, "You're early today."

As in Dickensian London, cats prowled the area, darting under gates. The air carried the yeasty scent of baking bread, a late afternoon signature for Fells Point. H&S Bakery, supplier of hamburger buns to East Coast McDonald's, also churned out onion rolls and challah, shifting to the cinnamon-laced raisin bread by 4 p.m.

Further west, I'd pass the shuttered Allied Chemical Plant, closed after 140 years and awaiting a Superfund cleanup for its chromium waste. Its industrial silhouette glowed stunningly at sunset. One evening, a saxophone's jazz riffs floated from its shadows, beautifully scoring the rose-hued ripples on the water. Today, it's the Harbor Point development.

Music often graced the walk's midpoint, where Aliceanna meets the Fallsway. A bagpiper practiced near the Columbus statue (later toppled in a protest) by the Eastern Avenue pumping station.

On my evening walk, I'd pass engineers tuning sound for bands at the Pier Six Music Pavilion. Frugal music fans would catch free shows from the promenade east of the pier, where I enjoyed Daryl Hall, Willie Nelson, the Doobie Brothers, Carlos Santana and John Fogerty. When Steve Miller played, powerboats crowded the water.

A glance across the harbor revealed the glowing neon of the Domino Sugars and Natty Boh signs. Construction workers, wrapping up their day, crossed my path at the footbridges to the finger piers, toting small coolers as young skateboarders zipped by.

In the late 1980s, the Inner Harbor's eastern edge buzzed with summer tourists but quieted in winter, left to construction crews, skate rats and the occasional angler. Herring gulls, juveniles marked by chocolate streaks, claimed the sparse off-season turf, landing to deftly tuck their wings, shuffling feathers like a deck of cards.

Past the gulls, I'd pivot north and stride up South Street.

Fat Man & company

Beneath a heap of blankets, Fat Man slept soundly on a park bench across from the Little Tavern at East Baltimore and South streets. Wind-driven tears left gray salt crescents on his dark skin. He wore a burnt-orange knit hat topped with a blue one. His shopping cart brimmed with essentials: more blankets, a dry slice of white bread, an apple, Kent cigarettes, a balloon stick, bottled water and 5-gallon buckets tied to the side, a poor man's kitchen cabinets. He rarely ventured beyond a block to Calvert Street or two blocks to the harbor.

He stood apart from his bench mates — Tin Man, Scarecrow and Big Man — who carried nothing. Fat Man moved slowly, pushing his laden cart, crowned by a dark gold saucepan glowing with a charcoal fire.

Fat Man spoke little. "I ran a truck and different things," he said. "I'd work today if I could ... well, it's Sunday, I don't work Sunday." His age? "I don't know myself," he shrugged. His friends guessed 40 to 60.

Quiet and solitary, he was well-equipped to feed himself and stay warm on this small patch. No one disturbed him, and his fellow street dwellers looked out for him. "Fat Man's always by himself," said Tin Man, the group's most cheerful and boyish member. The cart set him apart. "He's a real hobo, he ain't no tramp," Tin Man noted cryptically.

Besides Frank the antique shopkeeper, panhandlers were the most likely to chat with me. I preferred buying Fat Man a Little Tavern burger over giving spare change, which back then often went to drink rather than drugs as in later years.

After a half-hour, I'd approach the back entrance of the *Sun* building on Guilford Avenue. Smooth tracks were embedded in the asphalt where rolls of paper used to come in by rail. Historians and economists note Baltimore's pioneering role in innovations like railroads. Its port, closer to the Midwest than Norfolk or New Jersey, worked with railroads to ship goods inland. Driving past the marine terminals, I'd see hundreds of Japanese cars offloaded or Jeeps bound for export.

Up on the fifth floor, plenty of crime articles crossed my Metro desk workstation. And early on, I attended a presentation for staff on personal safety. "The best deterrent to a break-in is a dog," a police rep advised. "Second best is a big, chewed-up dog bowl labeled 'Killer' on your porch. Third is a security system."

When a staff meeting focuses not on business but on preventing home burglaries, your city has a problem. But on the bright side, our employer was trying realistically to prepare us.

I got a puppy and per the police talk, considered him essential to my security. Thankfully, no one tested him in his early, overly friendly days or later, when after 18 months he took his watchdog role seriously. He was a boon companion on my obsession in my free time: visits to Patterson Park.

Birdwatching at the oasis

The gem of East Baltimore, Patterson Park is a magnet for just about everyone in the area. As I would enter by bike from the west, a sweeping vista unfolded: the park, a tilted bowl, sloped down from Pagoda Hill three-quarters of a mile. Beyond its eastern edge, the terraced rows of lilac, brick and Formstone houses marched into the Canton and Highlandtown distance. The four golden spires of St. Michael the Archangel Ukrainian Catholic Church gleamed south of the park. Three miles away, a dozen containership cranes nodded at Seagirt Marine Terminal.

The park's Boat Lake teemed with carp, mallards, red-winged blackbirds, widgeons, turtles and transient Canada geese, alongside water lilies and pussy willows. Urban wildlife somehow thrives amid floating Old Milwaukee cans, Wonder Bread wrappers and Dutch Masters cigar casings, discarded after being repurposed for marijuana. eBird records 223 bird species here, unsurprising given Maryland's position on the Atlantic Flyway running from Florida to Greenland. Less than a mile away, the Patapsco River hosts blue heron colonies. A birdwatcher told me herons traced a triangular path between the lake and a pair of river colonies.

My sharp-eyed brother once noted the Boat Lake's pond scum was so thick, nine baby wood ducks could walk on it — a result of stagnant water and invasive phragmites reeds. Later, I tackled the water flow by regularly clearing the lake's clogged drain.

In the 1990s, my journalism career — stints at the *Washington Post* (commuting by train), a return to the *Baltimore Sun,* and remote work from Baltimore for an Alaska outlet — limited my park time. By 2010, writing books on my own schedule freed me to indulge in a favorite pastime: morning bike rides to the 137-acre park's winding paths, sports fields and pagoda replica.

At the Boat Lake's north end, I'd sip coffee from a travel mug on a bench, watching herons, egrets and hawks among dozens of daily species. My Shetland sheepdog, leashed to my bike's seat post, got a good run. My succession of shelties were dubbed by neighbors as Lassie, Lassie Junior, a "toy collie," a "shelby," "Sheetland shepherd" or (my favorite) "borderline collie." Beau, my first, earned hugs from kids and dog biscuits from birdwatchers. He was called "sweet one" in Salvadoran Spanish and Polish.

Collecting trash

My late mother's grabber — a tool for picking up objects — came in handy to clean trash from the 2.5-acre Boat Lake, created during the Civil War as part of a grading project. Later, I bought two fishing magnets, one stronger than the other, lashed to boat anchor lines to dredge up electric scooters, eyeglasses, fishing weights, a snow shovel, a cash register and other finds. I practiced coiling the soft anchor line and tossing the magnet for distance, a fun morning ritual. Switching to my grappling hook worked for some items, unless it snagged phragmites stalks.

One day, a Hispanic woman released her goldfish into the lake. "What's its name?" I asked. "Virginia," she replied, an odd but memorable choice. Drama struck when a loose dog attacked ducklings, prompting a group of us to herd them into crates for a bird rehabber.

Park managers noticed my cleanup and had me lead high school groups to help out, though few students were motivated to participate actively. More lively were random passersby who sparked unpredictable chats. Shri from Mumbai praised his pressure cooker, sending me a link to his favorite model. "It will change your life!" he exclaimed.

An observant man shared a worthwhile trash-picking tip: "Press the trash and fold it against the side of your shoe," he said. "I'm not sure I should tell you this, but I did this in prison. Yeah, it was fun!"

A couple in their 40s walked down most days from Monument Street. Even though that was a rough area, and they knew the schedules of local soup kitchens, they dressed well in stylish parkas and boots. I looked for them many days, and they helped me haul heavy scooters from the lake. A 2018 photo captures them smiling alongside a dog walker. I often spent two hours daily at the lake with my fourth sheltie, Copper, who sniffed out trash and greeted friends joyfully.

Two sharp-eyed boys, Malik and Craig, taught me to spot fish through the glare, a skill requiring focus on their subtle shapes.

A lone pintail duck, smitten with a resident mallard, lingered. "Love will do that to you," said Bud, an older man critical of Audubon Society birdwatchers leading school groups. "Why don't he and the other bird watchers pick up trash?" he asked. "Or more to the point, the school kids?" I agreed.

On Mother's Day, a woman mentioned humorist David Sedaris, who cleans trash with a grabber for hours daily in West Sussex, England — a story I verified.

And two teachers by the lake's western arc debated Social Security's untouchability.

"Well they limit the increases, to prevent inflation from money printing where you get your increase but a loaf of bread costs $30," I said.

"They can't cut Social Security," one insisted. "We'd march on Washington." They held firm, dismissing inflation concerns, as the lake sparkled behind them. We chatted near a stand of birch trees, where I gathered peeling bark for my fireplace.

Baltimoreans were quick to engage in friendly banter, standoffishness rare except among some sullen teens. The city could be warm and welcoming – if it wasn't homiciding you.

In 2018, police cracked down on an afternoon "happy hour" (yappy hour, we called it) for dog owners at Patterson Park's northwest corner. Herding dogs raced in the setting sun's dappled light after drone operators' whirring devices.

The loose dogs made some mothers with strollers feel unsafe on nearby paths. The crackdown was an example of what Sam Francis called anarcho-tyranny: law enforcement hassling law-abiding citizens, easy targets, instead of criminals. After the yappy hour shut down, I shifted to cleaning the Boat Lake.

Park moods

Without admitting it, I'd always craved an outdoor job, and Copper, my sheltie, led me to an unpaid one: cleaning trash from the Boat Lake. The hard work I put into the Boat Lake could be seen in retrospect as uncovering a latent interest in and energy for rural life, that I would escape to after Covid-19 hit.

After a lake visit, a typical day then might involve prepping a room in my rowhouse for a short-term rental guest, planning an outing to one of the Southeast waterfront's 90 independent restaurants (no chains), or cooking with a roommate, often enjoying Peruvian chicken and sides for a house dinner.

I was active in our Upper Fells Point community group, collecting discarded items for dumpster cleanup days, designing signage and serving as secretary. Writing, editing and web design rounded out my days, along with bike rides, restaurant outings and dinners with friends and guests at my large dining table under a world map.

In December 2019, just months from leaving the city, I took some notes on a visit to the park so I would have a memory of one of its moods. I knew I was serious about leaving even if no one I mentioned this to believed me.

At the start of the bike ride, the sky was streaked with pink and cornflower blue, like a Maxfield Parrish painting. At the park I brushed Copper and sipped coffee.

I'd meant to replace my boot laces in the bright light beside the lake but forgot them. Exploring instead, I found a vagrant's bivouac — sleeping bags, tarps, belongings — on the brushy slope above the Boat Lake's north end, one of many rough campsites sprouting near the boardwalk. Fast-food litter on the bench got picked up, and the grabber pulled trash, leaves and branches from the lake's perpetually clogged southeast drain. A professional from an engineering firm offered to weld a baffle to keep it open. The worst find by the drain was urinal cakes, which I swiftly removed to protect fish and birds.

Damian, a park maintenance worker, was raking near the dog park. "I take everything in life, the good, the bad," he said. A blue-collar guy, he surprised me with knowledge of HAARP, an obscure Alaskan research experiment into atmosphere and weather. I showed him my found fish-cleaning knife left behind by someone at the lake's bench and asked his favorite park find.

Damian described returning a lost wallet to its owner, keeping its cash and earning a reward.

"I did what anyone would do," he said of keeping the cash, startling me.

Good lord, I thought — no honest person would keep the cash. Damian's view, echoed during the 2015 Freddie Gray riots when two men in a checkout line joked about looting sneakers, reflected a backwards street code.

Many Baltimoreans seemed to follow an intricate, unwritten rulebook, distinct from moral codes like the Code of Hammurabi or Biblical teachings. As an outsider, I learned its nuances through observation. To me, with a more standard view of morality, only narrow exceptions, like stealing for hunger, seemed justifiable, and Damian's city job suggested he didn't need a stranger's cash.

I told him, "I'm not corruptible," then added, "I could be bought with food," joking to keep the chat light. "I guess everyone's got their price."

Going to the sun

Entering Patterson Park along Gough Street's high ground offered sweeping daybreak views of East Baltimore neighborhoods. Often I was meeting a neighbor who walked his sheltie after finishing a night shift at 6 a.m. I saw a lot of sunrises, and thought of my ride as Going-to-the-Sun Road, evoking Glacier National Park in Montana.

Before high-profile murders struck nearby, I saw the Highlandtown area east of the park as a delightful spot with affordable grocery stores, Peruvian chicken takeout, thrift shops and a spacious new library. Dark events had struck just east of where Damian and I stood chatting, alarming homicides of regular folks in 2007, 2014 and later. But on that 2019 visit — one of thousands I made to Patterson Park — all felt serene.

On that Maxfield Parrish December day, with Patterson's painterly allure, Baltimore's decline faded from mind. You could push doubts aside, justifying why you stayed in Charm City. Yet years later, tallying the beatdowns — fatal and otherwise— in the architecturally cohesive neighborhoods around Patterson Park, it was difficult to judge if Southeast Baltimore was a fairy tale or a horror show. A harbinger arrived in 1995, with an attack on Sen. Barbara Mikulski.

Part II. Grim realities

A senator moves out

In the late 1980s, from my third-floor apartment window on Ann Street, I'd occasionally spot U.S. Sen. Barbara Mikulski coming and going from her rowhouse close by. In October 1995, her life shifted. She was mugged outside her iconic green door, while returning from a late dinner at around 11:45 p.m.

"I'm fairly street-smart, so I always look at the streets," she told the *Baltimore Sun*, "and so, all of a sudden, this figure is in front of me. I was absolutely shocked."

The 4-foot-11 senator was shoved to the ground, her finger dislocated, her purse stolen. "I've lost the sense of personal safety I felt in a community that's been my home for more than two decades," she said, describing crying through "three or four boxes of Kleenexes" in anger and grief.Her attacker, Robert E. Perlie Jr., outweighed her by 90 pounds and towered over her at 6-foot-3.

Like the Butchers Hill laundromat rapes during my first month in Baltimore, Mikulski's mugging signaled all was not copacetic. Yet the impact was muted. Such events didn't spark the urgent alarm among the public that they might have in Rockville, my safe suburban hometown. Instead, it being Baltimore, we talked about crime like we were rubbernecking a car crash – yakking but not with the survival-driven fear you'd expect. Friends and neighbors often treated high-profile crimes as fodder for conversation rather than existential threats. Those who took these issues seriously moved away.

Baltimore's disorder fueled a storytelling industry for filmmakers such as John Waters and Barry Levinson, author Laura Lippman, and producer David Simon. The streets fueled endless anecdotes for me to share on visits to D.C.

Many who had started off as Baltimore's fiercest fans, including charismatic young couples on my street, left when their kids neared kindergarten age. This was partly due to bad schools, but danger played a role. Parenthood sobered them up from sticking around for nuggets of local color.

They weighed the risks carefully and announced their exits, not staying around for more exciting adventures, and were deeply missed. They weren't about to prioritize sharing cocktail party tales, just so they could brag about living almost adjacent to the world of *The Wire*.

"I came after college for a finance analyst role," notes former Upper Fells Point resident Tim Howard. "While the crime was concerning, the professional experience was invaluable. At that stage of life, the risk-reward tradeoff made sense; for many others, especially those raising families, it does not.

"Baltimore has everything it needs to be great — culture, water, sports, passion, nightlife and affordability – but persistent danger remains a powerful deterrent to its full potential," he concludes.

A loss of security

Reading that Mikulski grappled with anger and grief post-attack, crying nonstop, I suspected an unmentioned racial element. Checking Maryland Judiciary Case Search, I found her attacker, Perlie, was a black man with a 30-entry rap sheet since 1983, known for extorting Fells Point parkers for "car protection" money. For a liberal Democrat and former social worker like Mikulski, who championed civil rights, being mugged by a towering black career criminal outside her home likely caused profound cognitive dissonance.

A potential mugger who read the newspaper might have recognized Mikulski's status as a U.S. senator — or her 1960s activism saving Fells Point from an I-95 bridge over the Patapsco —and left her alone or even watched over her. "You can't have this occur without having a great loss of personal security, particularly in a community that has the lowest crime rate, that I fought to save," Mikulski told *The Sun*.

In 2016, Baltimore City Council member Rikki Spector faced a similar attack to Mikulski's. She was mugged and carjacked in a Federal Hill parking garage near a luxury waterfront high-rise, home to Baltimore Orioles players. The 80-year-old councilwoman was thrown down, slapped and left with a black eye, requiring brief hospitalization.

"They opened the door and I look up and these two kids in school uniforms with school bags they said 'B—— give your car,'" she told WJZ-TV. "I said 'You son of a b—— get outta here.'"

The attacks marked a profound shift in racial dynamics. Any lingering Jim Crow-era restraint that once deterred attacks on prominent whites seemed breached — at least from my post-1987 perspective, with limited knowledge of earlier Baltimore. As the years wore on, street codes evolved further, and pitiless robbers killed their victims even if they had crisply complied with orders to hand over valuables. Fortunately, Mikulski faced only the mugging, not that darker consequence.

The attack prompted Mikulski's 1996 move from Fells Point to a secure high-rise in Homewood near Johns Hopkins. She abandoned her decades-long home for a fortress-like residence. It was a sign that things were changing, and worse was to come.

A firebombing and a curb stomping

In the 1990s, Baltimore's crime surged, bucking national declines. Homicides exceeded 300 annually, fueled by the crack epidemic, drive-by shootings, gangs and overreaction to trivial slights.

Against this grim backdrop, in the 2000s, a pair of especially shocking tragedies rattled the city.

The first involved the Dawson family. Carnell, Angela, and their five children, ages 9 to 14, lived in a rented rowhouse on East Preston Street in Northeast Baltimore's Oliver neighborhood, six blocks north and three blocks west of Johns Hopkins Medical. Having resided there since 1998, they paid a few hundred dollars monthly for a four-bedroom home, with a carpeted kitchen and an entertainment nook for VHS tapes and computer games. A 17-year-old daughter had recently moved out.

The "crime discount" — low prices for buying or renting in high-risk areas — enabled the Dawsons, despite unsteady jobs, to secure this affordable three-story rowhouse. Yet, this bargain proved to be their undoing. Oliver was rough, with trash-littered streets and a 97 percent black population. In 2002, seven of 11 rowhouses on their block were boarded up; recent images show only two vacants, despite nearby blocks still being dotted with abandoned structures.

Dealers stake their claim

Drug dealers claimed the Dawsons' corner at Preston and Eden streets, resisting efforts to displace them. Carnell Dawson tried to oust a dealer, who snapped, "You can't tell me to leave the corner," reaching into his waistband as if armed. That summer and fall of 2002, Carnell and Angela made at least 36 calls about drug activity near their home.

In hindsight, skeptics might question their actions. Baltimore had been steeped in drugs since the 1980s, intensified by the 1990s crack epidemic, persisting into 2002. While less desolate than parts of West Baltimore, Oliver mixed abandoned buildings with housing containing residents holding part-time or blue-collar jobs — or none at all. It was an area where a drug dealer could find patrons. Paradoxically, Carnell himself was arrested for buying drugs, found with four vials of crack, and received probation. This underscores the futility of their fight: Even those battling dealers to protect their kids sometimes purchased drugs. And the arrest of Carnell seems to be a misfire. Arrests of dealers are to be preferred to arrests of a family man trying to build a life for himself and his family, on an unfortunate occasion where he took a step back.

The Dawsons' resolve to shield their children, who rode their bikes around the block, from dealers deserves credit. A mile and a half south, we fought a similar battle along Pratt Street's corners at Regester, Ann, Durham and Wolfe streets. Despite our neighborhood's professional clout, progress was slow. Upper Fells Point's location — with one-way Pratt Street leading from downtown, fed by I-95 or I-83 — made it ideal for drug sales. Buyers from the suburbs could slow down unnoticed on our corners, just past downtown and the rough Perkins Homes, and buy a supply.

Periodically I shooed away dealers and loiterers on my steps, politely but firmly. Knowing all neighbors by sight, I could spot outsiders selling drugs or sex, or casing homes to burgle. Unlike Angela, who faced neighbors doubling as dealers or lookouts, I had an edge: A majority of our corner's runners and prostitutes were non-local.

As for the Dawsons' calls to the police, Carnell on Oct. 1, 2002 told the cops, "I'm going to court tomorrow for a guy that busted out my windows and all, and they let him out of jail. He's got reinforcements. The drug dealers are all around my house. ... My wife is terrified, and she's crying. ... They are all around my house, trying to do something to my kids and my wife. ... They said they were going to bust up the windows and shoot up my house."

Both parents had minor records. Beyond Carnell's drug arrest, Angela was once arrested after police officers saw her punching and kicking Carnell, per the *Sun*. Yet their relationship was reportedly "lovey-dovey," marked by pet names, hand-holding and affection.

Controlling the corner

Drug dealing on your corner breeds frustration. Police are ineffective, and dealers target kids with free samples. Worse, lookouts, runners and dealers engage in ancillary crimes — disputes over money that spark stray bullets, maiming or killing bystanders. I'd tell loiterers, "It's not just the drugs. We can't deal with the other problems you bring around here." Unable to dispute this fact, they often left, respecting the logic.

The Dawsons faced relentless dealing at Preston and Eden nightly until 3 a.m. The noise, activity and menacing glares — implying the residents themselves were the problem — were maddening. Confronting dealers, who were often armed and intimidating, was riskier than handling the runners, young middle schoolers. Angela's police calls escalated tensions, with dealers smashing the Dawsons' windows. Discretion — covertly calling police — and misdirection, staying neutral or cordial to the faces of drug dealers, was safer. Surprisingly, Angela seemed unaware of or ignored this. Police arriving at their rowhouse after her calls effectively exposed the Dawsons as informants.

Angela rejected the unspoken survival rules for coexisting with drug dealers in Oliver, *The Washington Post* reported. Like many in Baltimore, she seemed to believe the "crime discount" for cheap rental housing could come without danger. Before the 1980s crack epidemic, cities like Baltimore offered affordable rents and safe streets. Later, safety dissipated.

Angela likely hoped her activism could make a difference. She fought for a healthier city but misjudged survival. Had a neighbor who took exception to her efforts not been a sociopath, she might have been a hero. But *The Wire's* first season, airing June to September 2002, depicted the drug trade's grip, unshaken by politicians or police. A few weeks after Season 1 aired its last prophetic episode, Baltimore would see real-world punishment of a family taking on the drug trade.

On Oct. 3, 21-year-old neighbor Darrell Brooks, tied to a dealer Angela had testified against, threw two Molotov cocktails into their home. Angela extinguished her burning curtains, saving her family. The children stopped attending school, and the Dawsons hid indoors.

Police proposed witness protection, but Angela initially resisted. Over 13 days, she began reconsidering. Her hesitation adds another layer to the tragedy. From 1950 to 2025, nearly 400,000 residents fled Baltimore, even without Molotov cocktails. The Dawsons resisted this exodus, nobly but futilely.

The firebombing

At 2:20 a.m. on Oct. 16, 2002, Brooks kicked open the Dawsons' front door, poured gasoline on the floor and stairs, and ignited it. His calculated act blocked the only safe exit, leaving jumping from second- or third-story windows or the roof as a deadly alternative. With chilling nonchalance,

Brooks returned to his nearby home, where police later found a measuring cup and pickle jar of gasoline in a closet.

Neighbors heard Angela's desperate plea: "God please help me, help me get my children out." Firefighters arrived to find Carnell, gravely injured, on the sidewalk after leaping from a second-floor window; some thought he was already dead. A fallen door blocked the stairwell, thwarting quick rescues. It took an hour to control the blaze, which killed Angela and the five children.

Fire official Tom Tosh later told WBAL-TV, "Going through the third-floor window off a 35-foot ladder, (I started) to find the dead children everywhere." Carnell, with burns over half his body, a fractured pelvis and skull injuries, died a week later, never regaining consciousness. "I can only imagine the world he will return to," Angela's mother, Donnell Golden, had observed as he lay in the hospital. "If I was him, I wouldn't even want to wake up."

The tragedy was hard to face yet impossible to ignore. At the funeral, the police chief couldn't look at the children's smiling school photos, taken days before, displayed on their small caskets. Neighbors raised over $10,000 for funeral costs, collecting cash in a water jug on the charred corner, guarded by the community.

Showing remorse

Did the Dawson firebombing signal that drug dealers would commit any atrocity to silence witnesses and maintain their trade? Was it a scorched-earth response to snitching or residents confronting dealers? Brooks, the perpetrator, only partly fit this narrative, perhaps more a product of a broken life than a calculated enforcer.

Beaten as a child by his mother for unfinished homework, Brooks lost his brother to a shooting at age 12. He drifted between low-wage jobs and street life, dealing drugs and committing petty crimes, evading probation officers. He briefly worked at Fuddrucker's in the Inner Harbor, where I may have unknowingly crossed paths with him. At 21, he served as a corner lookout — a role typically for fifth-graders

— his mental state diminished by family trauma and a Coast Guard rejection

In court, Brooks pleaded guilty, receiving life without parole. Sobbing, he addressed Dawson supporters: "I will never, ever, as long as there is breath in my lungs, ever forgive myself ... I knew those kids. I loved them. I swear I didn't mean it, I swear." *The New York Times* reported that the act deeply wounded the city and sent a clear message that Baltimore remained gripped by chaos.

Baltimore's Alamo

The firebombing stalled, even reversed, three years of progress against Baltimore's decline. Elected in 1999, Mayor Martin O'Malley had cut serious crime, doubled drug treatment funding and boosted accountability with data-driven tools like Cititrack, an online system for city services. I noticed better city follow-up on trash and dumping, missed recycling and unpermitted construction, with case numbers ensuring accountability, trackable online.

O'Malley's "Believe" campaign, with its black-and-white signs dotting Baltimore, showed early promise. *The New York Times* reported that groups from Los Angeles to Atlanta inquired about the program. Then came the Dawson firebombing. Brooks did lasting damage to the campaign, the *Times* noted. O'Malley called it "our Alamo," keeping a photo of the Dawson children on his desk beside his family's picture.

The Alamo analogy fits: a devastating, hyper-local event that tarnished Baltimore's reputation. It echoed the 1969 Manson murders disrupting Los Angeles, or Philadelphia's 1985 MOVE bombing, branding the city as self-destructive. Like the 1989 Central Park attack, which brought an end to women jogging in the park in the evening hours, fallout from the firebombing quelled Baltimoreans' willingness to report crimes, serve as witnesses or convict on a jury.

Sometimes a horror is so profound, complete, and beyond words that it attains a grim perfection, observed David Montgomery in *The Washington Post*. He likened the

Dawson children to the four girls killed in the 1963 Birmingham church bombing, equating Brooks' act to Klan-level evil. White House drug czar John Walters compared the Dawsons to the biblical Daniel, unyielding to false gods.

Oliver resident Delores Best, a 63-year veteran of the neighborhood, frequented the Dawsons' corner. "There is no way the spirit of six or seven people can be upon you and you be at peace," she told *The Baltimore Sun*.

In 2007, a lawsuit against state, city, and police officials for failing to protect the Dawsons was dismissed after their attorney admitted they were planning to relocate. Police noted the landlord was aiding the move, with the family even considering returning to Carnell's native Oklahoma.

Leaving a home you love

The Dawson firebombing drove many to pull up stakes. "A lot of people are moving out of here due to the fire," Janice Rose, Angela Dawson's friend, told *The Sun* a year later. "I'm moving too. I have a 6-year-old. I want her to grow up and go to college." Rose loved her spacious, high-ceilinged home but felt trapped, refusing to let her daughter play outside.

I echoed her sentiment, wishing I could just tow my 1848 rowhouse to a safe locale. Great house, unlivable location. H.L. Mencken, Baltimore's sage, felt strongly attached to his Italianate rowhouse at 1524 Hollins St., where he lived for 67 years, beginning around 1883. "It is as much a part of me as my two hands," he wrote. Spacious and stylish homes in Baltimore can engender deep attachment. Mencken's safe, prosperous neighborhood made it enviable, though today, while his block remains relatively secure, gunshots echo from rough areas nearby.

The Dawson firebombing serves as a cautionary tale against lingering too long when police warnings — or a Molotov cocktail igniting your curtains — signal it's time to leave.

Baltimore's Hiroshima

If the Dawson firebombing was Baltimore's Alamo, the 2007 curb-stomping of Johns Hopkins financial analyst Zach Sowers was its Hiroshima, especially for Southeast. *Baltimore Sun* columnist Gregory Kane discerned the negative synergy of their combined impact. Despite differences in the details, I see these incidents as twin pillars of Baltimore's civilizational collapse, dragging the city far from a healthy urban ideal. Beyond Charm City's grim crime rates, the nature of these crimes — with attackers' whims edging into sadism — provides a dark rationale for fleeing the city.

When residents like the Dawsons and Sowers, innocent of criminal ties, are targeted, no one feels safe. Sowers' case is chilling: a stranger to his assailants, killed in a "random," "senseless" attack. Terms like a robbery "botched" or "gone bad" clutter headlines and fail to capture the depth of the inhumanity. Burning a family reporting drug sales to the police, and slaying strangers who hand over valuables, defies civilized norms.

The Dawson firebombing revealed rage against a perceived enemy: a drug lookout, feeling challenged, annihilated a family, letting them burn in agony. Professing love for the children he killed, Brooks embodied a twisted psyche. But Sowers was not known to his attackers. This college-educated, married professional was killed in a manner more typically seen when a gang retaliates with a vengeance. A new victim class emerged, unrelated to the crime subculture where most victims have rap sheets. After the first few slayings of these innocent targets, some of the random victims began to resist, as compliance was no guarantee of having your life spared.

These incidents in a major U.S. city defy comprehension unless civilization's guardrails are crumbling. References to Sowers' attack linger in online forums like Reddit and City-Data, especially for newcomers eyeing Southeast neighborhoods: Canton, Highlandtown, Patterson Park. It's still called a "horror," shaping debates about safe areas and crime risks.

Agenda: robbing someone

Just before midnight on June 1, 2007, Zach Sowers, a slender 27-year-old Johns Hopkins financial analyst, walked from a Canton bar to his home at 305 S. Robinson St. in Highlandtown, just east of Patterson Park and a mile from my former home. The area, with tidy two-story rowhouses built around 1900, was familiar from my bike rides to Canton's hardware and grocery stores. While Canton boasted upscale renovations, like one with an indoor pool owned briefly by Olympic swimmer Michael Phelps, Highlandtown remained humbler, attracting young couples seeking affordable starter homes.

That night, four teens parked on Robinson Street, two blocks from Sowers' home. "We went out to rob somebody," one told police, per *Johns Hopkins Magazine's* Michael *Anft*. Trayvon Ramos and Erik L. Price, both 16, approached Sowers. He was on his rowhouse's top white stone step, key in hand, one step from safety, robbery detective Phil Lassahn told me in an interview.

Ramos, reportedly from either Elkton (60 miles northeast) or North Decker Street, four blocks from the Sowers' residence, was out on bail for a February carjacking. Price, his lookout, lived in the 800 block of North Lakewood Avenue, a mile northwest in a tough area near East Madison Street. Wilbert Martin, from a half-mile east, and Arthur Jeter, from Dundalk four miles southeast, waited in the car. That three assailants lived nearby underscored Baltimore's block-by-block safety roulette, where Sowers' midnight walk carried risks.

Older rowhouses in these areas, including the assailants', risked poisoning occupants with lead paint, banned in Baltimore in 1951 but lingering on old walls and windowsills. Price reportedly had a language learning disorder tied to lead dust, which can fuel aggression.

Ramos, over 6 feet and 250 pounds, asked Sowers for a cigarette, a classic ruse, then unleashed a *Clockwork Orange* level of violence. A single punch knocked Sowers from the steps to the curb, Lassahn recalled. Holding a parked car's fender for leverage, Ramos "repeatedly slammed his foot against the back of Zach's head, which lay between the car and the curb," Anft wrote, causing a brain stem injury. Ramos towered over the slight Sowers, mirroring the physical disparity in Mikulski's mugging.

Ramos stole Sowers' Timex watch, cell phone and wallet. Zach's friend Fanya Workman told *The Baltimore Sun*, "He would never have put up a fight that would have caused him such terrible pain. This was just somebody [Ramos] who was out to hurt someone." Lassahn confirmed Sowers didn't resist: "He was blindsided by the punch, it was like one punch from the steps to the ground. There was never any fight."

It's unclear whether a call reporting Sowers' condition came from someone spotting the teens or coming across a still figure lying in the street.

A potential homicide

Police found Sowers' prone body and initially thought he was drunk, but "flipped him over and realized they might have a potential homicide," Anna Sowers wrote on ZachSowers.com. Unrecognizable, without ID, he was admitted as a "John Doe" to Johns Hopkins Hospital, ironically where he worked, his head swollen "to the size of a basketball," per Anna.

Unable to reach him, Anna cut short a Chicago girls' trip, found him at the hospital and watched him nearly die three times that night. "His head was so swollen and his face so smashed that she could only identify him by a scar on his right shoulder," wrote Ron Smith for *The Baltimore Sun*.

Days later, surveillance footage caught the attackers using Sowers' credit cards for gas and movie rentals. The four teens — aged 16, 17 and 18 — were identified after detective Lassahn distributed a "Wanted" flier to Essex patrol officers.

"The case was a red ball," Lassahn told me, a top-priority case due to media and political attention. Some of Sowers' attackers were remorseful, while others were indifferent to Sowers' grisly injuries or their own plight.

"Trayvon, there's something wrong with him, he has no conscience," Lassahn said. "That was one guy that if I was able to label a monster, he was it."

At the Baltimore City Detention Center, Lassahn and his partner presented Ramos with a DNA search warrant. "So if I don't give it to you, what happens then," Ramos said flatly. "The law gives me the ability to use reasonable force," Lassahn replied. "So you're gonna beat my ass?" Ramos asked. "My partner and I will be getting a sample," Lassahn affirmed.

Unlike Darrell Brooks' tearful contrition for the Dawson firebombing, Ramos displayed a chilling detachment, embodying the remorseless young killers criminologists warned of in the 1990s, evident in Baltimore by 2007. At a July arraignment, Anna noted on ZachSowers.com: "Trayvon Ramos sports an arrogant grin to his family as he enters, and all show no signs of remorse. In fact I see Trayvon glance back and laugh at a family member who says something to Trayvon, inaudible to me." As trial dates were discussed, she observed, "They are handcuffed again, and are led out the courthouse door. I notice two smiling and acknowledging their friends or family."

Anna added, "Clearly these children are not the least bit sorry for their actions, and what's more disturbing, it seems the friends and parents believe this is not a serious matter. Do they think it's OK to laugh and make jokes during an attempted murder arraignment with Zach's wife, family and friends in the room?"

This echoed my warnings to my short-term rental guests: "Be very careful when on foot and avoid teens, especially in groups. They'll kill you for fun." The teens' courtroom levity underscored my point.

Comatose and severely injured, Sowers could only open his eyes vacantly. Anna faced overwhelming financial and emotional burdens, becoming an activist for justice for Zach and other victims. She pushed for the teens to be tried as adults and for legal reforms to allow murder charges if a victim later died from injuries.

The plea deals

"Official Baltimore did what it does best: ignore uncomfortable circumstances until they go away," Ron Smith wrote in *The Baltimore Sun*. This included blindsiding Zach Sowers' family with a plea deal. In December 2007, prosecutor Patricia Jessamy's office secured pleas from Zach's attackers. Trayvon Ramos pleaded guilty to first-degree attempted murder and robbery, receiving 40 years with parole eligibility in 20. His co-defendants each got eight years, eligible for parole in four. As of this writing, at least two who had been released have reoffended.

At a December hearing, Anna Sowers testified about the harm caused. Zach's attackers chatted with their attorneys, ignoring her, while Ramos' mother mumbled and left the courtroom, Anna noted. Of Ramos, her take was identical to Detective Lassahn's. "I looked into his eyes, and he seemed like an evil person, completely soulless. I don't know if 20 years will rehabilitate him," she wrote.

The plea deal roiled Canton and nearby neighborhoods, costing Jessamy her 2010 Democratic primary. Plea bargains obscure crime details, as no trial means no public record of the defendants' motives or backgrounds, hindering crime prevention and understanding. Victims' families, like Anna, are left grappling with unanswered questions, while city officials fail to provide the clarity needed to feel justice was served or answers on how to ensure public safety.

Hopeless juries

Why the plea deal? Fear of jury acquittals, driven by distrust of police and retribution concerns, loomed large. Over-policing during O'Malley's tenure and police corruption fueled juror skepticism. "Everybody's still afraid of the jury saying 'not guilty,'" Anna Sowers told *The Baltimore Sun*. "I was told the likelihood of a jury finding Ramos guilty of attempted first-degree murder was zero and about 5 percent of finding him guilty of attempted second-degree murder."

Lax prosecutors and juror distrust, especially in Baltimore's 60 percent-plus black jury pool (as of 2024), often favored black defendants, particularly against non-black victims. A 1993 case mirrored Sowers': Joel Lee, a 21-year-old Korean-American Towson University student, was shot for not quickly surrendering his wallet.

Despite the assailant's confession and eyewitnesses, a jury — 11 of 12 black — acquitted the 20-year-old black defendant. This likely spurred prosecutors' caution in Sowers' case, leading to the plea deal. Lee's acquittal sparked Korean community protests, and marked a step toward a parallel justice system where black juries hesitated to convict black defendants.

Circuit Court Judges John C. Themelis and John M. Glynn noted juries often failed to convict clearly guilty defendants, citing distrust of police and witness reluctance. I personally experienced this unease in a cramped Baltimore courtroom during jury selection, revealing my neighborhood and profession just six feet from a glowering defendant who seemed to memorize my details. Disclosing my job felt risky, as it could help someone with a vendetta track me down, despite living far from the accused's network. I was relieved to not be selected.

As jury forelady in another case, I encountered a skinny older black woman in a worn navy parka who rocked in her jury room chair, chanting, "Po-lice LIE, they LIE." Initially, I dismissed her as paranoid, but later, with Baltimore police corruption exposed, depicted in HBO's *We Own This City* based on real events, I saw her point.

Jessamy's office feared taking this case to a Baltimore jury, Anna told *Baltimore Magazine*, citing the harsh reality that Baltimore City jurors tended to be lenient on black defendants. A 2008 Abell Foundation study found Baltimore City juries were 30 times less likely than Baltimore County juries to convict on the gravest charges. Leniency by black jurors to black defendants has been confirmed by other studies in Florida and the United Kingdom.

Anna wrote to the *Baltimore Examiner*: “It’s no secret that Baltimore City juries are notoriously biased against prosecutors and cops. The notion is that the mostly black jury pool distrusts the mostly non-black justice system, and freeing black defendants is their way of settling old scores.” In Baltimore, racial dynamics tied to the victim’s race likely contributed to the stark sentencing gap between the Dawson firebomber (life without parole) and Sowers’ attackers (accomplices became parole eligible in four years).

Triggering departures

Like neighbors who fled Baltimore after the Dawson firebombing, Anna Sowers noted friends leaving post-Zach’s attack. She told Ron Smith some sought suburban space for children, while others feared for their safety. Speaking to *Baltimore Magazine*, Anna voiced a sharp insight, later echoed by others, that lower crime stats don’t ease fears: “The homicide rate might be lower, but I don’t feel safe, nor do my friends.”

She put her finger on the dread imparted by the potential for a street encounter to turn fatal given remorseless assailants. While robbery on its own is an outrageous violation, murdering a compliant, law-abiding stranger is barbaric.

Anna, Zach and their friends embraced Canton’s DJ-and-drinking scene, proudly buying homes within walking distance of bars to avoid drunk driving. I relate, having selected Upper Fells Point for its walkability, though I skipped the bar scene.

That June night, Zach drank at J.D. Smokehouse and Grill, an easy 15-minute walk from home. Transplants from quieter Frederick, Maryland, Zach and Anna understood drunk-driving laws better than Baltimore’s brutal street codes. Zach’s brother-in-law, William Cheng, expected them to leave J.D.’s together that warm night, but Zach slipped off alone. Even a bulkier, martial-arts-trained male would’ve risked danger walking solo – let alone a slight financial analyst and part-time DJ.

Understanding right and wrong

Zach Sowers lingered nearly 10 months, passing on March 25, 2008, at Bayview Medical Center, surrounded by family alerted to his waning strength. On July 24, Anna Sowers rallied on Calvert Street outside the courthouse, with myself and a neighbor in attendance. She demanded a retraction of a claim by a prosecutor's office spokeswoman that Zach, hospitalized, resembled "a sleeping baby," suggesting his injuries stemmed from a fall, not a curb-stomping.

"He did not look like a sleeping baby," Anna told *The Baltimore Sun*. "I saw him in the hospital. He looked like a used piñata. His eyes were the size of golf balls. His head the size of a basketball." Anna, not recognizing the figure wrapped in blood-soaked bandages, walked past his room.

Three days after Zach's death, the *Sun* published a letter by Lisa M. Cooper-Doerr of Parkville, capturing the dismay of decent Baltimoreans at Ramos' attack, which upended middle-class morality.

From a young age, she wrote, she understood right from wrong, recognizing that stealing candy or hitting a peer for an insult could lead to trouble. By 16 to 19 – the ages of Zach Sowers' attackers – she knew beating someone, stomping their head, or standing idly by during an attack was wrong, as was stealing money or taking a life. She believed in helping those in need or calling 911, and resisted following a crowd's bad choices.

Cooper-Doerr questioned when society stopped teaching youth these distinctions and ceased valuing life and others, reflecting the dismay of Baltimoreans at the moral lapse epitomized in Ramos' attack.

Cooper-Doerr voiced a plea for civilized values, bewildered by the moral void among Baltimore's youth.

What to do about it was a vexing question. Anna Sowers reflected to *Baltimore Magazine*. "Sometimes, I think, why is this even my problem, I'm not a public official. I'm not the mayor. I have no idea what it takes to make a difference, to make the city safer."

Dysfunction in many flavors

The dysfunction in the Dawson firebombing — targeting not just anti-dealer parents but also their children, negligent probation oversight and sluggish relocation efforts — manifested differently in Zach Sowers' beating. Juvenile assailants, coupled with Baltimore's black majority's distrust of police and prosecutors, allowed defense attorneys to leverage jury trial demands, forcing prosecutors into a lenient plea deal. A white victim like Zach, with a Taiwanese-American wife, Anna, would pose challenges for a majority-black jury.

"Many of these jurors simply won't vote to find these kids guilty of violent crimes," noted Judge Glynn, in charge of the court's criminal division, to *The Baltimore Sun*. "If the citizens want to know what the problem is, I suggest they look at themselves. ... They don't testify against criminals. And they don't vote to convict the guilty." In an interview, Anna expressed shock at this mindset.

Jaded Baltimoreans recognized the street's dysfunction, as Judge Glynn, Anna Sowers and letter-writer Lisa M. Cooper-Doerr highlighted. Residents either fled, or stayed and put the rampant crime out of mind. Anna joined nearly 30,000 who left Baltimore between 2000 and 2009, a decision no one could fault. A family member contacted in 2026 described being "deteriorated for years" and a long, long road back to healing.

The Dawson murders haunted responding firefighters for decades and derailed Mayor O'Malley's reform efforts. Sowers' attack set a grim template for escalating street robberies in Baltimore. Transplants from safer climes often arrived without the extensive checklist needed to navigate this reality.

The Baltimore Safety Handbook

Knowing Baltimore's unwritten street codes wasn't just for criminologists. It was essential for rowhouse residents without gates or barriers, where the city's sizable criminal element could pass by at any time. Two neighbors politely dubbed these suspicious pedestrians "transients," later moving from Upper Fells Point to less-trafficked Canton to reduce risks.

Clashes with rough passersby could arise unexpectedly, making it vital to understand the street's governing rules. Baltimore's black majority — whites became a minority in the 1970s — across all economic levels seemed well-versed in street and prison codes. Multigenerational, blue-collar white ethnics in East Baltimore, as well as new Hispanic arrivals, also grasped these rules, particularly avoiding solo late-night walks. Transplants from safer suburbs, like me, often missed these cues, but I was fortunate to find mentors to relay the unwritten handbook.

Personal friction metering

Staying alert to racial tensions was crucial in Baltimore. Walking my dog to Betty Hyatt Park, two blocks north, offered a gauge. Closer than Patterson Park and safer at night, this small park sat amid Washington Hill's stacked apartments, resembling rowhouses, where most residents were black. The intervening blocks featured white, mixed-race and Lumbee Indian neighbors. Miss Shirley, a heavyset white woman, often sat on her stoop with mixed foster children. She ceaselessly complimented my roommate's dog – "'at's a nice poodle, hon" – undeterred by many corrections noting it was a cocker spaniel.

At Betty Hyatt Park, I'd exchange "hey, how ya doin'" with locals, with that mid-Atlantic drawl that also turned Baltimore into "Bawlm'r." Once, a boy on the playground's climbing structure shouted, "That's a white bitch!" – more shocked than hostile. Likely new and from a rougher area, he wasn't used to the mixed demographics. "We don't talk like that around here," I replied evenly.

National events shifted local moods. Neighborly warmth dipped after the 1991 Rodney King beating and during the 1995 O.J. Simpson trial, with clipped interactions. Friendliness grew post-2008 with the Obama election, but Trayvon Martin's 2012 death cooled things again. The 2015 Freddie Gray riots, with three black officers and black city leaders in the thick of events, didn't noticeably alter dynamics, perhaps due to muted racial framing.

One Halloween, crossing my lively, costume-filled street, I trailed a skinny black man by 12 feet, giving ample space. My 30-pound sheltie, sensing a unprovoked hostile vibe, barked. "I'll KILL your dog if he barks at me," he snapped. "You kill him, that will be the last thing you ever do," I shot back in a low, firm tone – not a real threat, but a push back against his intimidation. To outsiders, it might seem like overreaction, but Baltimore's street code permitted and in a sense demanded defending my dog's protective instinct on my block, my home turf.

Any appearance of weakness could be exploited. The unwritten rules, akin to prison codes, demanded standing firm. Countering pressure with pressure, rather than ignoring it, was often the only way to carve out space and deter targeting.

Tips from the janitor

Navigating Baltimore's streets demanded meticulous attention to personal safety. My knowledge came from mentors, notably a janitor in his dark navy-blue uniform at *The Baltimore Sun,* who'd stop by as I worked the night shift. A muscular black man, about 5'11" with a mustache, he'd chat while emptying Business Desk wastebaskets, sharing practical tips with earnest eloquence. Other black professionals — a *Sun* colleague with whom I played racquetball at Towson University, and an artist friend from West Baltimore — also shared insights.

Their advice, blended with my own experience:

- Walk near house fronts to shield one angle of attack; a curb-side route risks encirclement.
- Tuck your hand in a jacket or jeans pocket, mimicking a weapon's grip. Form an "L" with thumb and index finger to suggest a handgun's outline in your pocket.
- Hold a car or house key in your fist as a makeshift weapon, a tip familiar to many urban women.
- Never walk alone at night, especially if drinking and unsteady — a clear target. For example, in 2017, a Locust Point bartender's visible inebriation contributed to his fatal robbery.
- Greet strangers with a quick "how ya doin'" and a glance noting their height, weight, hair color and clothing for a potential police report, but avoid staring, which is disrespectful. With certain black residents, especially Southern migrants, a return greeting might be genuine and warm.
- Don't fall for women with baby carriages claiming they need bus fare to distant suburbs — a scam.

- Avoid buses or Light Rail ("Loot Rail") when schools dismiss in mid-afternoon, as aggressive teens crowd them.
- Don't "wear your money." Dress plainly, skipping jewelry or watches, but conversely avoid tattered clothes that suggest homelessness, which can make you a potential target.
- Wear runnable shoes, not heels or sandals.
- Keep your bike's U-lock on the handlebars as a heavy, legal defensive tool, not on a rear rack or in a backpack.
- Stay focused. No cellphone calls, texting or earbuds while walking or on your stoop.
- Don't pass between two people, or especially through a group, to avoid being surrounded.
- Trust your instincts. Allow yourself the gift of fear.
- Skip carrying laptops, pricey phones or jewelry to avoid nervous tells.
- Avoid low-traffic areas.
- Keep eyes up, not down.
- Carry a "drop wallet" with $40 and a single credit card to toss away from you, protecting your real wallet.

These strategies, though exhausting, became second nature, as ignoring them was perilous. Safety discussions periodically come up on the Baltimore subforum on Reddit, a massive online forum where users discuss content across countless niche communities. Posters emphasize the risk from teens especially: "It's the kids you have to watch out for" ... nine out of 10 times "the teenagers are the ones who rob you" ... avoid packs "of 12–19 year olds." While valuable advice, an analysis I undertook of murders of law-abiding Baltimore residents over three decades shows that, in fact, armed robbers in their 20s and 30s are also prevalent.

Cigarettes and canines

Another tip: when a stranger asks for the time, cigarettes or spare change, treat it as a potential robbery setup — a test of your vulnerability. I'd decline politely while briskly moving away, visualizing I was steps from greeting a burly neighbor named Rocky so as to project confidence. Zach Sowers' attacker, for instance, asked for a cigarette – a "shark bump," like a predator testing weakness, as a divemaster once explained to me.

When asked for change, I'd reply without stopping, "Sorry baby, I'm kind of light today. Good luck." This shows street smarts, respect and calm risk awareness, avoiding the mistakes of pausing, sounding dismissive or disrespectfully ignoring the request.

Dogs are helpful for safety. I studied dozens of outlier murders – regular, non-criminal Baltimoreans killed outside typical drug-related crimes – and only two victims were walking a dog. Of those whose homes were invaded, none had dogs to deter intruders. I never walked at night without one or two shelties; even a medium-sized dog was a strong deterrent and better than any burglar alarm.

I avoided having cash, purses or anything suggesting wealth on my person, occasionally carrying a knife or pepper spray. My athletic club offered Krav Maga classes, teaching Israeli self-defense techniques designed for street gang attacks. Avoiding encounters was an even better strategy. When walking my dog, I'd calmly redirect to avoid suspicious individuals, crossing streets or moving to well-lit areas, steering clear of dark tree canopies. I'd repeat a mantra to myself, "I'm moving deliberately, like I planned it," to avoid seeming nervous.

Criminals might've scoffed at me, a small, older woman, but walking with an alert dog and staying undistracted signaled I wasn't really the easiest of targets and knew Baltimore's safety codes.

For short-term guests walking the nine blocks from my house to the waterfront, I shared quick safety tips. "If you spot two or more teens with blank expressions, have a plan," I'd say. "Check who's on their stoop and join them to chat. Note lit-up restaurants or bars with open doors. Plan alternate routes to avoid the group." Teaching situational awareness was vital for those unused to risky areas.

If they seemed dismissive, I'd up the ante. "They'll kill you for fun," which was not hyperbole. I'd repeat this point as needed, and had notes and article links on fatal robbery victims and dates to back up the point. I'd often offer to walk them to the waterfront with my dog for added safety.

Geography lessons

In my decades in Baltimore, I noticed a warmth and racial openness among many residents, black and white, unlike the driven, Type-A vibe of Washington, D.C. Baltimore's Joe Sixpack persona made it more grounded and livable than white-collar D.C. Black locals, like *The Baltimore Sun's* night-shift janitor, generously shared advice, passed down from parents and friends, even to elementary schoolers. While tutoring fourth graders, I noticed they could articulate strategies about how to deal with verbal and physical attacks down to the last nuance.

Initially, I thought Baltimore had less racial friction than D.C., where anti-white hostility surfaced in bureaucratic or retail settings. In Baltimore, race and income seemed less entwined. Lawrence Brown of Morgan State University maps Baltimore's poverty as a "butterfly" pattern — east and west wings of black poverty split by a white "L" of affluent northern and waterfront areas. Yet, edges between these zones, such as the north edge of Upper Fells Point, often blurred, with racial demographics and criminal proclivities shifting rapidly. Blocks could turn from safe to sketchy in a step.

This patchwork allowed assailants, like those who attacked Zach Sowers or Barbara Mikulski, to vanish via alleys or arteries, blending into the city in nondescript clothing. D.C.'s black poor, historically, faced sharper boundaries, with Rock Creek Park dividing wealthier whites to the west from blacks to the east, and deep poverty south of the Anacostia River, before post-1980s gentrification spread. D.C.'s affluent black "Gold Coast" along 16th Street contrasted with Baltimore's broader mix.

Baltimore's poor included a good number of low-income whites — almost 13 percent in 2023, per WelfareInfo.org, versus D.C.'s 5 percent in 2021, per the Census Bureau. This fostered more class-based than racial tension. Mixed areas along Pratt Street and smaller East Baltimore side streets, home to two-story rowhouses for the less affluent, saw frequent black-white interactions, often amicable, unlike D.C.'s sharper divides. Baltimore's prosperous black middle class, rooted in pre-Emancipation freedmen, and numerous poor whites, often Appalachian, flipped typical U.S. racial-income norms.

On MTA buses, you'd see integrated scenes of working-class whites with worn clothes and poor dental health alongside black riders of varied means, defying D.C.'s clearer racial-income lines.

'Decent' vs. 'street'

In 2005, *Baltimore Sun* columnist Gregory Kane described a "war" between Baltimore's criminals and law-abiding citizens, fought in jury rooms, targeting witnesses, and seeping into daily life, especially nighttime movement.

Yale sociologist Elijah Anderson frames this as a divide within black communities between "decent" and "street." I learned the term "street" early on — a polite stand-in for "ghetto." You might say, "So-and-so? He's street," meaning unpolished, streetwise, but possibly OK otherwise. Anderson explains "decent" folks embrace family-oriented, mainstream values, while the "street" follows an "oppositional culture ... whose norms are often consciously opposed to those of mainstream society."

Even "decent" Baltimoreans had to project strength to avoid trouble. Anderson notes, "Youngsters whose home lives reflect mainstream values — and the majority of homes in the community do — must be able to handle themselves in a street-oriented environment." Tutoring a fourth-grader at Coleman Elementary near Mondawmin Mall, I saw this. A glasses-wearing math whiz, nerdy yet steely, he held his own among rougher peers.

Suburban transplants like me needed coaching in the codes, which the fourth-grader navigated instinctively. Black friends and acquaintances, often unprompted, shared insights — perhaps watching out for me.

Tenets of the street code

Street codes revolve around violence and respect, demanding toughness, fearlessness and readiness to counter threats to avoid seeming weak. Mirroring prison codes, they're learned through interactions, observation and peer guidance. Key principles include:

- Fight fiercely to survive and earn respect.
- Appear merciless to rivals, cultivating an intimidating reputation.
- Settle disputes directly, bypassing police or courts.
- Flash material goods to boost status.
- Beware that "snitches get stitches" — witnesses face threats or death for cooperating with police.

Prison codes, nearly identical but lacking material displays, have been studied since the 1940s, per criminal justice professor Meghan Mitchell. Mass incarceration from the mid-1970s, aimed at public safety and the war on drugs, backfired to an extent. With 600,000 people cycling annually through prisons, "these seemingly distinct cultures blend," Mitchell wrote in 2020. Street and prison codes merge as ex-inmates reintegrate.

This "stop-snitching" code ensnared Eric Price, the lookout for Trayvon Ramos during his attack on Zach Sowers, held in lockdown at Hagerstown's correctional institution for aiding detectives as they built a case against Ramos. Civilians felt it too. While planting caladiums outside my rowhouse, I heard drug dealers from nearby Regester Street mutter "snitches get stitches," in my direction. I ignored them, continuing to garden, though they likely sensed my quiet efforts to deter prostitutes and dealers. Some Pratt Street neighbors, too timid to step past drug runners on their stoops, would wait patiently nearby. They were too frightened to claim access to their homes, let alone snitch.

A revolving door in the worst 'hoods

In 2020, Baltimore contributed 6,000 residents to the state prison system, or 10 per 1,000 residents, per the Prison Policy Initiative. Neighborhood disparities are stark: Sandtown, Madison, Southwest Baltimore, Greenmount East and Upton had 25 per 1,000 residents incarcerated, compared to 2 per 1,000 in Fells Point, 1 per 1,000 in Canton, and under 2 per 10,000 in Roland Park. By total number, Roland Park (7,200 affluent residents, low crime) had one prisoner, while Midway/Coldstream (7,200 residents, high crime, 96 percent black), near Oliver, had 213. Roland Park, 9 percent black, boasts tree-lined streets, unlike Midway/Coldstream's dilapidated patches, though a soccer teammate's street there was tidy during my visits.

High incarceration in places like Midway/Coldstream fuels the merger of street and prison codes. Baltimore's criminal presence showed in subtle ways. At a 2018 unemployment workshop I observed, the facilitator advised ex-offenders to refine resumes and swap "street" email addresses (e.g., juicybootylicious69@aol.com) for professional ones. She highlighted job fliers for roles like deep-freeze food distribution, suited for those with criminal records.

Even Baltimore's black professionals, like some of my friends, often had a "Cousin Terrell" — a drug-using relative who'd pilfer valuables during visits. Nearly everyone had or knew a Cousin Terrell, and close relationships overlapped between criminals and "decent" residents.

Safety along murderers' row

In dangerous neighborhoods, law-abiding residents learned to mind their own business and get inside by dark.

Baltimore Sun reporter M. Dion Thompson, a former colleague who is now a minister, followed up with residents near East Preston Street, the Dawsons' neighborhood, to examine their lives after the firebombing,

"It can be a safe street, as long as you mind your own business," he wrote. Soup kitchen volunteers indeed went about their work and were not afraid of the neighborhood, apparently counting on rational neighbors who were aware of their good efforts. Other residents kept silent about what they might see going on. Or they went to work, came home and stayed indoors.

It sounds extreme, but staying inside is essential for the worst-off neighborhoods, and at least partly applicable nearly everywhere. I recall being alarmed when a visitor went out on my front steps to smoke a pipe after midnight, with the rest of the block silent, empty and deceptively peaceful. He would have been a sitting duck for someone with bad intentions abruptly barreling around our corner from the blind side, Pratt Street, which I'd seen enough times to make me wary.

Ready to die

In "The Code of the Streets," Elijah Anderson portrays hard-core street youths who prioritize avoiding "disrespect" over life itself. To be unafraid of punishment or even death, "gives one a real sense of power on the streets," Anderson writes. Without projecting a ruthless persona, you can't gain street-code respect.

These fearless criminals pose unpredictable threats to law-abiding residents. Trayvon Ramos curb-stomped Zach Sowers' head, likely aware of the brain damage he inflicted — a stark street-code power play. Unprovoked, Ramos used Sowers to showcase dominance for his peers.

Anna Sowers witnessed another aspect of brazenness at the attackers' arraignment, where the shameless group flouted decorum before the judge and victim's supporters. Psychologists say sociopaths delight in others' suffering, often mocking victims' testimony.

Street codes view prison not as punishment but prestige. "The toughening-up one experiences in prison can actually enhance one's reputation on the streets," Anderson observes.

With incarcerated friends or family available for reunions "on the inside," prison can feel inviting — a warped reality.

Suburban parents of young professionals relocating to Baltimore from safer locales should adopt Anderson's guidance for "decent" black parents: Cultivate a relentless focus on avoiding trouble and instill constant awareness of dangerous people and situations. Local colleges and places of employment should do the same, and appear to be moving toward orientations that caution incoming students.

Avoid, avoid, avoid

Cooperating with robbers in Baltimore offers no guarantees — you might still be knocked out, curb-stomped, stabbed or shot by showboating assailants. Victims don't control whether they go home, to the hospital or to the morgue, making avoidance and deterrence critical. Over time, law-abiding residents resisted more, but arming themselves proved risky. In 2022, Timothy Reynolds, and in 2023, Darrell Benner, confronted juveniles with respectively a baseball bat and a gun, and were fatally shot, showing counterforce's limits.

Ramos' curb-stomping of a knocked-out Sowers signaled that even unconscious victims could be "overkilled," a term referring to a victim with multiple potentially fatal injuries. Street codes grew more sociopathic, spawning copycat crimes. Attackers targeting innocents showed no regard for civilized decency or fear of prison.

Why, unlike pickpockets in Europe's capitals, do Baltimore's thieves kill? Baltimore's sociopaths don't stop at wallets. They extinguish lives, as if drawn to snuff out happiness or beauty, with stolen goods an afterthought.

Ramos' crew feared no retaliation from Zach's friends or family, unlike in rougher areas where a victim's "crew" might strike back. "The convict code holds the aggressor responsible for his actions and thus liable to retaliation," writes criminal justice professor Alan Mobley. "A vengeful crew helps with garnering respect, toughness, and retribution," notes criminologist Dan Mears. Zach's supportive friends, while numerous, weren't street enforcers. Attackers might hesitate with other potential victims tied to felonious networks.

Former Baltimore Health Commissioner Peter Beilenson described the city to *The New York Times* as a unique blend of small-town intimacy and big-city scale. He explained that violence feels deeply personal because residents are often connected through family or close acquaintance, making retaliation swift and certain for any act of aggression.

This applies to street networks, not young professionals.

The Mikulski and Sowers attacks also signaled a fading avoidance of white victims. Data backs the street perception that police prioritized cases with white victims. The Sowers case, deemed a "red ball," was a top priority, suggesting Zach's assailants knew the risks of targeting him yet acted anyway.

A 2022 CBS News analysis of FBI data nationwide showed stark disparities: In 2020, murders of white victims were 30 percent more likely to be solved than those of Hispanic victims and 50 percent more than black victims. Despite this, after 2007, Baltimore saw random murders where a victim's lighter skin offered no deterrence. The Sowers attack may have signaled to gangs that targeting whites marked the boldest criminals, undeterred by the heightened risk of capture.

Once America's second-largest city in 1830, with grand mansions later used in *House of Cards*, Baltimore was drifting from civil society. A college-educated black friend, not "street," jolted me by saying black-on-white crime thrived because "whites are easier targets." I thought she was justifying robberies, but in retrospect, she was just explaining how criminals size up marks. To Trayvon Ramos, Zach was just that — "like him right there," he told Eric Price — they locked on their target, a skinny young professional steps from safety.

Ramos twisted the street code's demand for toughness into a vile new protocol of violence as a credential. Two years later, this credo would touch a young man I mentored.

Baby Boy

"Pop-pop." Pause. "Pop-pop-pop-pop-pop." Gunshots echoed into my rowhome after 7 p.m. on Dec. 26, 2009. A friend and I sprang into action. He called 911, pinpointing Pratt and Durham streets. I rushed to my roof deck, peering cautiously.

The sidewalk, lit by stark streetlights and Pratt Street Liquors' window, was empty — no pedestrians, no fleeing drug dealers, just a few cars, with Johns Hopkins students away for the holidays. No fireworks' smoke or sparkle; the sharp sound was indeed a shooting.

Downstairs, I stepped onto Pratt, peering around for a gunman. An ambulance and police cars had arrived, officers taping off the scene. A still figure lay before the liquor store, a drug hotspot we'd long complained about.

"It's Baby Boy," said neighbor Robert. Approaching, I was waved back by police. Neighbors lined the perimeter as medics tended the victim, motionless, no reassuring hand wave like a buffeted NFL player signaling he is OK.

Police deputy major Bill Davis confirmed it was Baby Boy. "Pretty bad," he replied when I asked how he badly he was hurt.

"I've known him since he was a little boy," I replied, stunned, hoping he'd make it. On the gurney, an oxygen mask hid his face, but that smooth forehead and bristly black hair signaled it was Kinlaw Craig Jones, a 21-year-old Lumbee Indian. My stomach sank.

"I loved Baby Boy," I told Robert, the words spilling out. "We watched him grow up," he shrugged. "That's why we called him Baby Boy."

Born in 1989, two years after I arrived in Baltimore, Baby Boy was pronounced dead at Johns Hopkins Hospital shortly after midnight.

A Lumbee child

Baby Boy was among 10,000 Lumbee Indians in East Baltimore, with common surnames like Kinlaw, Locklear and Jones. He and his brother, James, lived with their grandfather at 109 S. Ann St., a block away, rather than their parents, who also lived nearby. I learned his family called him Craig, his middle name, and I did the same to distance him from his street moniker, though here I'll use Baby Boy, as neighbors and news reports did.

Childhood lead poisoning stunted Baby Boy's height but not his strength or wit, catching my attention. I asked his father's permission to hire him to run a refrigerator circuit in my rowhouse, where rehabbers had overloaded the kitchen wiring. The crawlspace's tight 60-foot path under heating ducts was too narrow for me, but Baby Boy's small frame, courage and smarts fit the task. With his father's approval, I draped an old T-shirt over his clothes, gave him a flashlight and 12-gauge wire, and he threaded it from below to the kitchen's baseboard. Emerging covered in 1840s Maryland clay dust, he stood still as I brushed him off with a broom. I paid him cash, advising him to check with his mother whether he could keep it or alternatively contribute it to household expenses, and he left with a nod.

Baby Boy and his friend "Fat Mike" Cuffley — politely "Big Mike" to his face — tackled more rehab jobs that summer. Mike, a taller, heavier Lumbee raised by his grandmother Miss Linda on Pratt Street, had an absent mother with drug struggles. Years later, a slimmer Mike found me on Pratt to introduce his wife, sharing he worked at an Ohio auto shop — a warm, respectful exchange.

For one job, Baby Boy and Mike demolished plaster on my central stairway, wielding a Sawzall like a lightsaber, dust masks on.

Their limited schooling showed when tasks required literacy or math. Pointing to wood vises, I said, "Put them in the drawer labeled 'vises.'" Baby Boy struggled to spell, needing additional guidance. Another time, I asked, "You worked six hours at $5 an hour. What do I owe you?" Neither could calculate it.

Big Mike's essay

In October 2000, Big Mike shared with us a school essay he wrote on lined notepaper. His grammar, a delightful tangle that mirrored the Chaucerian chaos of Baltimore-ese, revealed a 12-year-old's unfiltered view of the city. He showcased a precocious mastery of street codes that left me quietly awed.

The essay reads:

An amateur's way to get out of the ghetto if you don't know it very well

The way you get out of the ghetto if you don't know it is,

you don't get there to know it. But if you come to a place called the ghetto, it's bad. A ghetto is a mostly a black residential neighborhood where no-income people live and the people that live there are not really bad people but they will try to get out of towners.

So watch it. And the first step in going into a ghetto is lock the doors of your car.

The next is to always look for strange people coming up to your car. Usually the person that wants to jack you would get you at red lights and stop signs. So be careful when stopping at the stop signs and red lights. And after reading this I guess you're wondering, "What if you get jacked, what do you do?"

Well. If you get in a little predicament you hit the accelerator and you hit the main street and you stop and calm down your passengers and yourself and you get directions to your destination and you get there in one piece. And i guess you're saying to yourself, "What if he has a gun?" Well, you do the same thing I told you to do the first time or do it your way and the conclusion is your own fault.

And that is how you get out of the ghetto if you dont know it very well.

Though weak in math and spelling, Big Mike and Baby Boy mastered the survival code. And they shone in other ways, particularly in their enjoyment of rap and food. Big Mike obsessed over DMX's *Ruff Ryders, Ryde or Die Vol. 1*, bringing its tattered CD daily to play while working. My old-school rap picks bored them as they awaited DMX. A black friend was horrified when I, swayed by exposure, played DMX's gangsta tracks, tweaking one lyric to "I love my shelties, but where's my corgis?" to dodge slurs in the original.

In the summer of 1999 – the "Summer of Ruff Ryders" – we lunched daily at Highlandtown's McDonald's on Highland Avenue. Once, Baby Boy snapped at Mike, "Give me some fries n-----." I explained why the n-word was harmful, but their beloved rap lyrics normalized it. They humored me, avoiding it in my presence.

Mike worked sloppily, but Baby Boy was precise and driven. After finishing the stairs, I gave Baby Boy more tasks, like flawlessly cleaning the kitchen floor. Often, he'd say, "Miss Jeannette, will you hold my money?" I'd store his cash in an envelope labeled "Craig" — a makeshift bank for a kid vulnerable to robberies on the city bus to school.

At 11, Baby Boy's street smarts, petite size and youth made him a prime drug-runner recruit, safe from adult sentencing. At McDonald's, I warned him: "Craig, you're smart and strong. Drug sellers will want you to work for them, using you to make money while you take the risk. If you need cash, come to me for work." He listened and nodded.

Freestyle rapping

Baby Boy grew more cheerful working with me, often chuckling during our projects. Driving to grab supplies, we hit the North Avenue Taco Bell drive-through, where I freestyled a rap comparing our order to McDonald's. Baby Boy giggled, urging "More!" with his usual brevity. Once, he quipped, "Ain't that a mother," to my grumbling, sounding unintentionally grown-up.

A friend took him to play soccer twice, noting Baby Boy's openness to novel experiences compared to hardened street kids. One snowy night, he and his brother James borrowed my shovel to earn cash clearing pavements. They returned soaked but pleased, and I gave them oversized clothes and belts while their outfits dried, serving hot chocolate as we chatted in the dining room. They'd adopted me, like stray cats, basking in the care of a sober, kind adult.

Another winter evening, Baby Boy asked to rest after a visit. Exhausted, he wouldn't stir on the living room trundle bed when I tried waking him. I draped a blanket over him, letting him sleep. I briefly wondered about fostering him, but with his parents nearby, I dismissed it.

His grandfather relocated to Erdman Avenue's grim public housing. I drove Baby Boy there once to visit the solemn, high-cheekboned man, now mute from throat cancer. He pointed to baby photos of Baby Boy and James: bristly-haired, black-eyed, like tintype papooses. After Granddad's death, Baby Boy drifted, his anchor of stability gone.

The streets win

As the years passed, Baby Boy's street earnings from drug dealing outpaced my job offers. By 2002, he was actively selling on our corner, led by a dealer named Dewitt, with a female accomplice. We learned 911 scripts that worked to efficiently get a police response, like "disorderly teens leaning on cars," "crack seller with vials in front pocket," or "suspicious strangers watching workers." We'd detail appearances, actions and where drugs or weapons were hidden.

Operators often asked, "Are they black, white or Hispanic?" Frequently, we'd reply, "Black, white, Hispanic and Native American," reflecting Baltimore's diverse crime scene.

In August 2004, Baby Boy committed armed robbery and vanished into the criminal justice system. He returned a summer or two later, bulked up, tattooed, sitting on a jersey barrier by Ann's Convenience Store. Spotting me with my dogs, he hid his face under his T-shirt. "Craig, is that you?" I called. No reply. "Craig, I know that's you." Silence.

Days later, on the bookstore corner with a hulking friend, I said, "Hi Craig." He didn't hide. "You know what you're like? A salmon — a fish that always returns to the place it was born." He smirked faintly.

His rap sheet grew: drug charges in August 2006, and in June 2007, he was linked to the killing of a U.S. Marine on leave, a few blocks north. Emails with neighbors noted he was pimping young prostitutes near Ann and Lombard. One neighbor feared Baby Boy's "fearless" path, with no dread of consequences or violence. More drug busts followed: November 2007, July 2008, August 2008.

Missed shot at redemption

In September 2009, East Baltimore prosecutors sought a community impact statement for Baby Boy's Oct. 21 sentencing, following a driving violation that landed him in jail on a minor charge. At an Upper Fells Point community meeting, they urged input to extend his sentence, but our community group declined, leaving them disappointed. The mood was almost comically contrary to their goal.

James, left, and Kinlaw Craig "Baby Boy" Jones
(Photograph by the author)

Neighbors reminisced fondly about rewarding Baby Boy and his brother James with quarters for spelling words correctly, recalling their endearing childhood selves. We sounded like mothers excusing a wayward son, calling him "a good boy." The Marine's 2007 killing, blocks away, felt distant — like it happened on Mars — while Baby Boy, a beloved local kid, remained close to our hearts, despite his crimes.

Unlike brash outsider dealers, Baby Boy dealt drugs discreetly, slipping through Ann and Pratt streets' shadows. We prioritized jailing the bolder intruders, and rationalized that his violent acts occurred off our turf. In hindsight, a condemning letter might have kept him locked up, possibly saving his life three months later, offering a shot at redemption.

Final encounter

In the summer of 2009, I last saw Baby Boy at Pratt and Durham's southwest corner, steps from where he'd later be killed. Walking my giant sheltie, Pierre, I smiled, and we hugged. "How you doin'," he said, his voice now pure street, echoing his old favorite, DMX. I trusted our bond – forged before his grandfather's death – guaranteed loyalty under street codes. Neighbors were split, some fearing him and others not, remembering his childhood goodness.

Yet, he was on a fatal path. Reading he'd been found with "gunshot wounds to his head and upper body" jolted me. *The Baltimore Sun's* grim headline, "City surpasses '08 homicide total," detailed his death at Johns Hopkins Hospital at 12:30 a.m. on Dec. 27. Baby Boy's rap sheet was long: convicted of drug distribution in December 2008 (10-year sentence, mostly suspended), acquitted of attempted murder in June 2008 but guilty of assault and weapon charges (five years, mostly suspended), and a probation violation in October 2009 (two years suspended). Our community's refusal to push for a harsher sentence, clear only in hindsight, left him free.

Homicide detective Joseph C. "Jay" Landsman, inspiration for *The Wire* character using his name, led the case. He pinned the shooting on Antonio "Dollar" Edwards, 26, from Cockeysville. "Witnesses said the men were arguing when Edwards pulled out a gun and shot Jones several times, then stood over him and continued to fire," Landsman wrote in his report, per the *Sun*.

The real 'Corner'

I dubbed Ann and Pratt streets "the Real Corner," a microcosm of drug dealers and world-class Johns Hopkins medical researchers and top department chiefs, clashing just three miles east of the West Fayette and North Monroe drug markets featured in HBO's *The Corner*. Visitors to my roof deck — publishers, carpenters, friends, renters — watched the corner's drug trade, foreseeing its players' grim fates.

Police were philosophical about Baby Boy's death, Baltimore's 235th homicide of 2009. Sgt. Anthony Zayas told me he'd warned Baby Boy days earlier of a Pratt Street turf war, urging him to steer clear. Defiant, Baby Boy kept dealing and paid the price.

A friend's Facebook post echoed my grief: "I took him to play soccer when he was tiny. He was a good kid. Those who led him astray should be ashamed, but they won't be."

Baby Boy's father sought funeral funds, but suspecting a diversion to drug purchases, I delivered my contribution and neighbors' checks directly to the funeral home. His gangsta funeral at a Broadway storefront church featured a baby mama and young half-black son I hadn't known about, plus T-shirts with his image, name and years on the planet — a Baltimore homicide tradition. His mother, Robin, and weeping kin passed a microphone, turning it into a chaotic spectacle.

Why didn't Baby Boy's or Zach Sowers' killings drive me from Baltimore before 2020's carjackings and Covid-19? Perhaps I rationalized, "It won't happen to me if I follow the safety protocols I'd been taught." Two execution-style slayings near my doorstep —a Hispanic man in 1999 and Baby Boy in 2009 — didn't immediately dislodge me, just as neighbors who had been carjacked stayed put. Maybe we're all salmon, clinging to familiarity, unable to admit, "This isn't normal."

After I posted an early version of this chapter on my blog, a weathered man with deep facial lines approached me at Ann's Convenience Store, right on our corner. He said inmates at Hagerstown Correctional Institution had somehow found the article, printed and shared it, finding its tone respectful to Baby Boy. "I'm glad you appreciated it," I replied.

Parachuting into a maelstrom

Events like my conversation with an ex-con about my tribute to Baby Boy took place right on my corner. I'd arrived in January 1990, after three years in Fells Point. I bought a house and moved to Upper Fells Point, five blocks north and still on Ann Street. The street was classic, a simple name, endlessly pretty blocks, three-digit house numbers, so different to a suburb.

When looking at properties for sale, the first four properties had choppy layouts. The fifth visit, to 203 South Ann Street, was different. The Polish rehabbers had transformed it from three tiny rental units into a spacious home. I loved it even before seeing any of the amenities farthest from the entrance. Winter light played on the living room floor of soft pine and on the exposed brick wall. I formed an immediate emotional attachment.

Above the ground floor, with its living and dining rooms and kitchen, were two suites, each with its own en suite bathroom, on the second floor, and a third master suite taking up the entire third floor.

The property had a logical, clean layout with all rooms accessible from the narrow central staircase. Grandfathering that staircase built in 1848 kept all the abutting rooms huge; rehabbers who built wider staircases to code ended up with smaller bedrooms.

An original stained-glass transom read "203" over the front door. The roof deck offered a 360-degree view of the Patapsco, downtown, nearby church steeples and Johns Hopkins Hospital. My sister living in the D.C. suburbs called it "magical," as every suite had delightful features, either a cathedral ceiling, skylights, a brick chimney or fireplace.

When I landed on the 200 block in 1990, I unknowingly parachuted into Baltimore's wildest socioeconomic crossroads. My three decades there swung between calm and chaos, like navigating Antarctica's Drake Passage — clashing oceans, towering waves and metaphorical shipwrecks. Just 10 steps from the nonstop improv theater of Pratt Street, my front door sat at what an online friend called the city's most turbulent corner.

Hopkins rock stars

On Ann Street, there were Johns Hopkins researchers, a T. Rowe Price financial analyst, chefs, library managers, realtors and landlords. My own home housed rock stars in the medical firmament, including the leader of the Doctors without Borders medical team that handled the 1995 ebola outbreak in Zaire. Razor-sharp professors of nursing and public health also stayed with me, commissioned to teach at Hopkins, arriving from D.C., Wisconsin, Ohio and such distant points as Uganda. Nursing school and medical residents might sit around my Ikea dining room table of an evening, eating a communal meal and chatting.

What I learned from all of them was that anyone who managed to pass Hopkins' stringent entry requirements was top tier at problem solving. If they had a problem in the morning, they had a solution by the evening. I admired them.

My rowhome was wedged between newsmakers unconnected to Hopkins. At 201 S. Ann St., Bernie Gietka hit the Mega Millions jackpot. On the other side, at 205 lived the affable Paul Cawley, a business analyst who went to federal prison after cashing his dead mother's Social Security checks for 15 years. I didn't see either event coming.

Paul's sister Lee, with her Bonnie Raitt-red hair and grey roots, was Baltimore incarnate. Her accent stretched "o" into "ooh," and turned "s" into "sh": *shtreet, shoda.* She'd whip up crab soup, with ingredients bought with food stamps, hollering from our shared alley as she set a container for me on a shared cement block wall.

Once, I mentioned the Inner Harbor, 12 blocks away. "Ooh, I've never been," she said. Her world map was limited to our block and the way to Broadway Market and Santoni's, folding trolley in tow.

Lee seemed to rely for money on what she called her flea market — putting a card table out front and selling gewgaws and cheap jewelry, during the Fells Point Festival or on random weekdays.

For a while, she was dating a tall man, a heavy smoker, named Junior. "He's a good painter ... when he's sober," she said with a half-smile. I appreciated her concise way of summing up people.

Then there was Pratt Street.

Helping an assault victim

On the early-'90s stretch of Pratt near Ann, you had squatters, vacant rowhomes, weedy lots, seedy bars, an abandoned shoe warehouse, drug dealers and users, and households of grandkids living with their grandparents — the missing generation lost to jail or rehab.

Free entertainment was everywhere. Neighbors dragged out lawn chairs, a six-pack of National Bohemian and steamed crabs to watch house fires and evictions. A large crowd gathered, with a carnival-like air of expectation, to watch a young man, the son of a drug dealer, threaten to jump off the Pratt Street liquor store roof. He was talked down safely.

Another staple was door-to-door scams, such as skimming funeral donations, a practice seen in the Third World and yes, Baltimore. One day a trio of kids brought a small goldfish bowl to my door, asking if I knew Cricket, an older woman found dead in her mid-block rowhouse. A misspelled card taped to the bowl read "Crickets fonral."

Suspecting a scam for drug money, I'd asked which funeral home was involved. The kids, unconnected to Cricket and vague about the funeral home, were likely exploiting neighborhood gossip. Similarly, children would knock and present crumpled pizza kit order sheets, which appeared to be plucked from a trash can, and claimed school charity drives, saying, "You're a nice lady, would you like to order some pizza?" I'd cite a dietary restriction and politely decline.

My Pratt Street neighbor Dalia and I shared bemused anecdotes. She once overheard an exquisitely detailed conversation about whether you could bring cigarettes to jail. Another time she watched in amusement as two overweight women tried to dislodge a manhole cover, attempting to stage a pretend fall into the sewer and lodge a fraudulent personal injury claim against the city.

She and her husband liked to go on camping trips, and didn't want burglars breaking in while they were away. As if on a top-secret military mission, they would gradually sneak their gear out to their car at night in small totes covered by blankets.

Criminals in fact did prowl the area. A Good Samaritan role was thrust upon me when a neighbor got robbed and beaten in a street attack. It was around 2 a.m. when I heard scuffling out front and, with my big sheltie Pierre leashed, stepped outside.

The attacker raced past me, in a corduroy knee-length coat and unkempt Afro, eyes huge and spinning like pinwheels. He leaned into the corner and sprinted up Pratt Street.

The night manager of nearby Honey's Lounge, likely thought to be carrying the night's receipts, was rolling off the hood of a parked car and falling face down to the sidewalk. The manager was bleeding profusely from a head wound. I called an ambulance and told him with outward confidence and inner alarm that he'd be fine, that the scalp bleeds easily.

Weeks later, he and his girlfriend visited me, dressed in their Sunday best, to thank me. "You saved my life," he said. I was deeply touched. They sat bolt upright on my sofa, hats in hand, formal and solemn. He brushed up his crew cut to show a long row of stitches in his scalp.

Shoutout to other Good Samaritans who comfort victims of street crime — it's a brave move to be outside in a silent Baltimore night, solitary except for you and an injured neighbor.

'Pratt Street forever'

Pratt Street teemed with vivid characters. The block's atmosphere? A little bit Dickens, a dash of *Hairspray* and a sprinkling of *The Grapes of Wrath.*

Cissy and Bob, an older couple, were stoop-sitting fixtures on the north side of the 1800 block when weather allowed. Hefty Cissy's foghorn voice summoned her grandsons, Karl and Bonzo, from mischief.

Rail-thin Bob, a West Virginian with a prominent forehead shaped like a light bulb, couldn't read or write. He would bring over food stamp applications for me to fill out, and order forms for Time-Life country music CD anthologies. The food stamp application gave me pause. I was working so hard, commuting to D.C. to work a demanding job at *The Washington Post.* Meanwhile my Pratt Street neighbors took it easy on public assistance and arguably had a better life, if a more run-down home. My *Post* salary afforded me nicer digs but endless office headaches. It made me wonder about the hamster wheel I was on; stoop sitting seemed more fun.

In the '90s, Cissy was catching wind of the World Wide Web — she called it "the intercom" during a memorable conversation in which I fought to keep a straight face. I loved the million miles away my Pratt Street conversations were from my day job in the *Post* newsroom.

Then there was Erica Ammenhauser, built like a sumo wrestler, a teen who ruled the block. One Sunday afternoon, I watched her unbuckle her studded belt and whip a smaller girl from Dundalk, curled in a fetal ball right in the intersection.

"PRATT STREET FOREVER!" Erica bellowed.

Full points for loyalty to the 'hood. Her declaration became a running joke with a friend — a nurse from South Carolina — who rented an apartment on Pratt and also saw nearby blocks as perpetual theater.

I expected that Erica would face an arrest for assault, but the victim's mother not only didn't press charges, she blamed her own daughter for crossing into Upper Fells Point — Erica's turf.

In 2008, Erica along with Baby Boy was convicted of plotting that led to the murder of a Marine reservist in the wake of a conflict in front of the corner grocery store. She served time in the big house and now lives quietly in Ohio, along other friends from the 'hood who relocated. I was told Ohio was a draw for welfare benefits that are easy to access.

An invisible epidemic

Erica's best friend didn't escape to Ohio. Ginger Myers, a 5-foot-tall mother of three, posted on Facebook in 2017: "Life's a gift, death's a promise." Suffering from depression, she battled the darkness for the sake of her children. Yet in 2019, she died of an overdose.

"Please be mindful of her children and do not come asking how Ginger passed," her viewing announcement read. A friend wrote, "RIP Ginger Myers I saw the pain in your eyes. Prayers to her family, especially her children."

Ginger was one of 1,652 Baltimoreans lost to overdoses in 2019, a year when the city also saw 348 homicides. Per day, that's nearly one murder and more than four fatal overdoses.

Depopulation was inevitable with 2,000 premature deaths annually, even with no moving vans involved.

The New York Times reported in 2024 that Baltimore's drug epidemic was the deadliest ever seen in a major U.S. city, with an overdose death rate from 2018-22 nearly double that of comparable urban areas. A commenter named Amy fumed at Mayor Brandon Scott's lack of awareness: "This is the same city as the [Johns Hopkins] Bloomberg School of Public Health. They can't find a few people who can make sense of this? That's pathetic."

I shared her shock — how could city officials and a top public health program miss this?

The author at left, Ginger Myers in headband at right

Erica and Ginger ran with Baby Boy and his brother James, kids I photographed as preteens on Ann and Durham streets. Only Erica, the toughest, survived the maelstrom. Pratt Street was not forever for many of her friends.

Long arcs of relationships

Relationships with neighborhood characters ebbed and flowed, tracing long arcs — ideally upward — or fluctuating like sine curves. Ginger was a case in point. As a cocksure and aggressive kid, she pelted my front door with rocks. Furious, I chased her off, only to flee her quickly assembled gang's retaliation. I sprinted to the corner grocery, hiding behind the rear shelves. The Sri Lankan proprietor covered for me, claiming I wasn't there, called the police and signaled when it was safe to return home.

Years later, Ginger, now a mother, softened. In her gentle voice, she respectfully called me "Miss Jeannette," asking me to be a big sister to her daughter, Rosalie. I was touched. She also invited me to see her son perform at a Wolfe Street Academy event. In retrospect, my lingering affection for the original neighbors, wayward as they were, was not shared by newer arrivals, who found them nuisances. I had a foot in both camps.

Likewise, another neighbor once tried to run me over — deliberately — during a zoning dispute over a garage. I took him to court for a restraining order. But with time, he too mellowed, and it may have been my stalwart pushback that straightened out the situation. In the end, he offered thoughtful advice on my move West and became, improbably, a kind of friend.

Of everyone, Rick Kirven was perhaps the best example of the long arc.

Rick orders mocha

For the Upper Fells bourgeoisie, such as we were, on Ann Street, Rick was our least favorite petty criminal of the Pratt Street contingent.

Public Enemy No. 1 was 5-11, with a salt-and-pepper beard, a loud and raspy voice, and two missing upper front teeth, said to be a signal he had been a prison bitch, although it could have actually been from a fight or poor health.

By 2007, at age 50, his house squatting and drug-dealing peaked. He built a lean-to behind a Pratt Street abandoned house, shacking up with a druggie girlfriend. He shunned his sister's Durham Street abode, where he would have to shape up and follow rules, to instead keep his criminal life. Like many homeless hustlers, he roamed vacant houses, styling himself an "unofficial watchman" for renovation properties, crafting hobo havens with discarded mattresses, tires for tables and scrounged camp chairs.

From 1998 to 2012, Rick racked up a dozen charges: drugs, theft, forgery, trespassing. In 2008, he was nabbed for littering after pocketing a contractor's cash to haul debris, only to dump it a few houses down. He did this over and over. We were tearing our hair out; "What to do about Rick" was a constant topic and energy drain.

In 2012, a burglary charge came with an alias, Walter Bogdan — a "Breaking Bad" nod, hinting that one of his squats had cable. The neighborhood sighed in relief when he was jailed; the quiet was palpable.

Post-release, from his drug-selling post in front of the liquor store, he spotted me, turned his face to a scowl and started recording with his phone. I countered with a goofy Zumba sidestep, making him guffaw. From then on, we were frenemies. I'd miss our chats when he was locked up, enjoying our little convos when he was freed.

One cold, rainy night, he knocked on my door. "Something warm to drink?" I offered. "Coffee or hot chocolate?"

"Can I get both?" he asked, hopeful.

"You want mocha?" I teased.

He beamed.

Rick's arc bent upward. He stayed clean for a good stretch, you could tell by his skin, hair and eyes looking healthier. He was friendly and sincerely warm when we ran into each other. Then he vanished. Word was he died in a motel room out Route 40, one last dance with a hooker and blow — for Rick, a fitting and perfect exit. We neighbors saluted.

Baby Boy, too, traced a long arc, his twinkly-eyed boyhood giving way to ruffian ways, yet our bond held fast.

As time passed, the colorful neighbors moved on or died. The devil-may-care vibe of the heritage Ann and Pratt Streeters was supplanted by scolds who overshared their politics. Up cropped a ubiquitous "Everyone is welcome here" window sign in eight languages. Another popular sign was "Lack of health care is violence," and after 2016, "Resist."

The "Everyone is welcome here" sign was the biggest paradox, posted by comparatively bland and forgettable residents. The companion "Resist" signs hinted that certain political viewpoints were in fact not welcome. The newer neighbors lacked the panache of the wildly individualistic Pratt Streeters, who never put sloganeering in their "windurs."

Pratt Streeters did not need to state who was welcome. If you were tough enough and wily, you would be tolerated, maybe asked to fill out food stamp applications, possibly even liked. If you weren't welcome, Erica might see fit to remove her studded belt and hold up traffic while she whipped you.

Peak Pratt Street was a book waiting to happen, with its daily dramas and character studies. I discussed this with Rafael Alvarez, a *Baltimore Sun* reporter with a knack for local color, his workspace adorned with an "Elvis on Other Planets Weight Chart," fitting for a city where the King reigns eternal.

"It's almost too easy writing about Baltimore," I said. "So many stories and anecdotes and ideas."

"They're laying all over on the ground, just for the taking," Rafe replied, squinting with his wry smile.

"It's just a question of which one of the millions of stories to write about," I said. "Like shooting fish in a barrel."

And some of the stories were all too real and lacked happy endings. As rough as Pratt Street could be, a far more ominous pattern was emerging not that much farther away — a map where unlike the Honey's Lounge night manager, who survived his robbery, you could give up your wallet, phone and bicycle, and yet, merciless boys barely out of middle school would not spare you.

A steep price for an uphill bike ride

For 33 years in Baltimore, I went car-free, saving on transportation expenses to fund travels from Italy to Madagascar and avoiding parking hassles in a neighborhood built for horses, not vehicles.

I biked everywhere — Safeway in Canton, research libraries, Peruvian chicken spots, social gatherings — pedaling past Linwood and South Robinson Street, zipping along Boston Street's 2500 block, or up North Lakewood to a Patterson Park library. Southward, I'd hit the H&S bakery outlet by the Tattoo Museum on Eastern Avenue. West and north, I'd pass a French patisserie near the Shot Tower, or cross Mount Vernon and St. Paul Street to access Johns Hopkins' undergraduate library.

My routine destinations hid a dark tale. On the exact spots I often frequented, all bike-able or walkable from my Ann Street rowhouse, regular folks with good families and jobs, and with no criminal connections, met violent ends. In hindsight, it's like a modern Jack the Ripper tour, only visible after the fact. The streets I navigated with misplaced confidence traced a map of loss, each location a silent marker of lives cut short.

This reality subtly gnaws at you. You may not admit you're playing Russian roulette when stepping outside, but the danger's real. Crime surged predictably — night more than daytime, summer more than winter — often spilling downhill from housing projects to the waterfront. Robbie Ponsi, a waiter at James Joyce Pub, which I cycled past most days en route to my Harbor East athletic club, embodied this risk. Bright, kind and generous, he troubled no one. In January 2016, biking home through light rain and a chilly darkness, the waterfront and midtown were peaceful, and he almost made it home. The stillness of that night was deceptive in its calm.

His story made me reflect on my own experiences cycling in Baltimore.

Getting ambushed

Biking in Baltimore felt safer than walking. I'd cycle-toured in England, France, Portugal, the Netherlands, Belgium, China and Bali, and commuted by bike in Maryland, England and Alaska, using a lightweight handmade bike or a sturdy hybrid. I felt at home on a bike and able to evade problems. Each ride carried the echo of those far-off journeys.

Navigating the city required more than good gear, experience and fitness — it demanded a military-style "sitrep" to assess threats. People, not cars, posed the biggest danger, so I constantly scanned for risks to avoid trouble.

One day, craving chocolate chip cookie dough ice cream, I rode to Bmore Licks in Canton, known for its 100 homemade flavors and a two-story cone mural. My route skirted Patterson Park's southwestern edge along Eastern Avenue's cracked sidewalk. Two youths on bikes maneuvered to flank me as I coasted downhill. Their cold, malevolent glares — boring into me — signaled they were sizing me up for an attack. I hid my alarm, and my downhill speed likely deterred them ... this time. Their eyes, devoid of mercy, lingered in my memory, a stark reminder that every ride was a gamble.

The incident with the two youths might seem overstated, but a 2014 helmet-cam video by cyclist Michael Bowman proved the danger — and the value of my gift of fear. On April 12, teens ambushed him in a bike lane on Guilford Avenue's 1600 and 1700 blocks in Station North.

"You can hear when they threw a bottle at me," Bowman posted, with laughter and whooping audible. He grabbed his bike lock for defense, and was punched and had his thumb stomped. Yelling "Help!" drew residents, scattering the attackers.

Commenters on Bowman's video reported similar incidents: a 2013 attack on a woman biking on Pratt Street, and warnings that Guilford's mile-long stretch between 17th and 27th streets was risky at night.

Some urged carrying firearms, pepper spray or a wrench, and avoiding teen groups. One wrote, "People get attacked all the time on foot/bike in Baltimore. Teens hang around in groups, wandering streets at night looking to pick fights."

Bowman's ambush was a mile north of my *Baltimore Sun* commute. A bike advocacy group noted five to 10 similar attacks nearby. Riding uphill, Bowman was vulnerable — slower and straining. Downhill, speed offered escape.

Yet, even downhill, I wasn't immune. Returning from Mount Vernon with pet food one midafternoon, a pedestrian near the *Sun* building on Guilford shoved me off my bike. Furious, I scrambled up, my temper flaring as I used my bike to push him away, so hard that he fell on his side. His surprise at my instant pushback gave me just enough space to speed off. That surge of defiance, a primal instinct to meet aggression with force, carried me away but left a lingering unease.

Riding past the projects

In 1988, the book *Historic Baltimore: Twelve Walking Tours* highlighted routes near Johns Hopkins Medical, now risky without leveraging Hopkins' armed private police and guard kiosks. Over the years, walking the city became less tenable. I stopped walking to my *Baltimore Sun* job and biked both ways, storing my bike in a secure Centre Street shed. I adjusted routes, avoiding Pratt and President streets after a man lunged at me one night, requiring quick evasion.

My routes prioritized downslopes for speed, assessed pedestrian demeanor, weighed vehicle traffic risks and favored bike lanes. Over time, biking grew dicier. In September 2015, I rode with a friend to an Orioles game for a hoodie giveaway, witnessing a rare double grand slam. But en route, kids from Perkins Homes housing project pelted us with rocks on Pratt Street — potentially a prelude to chases or beatings. I slammed my brakes, pivoted my bike 90 degrees and stared down the attackers. Counterintuitively, it worked; they scattered, showing only their backs and the soles of their sneakers.

Street code demands not letting yourself be punked. My Italian friend Valentina, talked into attending the game, stayed calm, trusting my judgment. At her 2019 wedding in Emilia-Romagna, her parents and 100 guests, many with limited English, warmly thanked me for keeping her safe in the U.S. Their gratitude, heartfelt across a language barrier, revealed that the main thing people an ocean away knew about Baltimore was that it was extremely dangerous.

Ambush on Old York

On Jan. 9, 2016, nearly two years after Michael Bowman's ambush, Ponsi finished his shift at James Joyce Pub in Harbor East. We might've crossed paths; I dined there with Icelandic and Brazilian guests after a water taxi ride. His manager called the 29-year-old a "genuinely good guy."

Ponsi lived near Waverly, 4 miles north. His 30-minute ride took him from 7 feet above sea level to around 250 feet, It is unlikely a native would chance this particular bike commute, tempting fate with exposure to night-time

Baltimore and climbing in medium gears on the steeper stretches. This ride was to test his endurance to the limit.

Like Zach Sowers, Ponsi was a transplant who underestimated the risks of solo nighttime travel. He had moved to Charm City five years earlier from Leesburg, Fla., northwest of Orlando. A high school friend recalled, "He was a REALLY nice kid. Smart, funny, talented, and extremely kind."

He had just another five to 10 minutes to go when he was attacked.

Around 9 p.m. at Old York Road and Venable Avenue, Ponsi saw eight teens robbing someone and stopped to help, his mother, Dawn, told CBS News. A vigil attendee, speaking on Ponsi's 30th birthday three days later, witnessed the assault: "He was waving his bike at them, trying to get away, but they kept circling, yelling obscenities and threats." Ponsi fell retreating, and the group swarmed, kicking and punching while shouting, "Take his f——— wallet!" and "Take his phone."

Athletic and resilient, a former Young Marine with survival training, Ponsi tried to defend himself. The youngest attacker, 15-year-old Prince Greene, went into a frenzy. With a large knife, he stabbed Ponsi's neck and chest 11 times and slashed him six more, only one fewer than Sharon Tate's wounds in the Manson family slaying.

The teens stole Ponsi's phone, wallet and bike.

Like a serial murder

The attack on Robbie Ponsi was "overkill," per forensic psychiatrists – excessive injuries far beyond what's needed to leave a victim for dead. *Forensic Science International* notes chest stabbings, as here, are typical, suggesting an "absolute will to annihilate," akin to serial murders.

In his rage, 15-year-old Greene stabbed accomplice Daquan Middleton, 16, twice in the calf, per charging documents, a frenzy hinting at sociopathy.

A passerby, fresh off an MTA bus, found Ponsi on the sidewalk after the attackers fled and called 911. Taken to

Johns Hopkins Hospital, Ponsi underwent trauma surgery but died at 3:30 a.m. Middleton was also treated there for his wounds.

At the vigil for Ponsi, his mother, Dawn, said, "There was no need to escalate it to this level." She noted Robbie would've given his attackers "the shirt off his back."

Photos of Ponsi's bright demeanor contrast sharply with the mugshots of Greene, Middleton, and Antwan Eldridge—menacing, defiant, with lowered eyelids and disheveled hair, radiating trouble. Even allowing for mugshot grimness, Baltimore's criminals appear chilling, drawn to the city's kind-hearted, productive citizens, whose obituaries highlight their warmth.

These attackers seemed to reject *logos* — Greek for light, order and reason.

"It's numbing to spend so long in this city, loving it, to have someone else's children do that to mine," Dawn told WBAL. "All we can do is hope for justice."

Residents leave

Sentenced as a juvenile, Greene served two years for Ponsi's murder, then beat and robbed a man at Mondawmin Metro Station after release. Eldridge faced re-arrest in March 2025 for attempted murder.

WBFF online commenters raged at lenient sentencing. "I don't care if we have to build a prison from Baltimore to the Pacific Ocean, get these violent people off the streets," one wrote. Another demanded lifelong isolation for murderers, citing El Salvador's model. The other teens in Ponsi's attack apparently evaded prosecution.

These sentences beg the question: if Baltimore's prosecutors and juries refuse to keep murderers, violent sex offenders and sociopathic juveniles locked up, what can be done? Can the state or federal officials intervene to whisk away those who pose a danger to law abiders? Without change, Baltimore suffers a perfect storm of exceptionally dangerous criminals operating in an exceptionally lenient environment.

Ponsi's murder drove some to flee Baltimore. Commenter Ryan McElroy, a Waverly resident who blogged as "The Chop," left in 2016, citing Ponsi's killing near their home: "We'd been chased by a gang of kids a block away. ... It could have been us."

As with Zach Sowers, accusations of racism emerged, with some black residents decrying outsized attention to a white victim's death. McElroy rebutted: "All murders are not created equal. Some victims are targeted for their choices ... But Robert Ponsi was targeted because violent scumbags thought he'd make a good victim. That's more terrifying and outrageous, and it's not racism to say so."

A former Federal Hill resident swore off Baltimore after dining a week earlier near the spot that became Ponsi's murder scene: "I vowed ... to never again patronize a city that does so little to protect its hard-working citizens," she posted online. Her vow crystalized the thought process behind the silent exodus of so many in response to dozens of victims like Robbie Ponsi.

An outlier among 2016's 318 homicides, Ponsi was a regular working man, not a criminal — the first of four such victims that year. Of 44 law-abiding Baltimoreans killed in similar circumstances since 1993, Ponsi fought hardest against steep odds. Street code might've warranted respect, but Greene showed none. Ponsi's desperate stand stood as a metaphor for every resident who begged for a safe city, only to fear the prospect of youth gangs wielding savage brutality.

Outnumbered

Law-abiding individuals like Zach Sowers, Robbie Ponsi and Joel Lee were killed by groups of black male assailants. Other Baltimore victims of homicides by two or three black males include NIH researcher Peter Marvit, body piercer Jim Forrester, bartender Kim Leto, coach Jordan Taylor and delivery worker Cheryl McCormack.

Four others — Stephen Pitcairn, bartender Alex "Albo" Wroblewski, photographer Alex Ulrich and innkeeper Larry Peterson — were killed by black males with female accomplices who punched or stole items. Contracts professional Timothy Moriconi was shot by a black male with a girlfriend driving the getaway car.

Bartender Sebastian Dvorak's lone killer in Canton was backed by a drug gang that supplied and disposed of the gun, with three members convicted as accessories.

Northeastern University criminologist James Alan Fox notes in "Teenage Males Are Committing Murder at an Increasing Rate" that group killings often cross racial lines. While only 11 percent of solo killings are interracial, 25 percent of group killings involve more than once race, with 71 percent involving black offenders targeting white strangers, often during robberies (60 percent). This mirrors many of Baltimore's innocent victims. The statistics, cold and unyielding, painted a grim portrait of a city where group violence became a haunting norm.

Stains on the sidewalk

In 2016, University of Maryland Baltimore County art student Amy Berbert began photographing each of Baltimore's 2016 homicide sites exactly one year after the event. On Jan. 9, 2017, at 9:10 p.m., she captured Venable Avenue at Old York Road, where Robbie Ponsi fought to live.

Her project, "Stains on the Sidewalk," extended into 2018, documenting 2017's 343 murder sites — another record year. Shared on Instagram as "An Exploration of Homicide in Baltimore City. Same Day. Same Time. Same Place. One Year Later," the series resonated deeply.

Robbie, an artist and photographer, would've likely approved, his mother Dawn told *The Baltimore Sun*. "I hope it wakes people up and shakes foundations," she said. "The murder rate is so out of control, it needs to be kept in front of everyone. Anything that honors Rob's memory with dignity, I'm fine with."

A colleague who worked with Robbie at the Pratt Street Alehouse noted that he would often type jokes into the food and drinks orders to brighten another employee's day. That's the best memory to emphasize for this gladiator.

When a neighbor wins the lottery

I'd settled into my Ann Street rowhome by 1990, a newcomer to Upper Fells Point's lively circus of the absurd. Next door lived Bernadette "Bernie" Gietka and her mother, Miss Kate. Their three-story home at 201 and mine at 203 shared a party wall dating to their joint construction in 1848. They were neighborhood fixtures — Polish, Roman Catholic, unassuming — until Bernie's life hit a jackpot bigger than a Pimlico bettor's Preakness trifecta.

Bernie, or "Chochi" to her nieces and nephews, was pint-sized, barely 5 feet, with fine brown hair and a sturdy build, like our senator, Barbara Mikulski. Raised above their family's ground-floor candy store, Bernie and her siblings, Jerry and Lynda, grew up with the store's pinball machines and comic books. Miss Kate ran the shop until an attempted robbery shut it down. Her profits funded gambling trips from Atlantic City to Reno, jaunts from Disney World to the Vatican, with Bernie often tagging along, hooked on slots and amusement parks.

Bernie tried convent school, dreaming of nunhood, but left to work at Montgomery Ward and the Social Security Administration, and as a rural letter carrier in Baltimore County's horse country — Phoenix, Baldwin, Hyde. She pet-sat, housesat and cared for the elderly, juggling gigs to keep her travel dreams alive. Miss Kate, meanwhile, was a character straight out of Baltimore's playbook: divorced, she remarried her ex, Ben, in 1992, sweeping down Ann Street in a puffy white veil, grinning like she'd won big at Atlantic City slots. Which is where a giant Gunther charter bus often took her and Bernie, directly from our corner.

We were neighborly enough. When I painted my house and opened windows, fumes leaked through our shared brick wall — a Fells Point quirk I hadn't anticipated. Bernie left a handwritten note in my mailbox, griping about the smell. I sent apology flowers; she wrote back, thanking me and begging my indulgence for their piano's muffled tunes, which I quietly enjoyed. She smiled softly at my sheltie puppy and gave me a decent trundle bed that I refinished and kept in the living room.

A neighborhood bombshell

On June 19, 2003, Bernie bought four Mega Millions tickets in Middle River, near her new Dundalk basement digs. The next day, she won $183 million, netting $76 million after taxes and taking a lump sum. The news hit Ann Street like a stray bullet at the Fourth of July fireworks. Our unassuming Bernie was the second-biggest lottery winner in U.S. history, Maryland's biggest ever.

WBAL-TV's Barry Simms knocked on my door, knowing Bernie's roots were in Upper Fells, not Dundalk. I gave a chirpy interview, saying her win might fund her dream of writing a pro-life musical. *The Baltimore Sun, Washington Post,* CNN — everyone covered it. Neighbors gathered on stoops, half-thrilled, half-jealous, boisterously brainstorming what *they* would do with such a windfall.

Bernie's win wasn't all roses. She told the *Catholic Review* she'd prayed to God in anger, frustrated by obstacles to writing her musical: "I'm so disgusted," she lectured the Supreme Being. "I know what you want me to do, but I don't have the means and never will. It's up to you. It would benefit you to make me really, really rich!"

To Bernie, God was framed as a rich uncle who would write a stupendous check if she complained enough.

Three weeks later, she won, calling it divine intervention. The archdiocese lapped it up, likely eyeing donations, but online skeptics on FreeRepublic mocked her materialistic prayer. The Catholic Catechism frowns on chasing limitless wealth, yet Bernie seemed to be embrace the evangelical prosperity gospel, and savored a windfall born of gambling not effort.

From neighbor to nuisance

Bernie's millions didn't just change her — they shook our block. Even before the win, she'd decamped to live with a family member, leaving 201 vacant, a decaying relic of her candy-store childhood. Rats overran it, chewing through pet food bags in my property until I got a metal trash can. I shoveled her 100-foot sidewalk after every snowstorm, unpaid, for years, while her family forgot our corner. Pratt Street's chaos — drug deals, teens chucking glass bottles at cars, neglected rowhouses collapsing like dominoes — was just constant background noise, but Bernie's willful neglect seemed deliberate and personal.

One summer noon, Bernie rolled up ready to battle the rodent invasion herself. There she was, a millionaire in a white hazmat suit, battling rats like a hero in a sci-fi remake of *Willard*.

Despite her millions, she skipped hiring a biohazard specialist, tackling the mess in sweltering heat with no power or water — utilities had been cut off. She was probably too embarrassed to let anyone else see the house's state. After cleaning up, hot and sweaty, she invited me inside. The front room still held a vintage soda fountain, counter, confectionery cases, and battered storage boxes, a museum piece of 1950s East Baltimore.

She spent wildly, once more a kid in a candy store, except now one who treated Baltimore County as her personal Monopoly game: 38 properties, mostly in Phoenix, 40 cars, a $6.4 million manor, even a 9-foot John Lennon "Imagine" piano that Yoko Ono signed in exchange for a donation to a favored charity. She chased celebrities — the Ravens' Ray Lewis, Donny and Marie, Jerry Lewis, Cardinal Keeler — buying access with charity checks.

Her brother Jerry's memoir, *I Like Me Now*, paints her as naive. She approved real estate purchases without bargaining. She snatched up houses and high-end vehicles only to leave them to rot, like a pack rat with a platinum card. She joined a country club but made no friends, a fish out of water. She read every line of her junk mail and hoarded it in stacks. Her fur coats, and an honorary doctorate finagled with yet another donation, screamed "I pay for prestige" louder than the glowing Domino Sugars sign.

Bernie's win didn't just change her bank account — it thrust her into a spotlight she craved, starting with a surreal night on Jay Leno's stage.

Her Leno appearance in July 2003 was peak Bernie. She glowed, tossing one-liners, claiming she'd written scripts and a musical — news to her brother Jerry. Colin Farrell playfully proposed; her father cringed, sensing mockery of our convent-girl millionaire. The spotlight brought a flood of money requests, overwhelming her charitable foundation. In Baltimore, single guys buzzed about meeting her, picking up an asexual vibe but chasing her cash anyway. Jerry wrote she couldn't trust anyone's motives, losing a true long-term friend after fame and fortune called.

Meanwhile, 201 S. Ann St. became my headache. I fielded city complaints about rats, water meters and storm drains. In 2008, the rear wall of her adjacent Pratt Street property showed deterioration, threatening my bike shed. By 2011, Bernie ordered a hand-demolition to avoid damaging my home, but her bizarre instructions baffled workers.

Jerry's memoir noted Bernie fancied herself an expert in plumbing, masonry, concrete work, zoning law and more, despite neither experience nor a knack for construction. The workers grumbled about her interference. I can't remember the specifics, but her directives were on the lines of suggesting using hammers to drive screws. Her "Bernie logic" made contractors and family members weep. I winced, descended from shipbuilders who valued precision, not Bernie's whimsical "expertise."

What might that shaking be?

In October 2011, a massive rumble shook my rowhome.

Pratt Street was no stranger to mayhem: shootings, prostitution, a marijuana farm filling an entire rented rowhome, and a rumored porn ring lurking in the basement of a corner house. Squatters hopped between projects, and boom cars blasted subwoofers. Traffic leaving the Fourth of July fireworks in the Inner Harbor had to dodge a hail of bottles said to be hurled by brothers Karl and Bonzo (legends), from their tarpaper roof on Pratt Street. A ranchera band's rehearsals above the liquor store provided the soundtrack, off-key and off-tempo.

A rowhouse collapse — we'd had three crumble partway through renovation — might have explained the racket. Initially, I didn't budge from my office chair, numbed by the street's steady disruptions. Curiosity won, and I squeezed to the back of my bike shed. A three-story stonemason's wall had collapsed, burying the Gietka's patio in bricks and propane hiss. Bernie had ordered the wall to repair a neighbor's house exposed by her demolition project behind my bike shed.

Traffic vibrations likely loosened it. The collapsing tons of masonry was a near-miss for a cyclist — and me, had it fallen toward my bedroom.

It was not lost on me that the more money the Gietkas had, the more likely their buildings around me would collapse. They were some funny millionaires.

While Bernie and her family members lived in mansions in and around Phoenix, Maryland, debris filled her former patio adjacent to my home.
(Photograph by the author)

A nurse friend living in an apartment across from Royal Farms on Eastern shared a similar tale: hearing gunfire from a police chase, she looked up, shrugged and calmly turned a page in her book. We'd all grown deaf to East Baltimore's constant drama.

The fight for 201

A vacant-house program kicked off in 2010. City housing officials targeted 16,000 derelict properties, including 201 S. Ann Street. Polish families often clung to old rowhomes, sentimental about the stoops where their mom raised them, but letting them decay as they moved to suburbs.

In 2012, the city sued Bernie and Miss Kate to force a sale or rehab, under a receivership law to curb nuisances. Millionaires don't usually own vacant rat nests, but Bernie was no ordinary owner. She fought back with top lawyers, dragging out hearings for two years. She threatened to demolish 201 out of spite, despite the fact this would cost her more than selling it outright to a flipper.

I worked tirelessly to save a house that wasn't mine, a farcical situation but essential. I feared a demolition would wreck the stability of my entire structure, given the likelihood of shared joists. Neighbors dreaded a vacant lot turning into a drug haven.

The Gietka house on the corner, my former house on the right, and 1805 E. Pratt at left, in 2009.

Through a relative acting as a proxy, Bernie offered to sell me 201 for $180,000; developers valued it at $125,000. Her family proxies, from their Phoenix estates, taunted us with silence and neglect — thieves stole bikes through her collapsed gate, her yard became a dump. In 2014, the Upper Fells Point Community Association begged the mayor to revoke her demolition permit, in desperation copying her pastor at Holy Rosary Church.

Her Catholic image — funding restoration of the church's stained glass while letting her house decay — felt as empty as the pews after the last Sunday Mass empties out.

I emailed her lawyer begging for a sale instead of a demolition: "Bernie is the one person in the entire city with the most means to take care of her property, and she does the absolutely worst job of it, in the view of most people around here.'" Jerry's memoir called her reasoning erratic, maybe inherited from what he called Miss Kate's "strange" side.

In 2013, Bernie considered a reprieve. She met my brother-in-law, a builder, with blueprints for 201, including Virgin Mary alcoves in all the second-story windows. He quipped, "Guess you're not renting to Jewish people," earning a chuckle, and urged her to sell. The blueprints also specified a ground-floor massage parlor. The clashing themes — saintly statues, incongruous services — would tank resale value. Many hours were spent with all the potential builders, crunching numbers and brainstorming ways to preserve 201.

Bernie's Virgin Mary alcoves and her birthday Mass with Cardinal Keeler, secured through yet another donation, didn't square with the rats she left us to fight or the anxiety she unleashed, as jarring as a Pratt Street building collapse at midnight. Her actions revealed a faith more performative than authentic.

Solving 'the Bernie problem'

On Aug. 18, 2014, I ran into Bernie's attorney outside 201.

"Bernadette had a heart attack by her bed, dead before she hit the floor," she said, her power suit an unfamiliar look on our casual block. Bernie had died Aug. 10 at her Phoenix home, age 65, after gambling the day before at a casino and packing boxes — work her millions could've outsourced. A police report noted a bruised forehead from collapsing in her bathroom; CPR failed.

The attorney and I walked to the Gietka's derelict patio, where a guerrilla gardener had planted a pollinator garden with bee balm, daisies and yarrow, and a stylized metal hummingbird on a stake. The flowers showed neighbors' efforts to improve our corner. Bernie lived in a 5,000-square-foot Phoenix home, sitting on less than half of her original $76 million, distant from our struggles.

The guerrilla garden in the patio of the former Gietka home.
My fence and kitchen wall are in the background.
(Photograph by the author)

The attorney sighed, "It was a difficult representation." We stood together quietly looking at the flowers. I felt her combination of frustration and relief.

I emailed Jerry, offering condolences. He said he and his sister Lynda were devastated. I'd last seen Bernie in June, when she paid me $200, peeled off a fat wad of cash, for minor tree-watering, overpaying but well-earned after years of shoveling her snow.

The news of Bernie's passing arrived late to me, and I missed her funeral at Holy Rosary, five blocks away but a world apart since the demolition friction had surfaced. Days later, the family green-lit selling 201, and I was asked to alert potential builders.

Neighbors were blunt: "I guess this solves the Bernie problem," one said. Another asked, "Does this help you out?"

Their open joy surprised me. As a newer resident, I expected the Gietkas' long tenure to earn respect, but it didn't. Despite our disputes, I'd once liked Bernie; others clearly didn't.

Miss Carm, our block's eldest resident, had called the Gietkas "trash" years earlier. "They came from trash and they were trash, and it was always trash in that house," she told WBAL when I escorted reporter Barry Simms to her parlor after he asked my suggestions for neighbors to interview about Bernie's win. Candy cost two cents at Miss Kate's store, not one cent as everywhere else, she recalled, hinting the overcharging funded their European trips. Simms stifled laughter and wrapped up; I'd had a ringside seat to an interview that never aired.

Bernie's death effectively ended the city's lawsuit. Miss Kate sold 201 for $130,000 to a developer. Bernie's estate — whittled down to around $32 million, from $76 million — included 38 properties, many neglected, and 13 cars, mostly left to her nephew, as well as celebrity memorabilia stuffed into houses and storage units. She spent on Steinway pianos, fur coats and Broadway cameos, where she would arrive late for makeup and costuming, a wannabe diva, and be led around the stage by hand.

Bernie was on her way to fulfilling a goal to burn through it all before she died, as Jerry's memoir notes. Her brother mourned a sister he barely knew, changed by power, not happiness: “My sister was a complete stranger to me,” he wrote.

Bernie’s win revealed her, as the saying goes: Money doesn’t change people, it unmasks them. Her Catholic devotion clashed with her neglect, her generosity with her spite. Her wealth built walls, not bridges to the neighborhood. Lottery studies have noted cases where winners harm neighbors, from neglected houses to gaudy fences and multi-day metal band festivals. Bernie’s 201 threats were a bigger stressor during my 30 years as an Ann Street resident than even the nearby homicides.

For different reasons, she and I had left our houses. Bernie’s millions won compliant responses from Jerry Lewis, Yoko Ono and an archbishop, but couldn’t buy her a place in our community’s heart. Maybe lotteries should limit themselves to a smaller payout of just a cool mill or so — enough for a house, a car, a boat, tuition, or a dream. That would’ve kept Bernie and many others grounded.

Few lottery winners are constituted to handle suddenly becoming the richest person they know. The fallout for many includes bankruptcies, lawsuits, loss of friendships, kidnappings, murder, arrests, betrayals, depression and regret. And in Bernie’s case, a heart attack possibly linked to packing boxes that she could have hired out.

Through her last days, with a fortune still to her name, Bernie continued to hit the casinos, squandering time she could’ve spent writing her musical or a memoir — a no-brainer for someone with her backstory. This book is the third mentioning her lottery win (as well as Jerry’s book, Miss Kate also wrote her memoirs). Only Bernie herself, who styled herself a writer of musicals, hasn’t weighed in on her intriguing experiences.

What’s a jackpot worth if you aimed to spend it all, never wrote that musical you prayed for (at the pearly gates, did St. Peter demand the lottery money back?) ... and your passing lifted a great weight off the neighbors?

Life in a permanent construction zone

After Bernie's death, Miss Kate sold 201 S. Ann St., the house next to mine, to James, a contractor from suburban Howard County. Most rehabbers in our Baltimore neighborhood, including James, commuted from counties a half-hour or more away. Had they lived in rowhomes themselves, they might have valued noise-proofing over aesthetic Instagram bait.

Our shared party wall — one brick layer thick — had exposed brick on my side and plaster on James's. I urged him to keep the plaster and add a brick veneer, providing both sound insulation and the exposed masonry appeal, offering to chip in. Both households would benefit.

James proposed a $5,000 double brick wall, which my research showed would be about as effective as tissue paper. His on-site supervisor admitted James prioritized "what sells," ignoring architects' warnings and residents' complaints about noisy exposed-brick rowhomes in places like Baltimore, Brooklyn and Philadelphia. Exposed brick looks charming but turns neighbors into unwilling eavesdroppers.

James refused my veneer offer. One day, masons at 201 broke through the single-wythe wall, and a workman's hand popped into my second-story room, occupied with guests, proving its thinness like a David Copperfield magic trick gone wrong.

A worker's gloved hand reaches through the damaged wall.

More changes followed. James added a deck, crowding my cherished Baltimore skyline view. My own deck — a personal Hanging Garden of Babylon with tomatoes, peppers, basil, spinach and potted palms — felt less private.

In 1990, mine was one of only three roof decks visible in any direction, overlooking delightful Mary Poppins-like chimneys and rooflines. Now, with four in a row, cheek by jowl, the experience lost its magic, as if my oasis had been hijacked into a communal party area — a role already filled by the sidewalk below. The sloppy deck teams sawed offcuts that rained onto my bike shed's shingles and squeezed balusters so close to property lines that maintenance became a logistical game of rowhouse Twister

James's deck had stereo speakers built into its base, pointing down to the roof — a nice touch if you had 140 empty acres to serenade, instead of Maryland's densest zip code. He also installed speakers in the living room wall, both sets turning our joint wall into a soundboard. This vibrated my house top to bottom while proving that in Upper Fells Point, silence isn't golden — it can be shattered by one household's blaring music festivals for an involuntary audience of several hundred rowhomes.

The block was changing, with newer residents hailing fewer derelict buildings and more renos as "better." But for someone noise-sensitive like me — who can hear a neighbor's phone call clearer than my own thoughts — these changes were a purgatory I couldn't mute.

Rowhome archeology

Ann Street could feel like a block-long slumber party on good days: kids chalking sidewalks, neighbors sharing crab soup, or hosting movie and pizza nights. But the bad days came loud and dusty. Aging buildings, cheek by jowl, meant long construction stretches — sledgehammers tearing up walls on one side of my refuge, then the other, then catty-corner. The clang of debris filling an endless series of dumpsters.

Lee Cawley's former home next door — on the opposite side to Bernie's — got a fancy renovation, but the new owners let their deck mold, and the hired power washers splattered my windows with grime, leaving permanent pockmarks. Suburb-friendly fixes turned thoughtless in these tight quarters.

As houses on three sides were gutted, I was sandwiched in a years-long construction zone. Granting workmen access to repoint the brick wall behind my patio unleashed choking mortar dust, piling two feet high around my bike shed. Formstone removal on both sides sprayed permanent reddish dust over my mortar, turning my own home's front into a dull monotone while neighbors' mortar gleamed.

These 1840s (Ann Street) and 1900s (Pratt Street) homes aged unevenly. My 1990 remodel uncovered archaeological layers: rose-colored carpeting, multicolored linoleum, planks stamped with the sawmill's name.

Investors chasing get-rich-quick dreams flooded in from the suburbs, tone-deaf to the historic urban vernacular. They were from out of town and built out-of-scale additions. They viewed us locals — reporting unpermitted work or hookers sneaking into their unsecured projects — as profit-killing nuisances. Their overdone rehabs turned Upper Fells Point into a suburban fiefdom of pot lights and pot-fillers, of vessel sinks in front of Agreeable Gray walls, and fake balconies offering a front-row view of rats, riots and drug runners.

Rowhouse living provided a sense of community and preserved delightful architecture, but its headaches go underreported. In a neighborhood of hundreds of very old, tightly packed buildings in various life cycles — some crumbling, others under renovation, a few quality rehabs in great shape — residents feel like they've moved into a rotating noise-fest you could call "Jackhammer Acres." The investors were tone-deaf to our historic fabric.

It's not only the jarring speakers everywhere. City attorneys and inspectors couldn't keep up with the shenanigans — hidden rentals squirreled behind side doors, entered off alleys or lacking plumbing; basement units without the windows needed for fire egress, as if landlords were hosting a citywide game of hide-and-seek with safety codes.

A well-off neighbor once offered to fund legal battles against housing code violations but quickly gave up. Landlords and developers were a bottomless pit of charlatans, focused on profits and heedless of the neighborhood's health.

In Maryland's packed 21231 zip code, disruption was relentless for noise-sensitive folks craving quiet. Some longtime neighbors bought adjacent properties to create buffers — a luxury I didn't realize the value of until my nerves pleaded for mercy.

Little did I know, my noise woes were about to hit a decibel level that would make even a Moonrise Festival crowd wince.

Beneath the surface at Under Armour

After James rehabbed 201 S. Ann St., he rented it out. In March 2016, three designers of athletic shoes — I'll call them Sid, Andrew and George — moved in. They worked for Under Armour, the athletic gear company headquartered in Baltimore.

As a University of Maryland alum, I admired Under Armour's founder Kevin Plank, who played on Maryland's football special teams, and the company's "Protect This House" campaign. I often visited their Curtis Bay outlet, now closed as the company retrenches, for shirts, leggings, backpacks, sports bras and socks.

Initially, I was intrigued by the tenants. But their housewarming party brought a skunk-like reek that may have been "loud" marijuana, a particularly potent type, and blaring hip-hop from the roof speakers, flooding the neighborhood.

Sid and Andrew hosted these parties on Bernie's former concrete pad, with partiers standing in the street to direct parking, like a mini Fells Point Festival.

A second party disrupted guests visiting as part of my short-term rental business. Two Taiwanese visitors couldn't sleep due to the noise, their jet lag no match for the decibels. I invited Sid into my home to listen. He pretended to be attentive, cocking his head like a dog hearing soft whispers. He weighed the sound leakage, then downplayed the issue and left. He knew how to deflect complaints, and was a maestro with cops showing up at later parties, contritely lying that the parties were a "one-time thing."

The parties forced me to offer discounts to later guests as well, as the keggers continued on every nice weekend. I lived in fear of bad reviews from short-term guests who couldn't have peace and quiet.

The word was spreading in our neighborhood and among my guests that Under Armour staff were inconsiderate of neighbors. George, the most mature and thoughtful individual, admitted he and his girlfriend fled weekends to escape the noise — yet neighbors had to endure it.

Bernie's pad now featured kegs, beer pong, a basketball hoop, and the "stump game," which I discovered when relentless hammering noises drew my attention.

Stumped by the stump game

Associated with tailgating and fraternity parties, the stump game involves tossing a hammer with backspin, catching it after one rotation, and driving a nail into a stump. The ritual was better suited for a stadium parking lot tailgate than a rowhouse patio. Dropping the hammer, missing the nail, or hitting another's nail required chugging beer, turning the contest into a peculiar variation of carpentry that could lead to hangovers and injury.

The drunken shenanigans were marked by bizarre, walrus-like groans — "rrrrrrrrrr-AAAAHHHHHHGGG—EEEEEEE—errrr." So much for peace and quiet on a nice spring evening.

By summer, the neighbors' guests grew ruder. One Saturday, a female guest in a striped dress mocked me on my landing, calling me out for having a dog companion and suggesting I needed a date. My social calendar was probably more full than theirs, just not as publicly loud and inebriated, or as the Brits say, "tired and emotional."

Her mean-girl tone and appearance — close-set eyes, thinning hair — didn't scream "charm." Sid or Andrew likely egged her on. Another guest crudely offered to show her "butt cheeks" and her "five nipples," as witty as a broken barstool.

Under Armour was not only a testosterone zoo, it had toxic femininity matching its toxic masculinity.

Their portable basketball hoop on the pad created a constant BANG-BANG-BANG, with balls hitting my fence, stucco kitchen walls, and crashing onto my bike shed's roof. I scoffed at their patio setup, and played basketball myself at the Cold Spring Elementary's public hoops, just steps away. *Sissies*, I thought. Every missed shot echoed like a challenge to the neighborhood's tranquility. Their hoop dreams were my hoop ordeal.

In East Baltimore's dense rowhomes, deck speakers and patio hoops were uncommon — they annoyed neighbors needlessly when both Under Armour itself and local schools had basketball courts, and a bar ambiance could be had at dozens of watering holes steps away.

The basketballs risked damaging my self-installed fence and newly recoated stucco, which they likely assumed were theirs. I also worried an errant ball might shatter my skylights, raining glass on me at night.

Despite Under Armour's gym and nearby pubs, they treated their home like a sports-entertainment hub, ignoring zoning and neighbors' rights to peaceful enjoyment. Their habit of pre-drinking cheaply at home before hitting Fells Point bars for pricy libations brought unwanted waterfront rowdiness to the more family-oriented Upper Fells Point.

When police responded to noise complaints, Sid lied smoothly, promising to quiet down, claiming each party was a one-off. His fawning, non-confrontational demeanor with officers seemed almost sociopathic.

The worst two nights

In 2017, the parties at 201 S. Ann St. persisted. On Feb. 5, I asked partiers to stop playing basketball at 1 a.m., two hours after Baltimore's quiet hours began. A guest threw the ball at me. Apparently, to these interlopers, "quiet hours" were just a suggestion, like a dash of Old Bay on a crab cake.

The next weekend, I moved my bed from under my skylights, fearing a ball might shatter them while I slept. That Saturday, a football crashed above my head, hitting my deck's metal spiral staircase. Footsteps followed as a partier trespassed on my roof at 1 a.m. to retrieve it, sounding like a break-in.

From my deck, I heard Under Armour partiers mock me with a fake rapper accent, yelling, "Go to bed Shawty" (Shorty). They were tossing footballs at a basketball hoop two stories below. One shouted, "What's up Worldstar, I GOT A FUCKIN' CANNON," as if their antics might earn them a spot on the Baltimore Ravens roster — or at least a viral video trophy. Two gave me the finger, arms swinging wildly for emphasis.

Across the street, houses stayed dark — neighbors likely slept in back rooms with earplugs, a solid survival tactic. One night, guests of the tenants played basketball long after midnight. Once again, I found myself on my own roof, in pajamas, 25 feet above the ground, politely explaining the city's quiet hours to strangers below. They apologized and stopped, a more neighborly response than the tenants themselves ever offered. The absurdity of my midnight rooftop diplomacy in sleepwear wasn't lost on me.

I shared interests with the Under Armour designers — namely sports and design — but their hostility born of a male- and youth-oriented outlook made a cordial relationship impossible. I had close male friends in the same late-20s age bracket, a nurse and a financial analyst, who were social and engaging, unlike these incurious designers who dismissed my older self as worthless. Years later, digging into Under Armour's culture clarified their behavior.

Would Under Armour care?

I knew Sid, Andrew and George were Under Armour shoe designers from our friendly introduction, where I quoted Outkast's "Hey Now" ("lend me some sugar, I am your neighbor") to Sid's amusement. But their disrespect demanded action. Without last names or bosses' details, I scoured social media and was eventually able to identify them and their chain of command.

With James an indifferent landlord, I targeted the tenants' employer, hoping Under Armour executives cared about their employees' local reputation. After the second chaotic party in February 2017, I contacted Charlotte James, then UA's senior footwear manager. On the phone, I explained that the past two weekends had nearly turned violent, with multiple police visits, stressing my disappointment as a UA customer and athlete.

I followed up with a letter on Feb. 14, citing a December 2016 incident where a drunk guest operated a city Bobcat excavator parked on the block from 2:30 to 3 a.m. Because nothing says "good neighbor" like heavy machinery joyrides in the dead of night.

Charlotte said Sid was leaving to coach in Africa, a relief, possibly explaining his boldness. She promised to address Andrew and the third designer's behavior. Regulating off-hours conduct is tricky — like many other employers, the code of conduct posted on UA's website bans workplace harassment but doesn't clearly cover external actions.

On April 28, 2017, I wrote a letter to UA CEO Kevin Plank, concerned that he needed to be aware of the dark hell-raiser ethos of his employees' next door. I wasn't given the courtesy of a reply, a silence that spoke volumes and a customer service blunder.

By March 1, the landlord ended their lease, and the tenants left, leaving behind a sidewalk covered in Under Armour shoe boxes, as well as party cups, clothes, golf clubs and gym gear. The legacy of discarded junk for neighbors to clean up perfectly encapsulated the UA bros' tenancy.

Wall Street Journal exposé

In 2013, three years before my first-hand UA encounter, online platforms such as Reddit Baltimore and Glassdoor had already warned of UA's aggressive, alpha culture. Commenters described it as a clique of "high school quarterbacks and cheerleading captains" and "Google for jocks." My athletic background — squash, swimming, soccer — didn't earn their respect; only elite UA-endorsed athletes might have.

In November 2018, a *Wall Street Journal* exposé revealed UA reimbursed strip club visits, limousines and gambling for executives and athletes, a practice most firms had long banned. Apparently, UA's idea of "team bonding" was more suited to a Vegas bachelor party than a Baltimore boardroom

The Washington Post quoted a professor noting this reflected a cultural "blind spot." The WSJ also reported women were chosen for a Preakness-eve event at Kevin Plank's horse farm based on attractiveness, termed "stocking the pond."

Plank called the *WSJ* article "tough to read."

My April 2017 letter to him a year earlier had warned of UA employees' reckless behavior on the Harbor Connector water taxi, at the Cat's Eye Pub on the Fells waterfront, and at parties like those of the shoe designer tenants.

I urged mandatory off-hours responsibility training given the "reputational risk" of "really bad PR." The PR fallout was, in hindsight, a masterclass in what not to do. Had Plank heeded my letter — maybe he was busy with a last hurrah at the Scores strip club — or social media criticism, UA might have dodged the damaging publicity that hit alongside its business struggles.

Fueling the issues next door and the bad PR was Under Armour's "bro" culture, its frat-boy swagger, which may have also been a factor in generating uninspired products. By

2024, Yahoo Finance's Brian Sozzi criticized UA's decline, questioning how long stars with endorsement deals such as Steph Curry or The Rock would stay. He noted UA missed the super-shoe trend — advanced performance shoes for elite athletes — and lagged in quality compared to rivals. Sozzi highlighted upstart shoemakers Hoka and On outpacing UA's weak sneaker designs, implying my neighbors' work fell short.

Commenters on Sozzi's article and Reddit Baltimore called UA's products "ugly," unstylish and overpriced. They slammed an outdated aesthetic and toxic work environment, marked by harassment, drinking and a "douche frat bro" vibe. One likened UA's image to Marvel's vengeful and dark Punisher character, reflected in tense, unappealing models on its website and garish products like a red Steph Curry shoe.

UA's iconic 2003 "Protect This House" ad energized jocks but fostered an "Us-vs.-Them" mindset. Rewatching it years later, I saw how its locker-room rallying cry bred entitlement in the UA tenants. They acted like they owned the place, clashing with me, a longtime homeowner, each of us feeling like the "home team." In our turf war, my own rallying cry was, "Can You Keep It Down?"

Noise and stress disorders

Rowhouse living grew unbearable for me each weekend with the noise from Under Armour tenants, highlighting how closely packed homes amplify clashing lifestyles. And how bad corporate vibes don't always stay in the boardroom.

Thoughtful neighbors like the Johns Hopkins researchers on the other side of my rowhome were a contrast to these self-proclaimed alphas who treated every interaction like a showdown. The Hopkins guys politely mentioned to me that they would be having a dinner party — hoping it wouldn't be a disturbance, as if their cheerful backyard chatter could ever rival the UA tenants' midnight basketball tournaments, which had swept the championship for Upper Fells Point's loudest nuisance.

I would have rallied more neighbors against their parties, but many slept in quieter back rooms. Or they weren't as noise sensitive. Philosopher Arthur Schopenhauer called noise a particular torture for thinkers, disrupting thought — a pain less felt by uncomplicated souls. Psychologists note highly sensitive people are noise-averse, and we risk being labeled a Karen for complaining, a title I was apparently auditioning for every time I stepped onto my roof in pajamas to negotiate peace at 1 a.m.

Options were grim: Sell my home, ignore the racket, or leave during parties, risking unwitnessed property damage. In hindsight, my sensitivity meant perhaps I should have surrendered and departed. While I outlasted the Under Armour bros, a more peaceful life was beginning to beckon.

The Providence Noise Project declares "noise is the new smoking," citing its harm to sleep, stress and heart health. Police rarely enforce quiet laws effectively, and violators exploit this.

Triggers like loud music or car horns plagued our area, alongside the police helicopter's thwap-thwap-thwap. In 2005, the chopper directly overhead startled a new kitten I got from a shelter in quiet Annapolis, and reminded me of how much background noise I was subject to. Noise denialists claim cities are inherently loud, justifying more noise.

Despite Under Armour's "Protect This House" ethos, these tenants didn't protect our community. If they were more mature, these strapping young men could have been a godsend, maybe even starting a neighborhood watch that doubled as a fitness boot camp — though I suspect their version of "protection" would've involved flagrant fouls on seniors instead.

The charm of the Upper Fells Point I first encountered was a subtle, quirky street symphony, harness bells on an arabber's horse or the Orioles on AM radio. The Under Armour bros hooping at all hours drowned out these nostalgic notes carried by harbor breezes. With less stump game and more stories swapped on our abutting decks about their work as shoe designers, they could have been a bridge to the community for their wayward company. That free throw was missed.

Part III. The Outliers

Stephen, Kim, Marilyn and Freddie

My first 15 years in Baltimore felt like an extended honeymoon, shattered in 2002 by the Dawson family tragedy, signaling trouble in Charm City. And the 2007 Zach Sowers attack, just a few neighborhoods east, hit closer to home. Were these isolated horrors or harbingers of decline? Could my neighborhood escape their shadow?

The fates of four figures — Stephen Pitcairn, Kim Leto, Marilyn Mosby and Freddie Gray — and events in the lives of each from 2010 to 2023 shed light on these questions.

The best known is likely Freddie Gray. In 2015, Gray, a 25-year-old, died from a neck injury sustained in police custody, sparking riots and accelerating Baltimore's population decline. The riots attracted international attention.

But my own focus was firmly on Johns Hopkins researcher Stephen Pitcairn and bartender Kim Leto. If the Dawsons and Sowers tragedies had ended my honeymoon, with Pitcairn and Leto, the possibility of divorce began to take shape. Their murders signaled a growing threat to Baltimore's law-abiding residents. And they were creeping closer to me.

What happened to Pitcairn sent shockwaves through Charles Village, the city and even the state, and played some role in driving 15,000 residents away in the following year, a bigger exodus even than after the Freddie Gray riots.

'I feel safe with you'

At around 11 p.m. on July 25, 2010, Stephen Pitcairn was walking to his home in Charles Village from Baltimore's Penn Station.

The 23-year-old was a friendly, thoughtful and bright individual, who treated his lab mates to his eclectic musical taste. He learned Japanese during a year studying stem cells in Japan. As a child, he played the piano, took apart telescopes, was riveted by bats and iguanas. As he matured, he constantly looked for opportunities to volunteer and mentor.

Many in his orbit thought he was going to be a phenomenal force in breast cancer research.

Stephen was returning from a visit to New York with his sisters. He was on his iPhone with his mother, Gwen, telling her about the visit. He asked his mother to continue the conversation until he got home. He told her, "I always feel so safe when you're on the phone with me."

But his distraction and visible iPhone made him a target. Johns Hopkins advises students against walking alone at night, but it's unclear if researchers such as Stephen also received this advice.

As a former Penn Station commuter, I wouldn't have walked his route alone after sunset. As he neared the safer heart of Charles Village, walking along St. Paul Street, two career criminals, John Wagner and Lavelva Merritt, followed him. They had planned a robbery earlier at their apartment nearby, telling their roommates that they would look for someone who appeared distracted. From their lookout in a bar, they spotted Stephen exiting a Bolt bus at Penn Station, tailed him for eight blocks on St. Paul, and attacked in the quiet 2600 block.

Had Stephen known street-safety strategies, he might have avoided walking alone at night, unarmed, on a quiet block, distracted by his phone – a risky combination.

"Much was said at the time about Stephen on his cell phone and how unwise that was," poet and Charles Village resident Shirley J. Brewer noted in an email to me. "I agree, but here are some thoughts. Stephen's bus was late getting in to Penn Station from NYC. It was a gorgeous summer evening, still warm at 11 p.m. with a perfect full moon. Stephen called his mom from the bus stop. She suggested he take a taxi.

"But he'd been cooped up on a bus for several hours and the evening air was a balm. Stephen had a ritual with talking to his mom when on a long walk. It was a way to stay connected. They were very close. The walk to Charles Village was only about a mile. It wasn't wise considering it was Baltimore. But Stephen was used to Florida and Kalamazoo."

Indeed, Pitcairn's focus on his mother made him a target, his warmth taken for vulnerability by Wagner and Merritt.

The pair confronted him, demanding money. Gwen overheard her son offer his wallet, followed by a hateful "Shut up!" and sounds of violence. Wagner stabbed Stephen in the left ventricle, and Merritt punched him in the head and took his iPhone, disconnecting Gwen's call.

Neighbor Reggie Higgins, witnessing from his window, saw Stephen collapse and called 911. "Hang in there, the ambulance is coming soon, you're going to make it," Higgins told the young researcher, holding Stephen as he whispered "Mom." Medics rushed Stephen to Johns Hopkins, but he was pronounced dead at 12:05 a.m.

Wagner and Merritt sprinted to their apartment on Maryland Avenue. Wagner told Merritt, "I think I stabbed him twice. I think I hurt this white boy pretty bad."

They took off their bloody clothes and cleaned the knife. Reality set in. Shaken by the amount of blood they'd witnessed at the scene, Wagner began sobbing. On one level, his tears were absurd; what did he think would happen when he stabbed a man? On another level, the reality of Stephen's murder was not a TV drama or a video game, it was a nightmare and it was real. Merritt believed that Wagner came to realize what he'd done was wrong.

"All that over a phone, I didn't mean to do it," Wagner said. The statement is baffling, did he mean to just wave the knife around menacingly, but the knife somehow landed in a victim's heart?

"I think I stabbed him twice ... that was a lot of blood." Merritt told Wagner not to worry, that "he's going to make it." Wagner had a second episode wracked by tears.

These were the crocodile tears of a cold-blooded killer feigning regret in the immediate aftermath ... tears that evaporated quickly as he moved on to using Stephen's stolen credit card for drug money.

As his chilling, emotionless denial at trial and sentencing ("I didn't do it") made clear, there was no true remorse, only the actions of a vicious predator who stalked Stephen for blocks and made the deliberate choice to escalate a robbery into murder over a phone and wallet.

The worst finds the best

A total of 44 "Outliers," law-abiding victims in Baltimore' homicide tallies from 1995 to the present, made varied contributions to the world around them, but it was the scientists — Pitcairn, along with Peter Marvit and Molly Macauley — who were particular losses.

Former Hopkins president William C. Richardson said that "of the thousands of students, [Pitcairn] stands out in my mind as the most complete person," after crossing paths with Stephen at Kalamazoo College in Michigan. "He was just an extraordinary young man."

Emily Pitcairn, Stephen's sister, weighed the toll exacted. "Our whole family has been shattered. The family I used to have isn't there anymore."

A fellow economics major at Kalamazoo, Julia Anderle, said, "It is so unjust. He was the one (in our class) who had the most potential."

Did criminals like Wagner and Merritt target not just distracted victims, but those like Pitcairn, whose talent and promise shone brightly in Baltimore's gloom?

Gwen Pitcairn noted Wagner's hateful tone, and the senseless stabbing suggests sociopathy, possibly rooted in childhood trauma or simply evil, as some psychologists concluded about serial killer John Wayne Gacy.

WBAL host Ron Smith, in his essay "Not All Murders Are Equal," questioned why Stephen was killed despite complying with the robbers, suggesting impulsiveness or malevolence. Maryland Comptroller Peter Franchot was haunted, unable to fathom why Stephen, talking to his mom, wasn't permitted to survive after surrendering his belongings. Smith addressed racial critiques, noting that unlike drug-related black-on-black homicides, Stephen's murder stood out for his promise, regardless of race.

Poet Shirley J. Brewer, living near the crime scene, wrote 13 poems about Stephen's death, reflecting the deep scar it left on Charles Village, much like how Zach Sowers' killing shook Highlandtown and Canton.

Did you feel anything
when you took my life?

Your blade broke through
skin and muscle, tore my young heart. ...

You carried away my wallet, my phone —
possessions I had already offered.

I imagine your hearts
black canyons unable to bear

the lightness you heard in my voice
as I talked to my mom.

Brewer may have figured out exactly what enraged Wagner — the happy mother-and-son bond overheard as he stalked his prey. Her poems, daily visits to the tree where

Stephen's spirit left his body, and community vigils kept Stephen's memory alive, a quiet defiance against the city's traumas.

"There was a kindness in his eyes," Brewer told the *City Paper*. "He was such a handsome kid. He was only 23 and had his whole life in front of him. He wanted to find a cure for cancer."

Brewer attended Wagner's trial and met Stephen's family. Wagner faced the Pitcairns in court and refused to take responsibility, Brewer recalled. "He said something to the effect that he was sorry for their loss, but that the real killer was still out there. I was disgusted."

Brewer and Good Samaritan Reggie Higgins met at Pitcairn's memorial, and became and remained friends. Their friendship over the years is remarkable, and it speaks volumes about the ripples of humanity that persist even amid such loss.

The body count

From 1993 to the present, Baltimore has seen a disturbing trend of 44 innocent individuals, including at least eight in science, technology and finance, killed, often during routine street robberies. Beyond Sowers and Pitcairn, as many as seven such "Outlier" murders have occurred annually, with career criminals, some as young as 14, targeting the city's promising newcomers, devastating families. Where other cities might suffer one or two such high-profile tragedies, Baltimore has dozens.

Letters to *The Baltimore Sun* expressed despair: Therapist Myra MacCuaig described a "seething monster" beneath Baltimore's charm, claiming victims like Pitcairn, while Parkville resident Philip Kerr lamented career criminals like John Wagner, who, despite a long record, faced little jail time.

Sun columnist Dan Rodricks noted Wagner's recent charges of robbing a gas station were dropped, giving him the freedom to roam the streets and kill. Pitcairn's death, like Sowers', damaged Baltimore's reputation, with the news spreading around the country. Criticism mounted against State's Attorney Patricia Jessamy for failing to lock up violent criminals, leading to her election loss. Safety fears deterred many in the medical field who rejected Johns Hopkins despite its prestige — I witnessed this first hand among potential medical residents on site visits, including a married couple from Alabama that stayed with me. In a roof deck conversation, they admitted their qualms about coming to Hopkins Medical.

Zach Sowers' neighbor

After Pitcairn's murder shook Charles Village, another tragedy in 2014 struck closer to our world in Southeast Baltimore.

Kimberly Leto, 51, was a popular bartender at O'Donnell's Pub in Canton who lived on South Ellwood Avenue, three blocks from the former address of Zach and Anna Sowers.

Friends described Kim, petite and blonde, as always smiling and laughing. Her warmth drew people close but may have provoked the resentment of two sullen teens.

She was sleeping on the sofa in her rowhome in the Patterson Park neighborhood on Jan. 31, 2014, when a 16-year-old and a 14-year-old pushed a chair up to an unsecured kitchen window in the rear of the structure.

Awakening, Kim may have recognized the 14-year-old from a home invasion months earlier. During the followup attack, they smothered her with a pillow and stabbed her 11 times, stealing change and electronics. She was found dead in a pool of blood.

Her murder shocked the community. The *Baltimore Sun* called it a "burglary gone wrong," prompting MacCuaig in a second letter to *Sun* editors to criticize society's tendency to excuse brutality.

Friends, like Kevin Carrick, questioned why the teens killed her instead of just stealing what they wanted and departing. Following Sowers' death by seven years, the murder deepened Southeast Baltimore's unease. The 14-year-old killer casually mentioned his daughter at his hearing, while the 16-year-old's lawyer suggested mental incompetence.

In 2014, as well Leto's murder, *Baltimore Sun* editor Jon Fogg was brutally attacked 10 minutes to the southeast near his Canton home.

A 20-year-old asked for a cigarette, then threw Fogg down, smashed his head with a brick, and stole his car, keys, laptop and wallet. Fogg survived with six skull fractures, lost teeth, broken fingers, a lisp and lasting fear.

Keeping a list

The murder of a middle-aged, harmless woman a mile east of my house was distressing. Leto's South Ellwood Avenue home would be in my field of vision whenever I ventured by bicycle to the library, the Peruvian chicken joint or the grocery store in Highlandtown.

That regular people with no ties to crime could be killed as they cooperated with a robber or slept on the sofa spelled personal danger to me. I opened an electronic Stickie note on my Mac Mini computer, where I did most of my writing. As of 2015, it read:

BALTIMORE ATTACKS
2007 Zach Sowers
2010 Stephen Pitcairn
2014 Kim Leto
2015 Robbie Ponsi

The combination punch of Sowers and Pitcairn broke through the armor of city living, particularly for neighbors, friends, family and colleagues, and more sensitive residents felt the accumulating losses.

My list would continue to grow over time. I thought of these victims as "the Outliers," homicide victims with a radically different profile to typical criminal-on-criminal slayings. These Outlier homicides showed Baltimore was lethally unsafe, with simple muggings escalating to deadly attacks. Risks surged, as these slayings evolved from rare to as many as seven annually.

Uproar and futility

Outlier murders left Baltimoreans desperate for solutions. A vigil for Pitcairn drew 100 Charles Village residents, where resident Marc Unger expressed community distress, shouting at city officials, "We live in fear!"

A packed Highlandtown church meeting after Leto's death proffered the same ideas that had been raised ad nauseam — tougher prosecution, more police patrols, mentorships — but officials offered no concrete plans.

The core issue was sociopathic criminals killing for trivial gains. As well, the *Maryland Daily Record* criticized the failure to jail Pitcairn's killer, John Wagner, despite prior crimes, highlighting a justice system letting criminals roam free. Mayor Stephanie Rawlings-Blake, sworn in days after Leto's murder, avoided tough action, prioritizing the city's image and economy, like the mayor in *Jaws* ignoring a great white shark terrorizing swimmers. Honesty from Rawlings-Blake about how residents needed to focus on self-defense and home security ("Get a dog and a taser, people!") could have better served residents, given the city's apparent refusal to lock up killers. Instead she focused on rocking Under Armour ball caps and other sassy fashion pieces at press conferences while the city deteriorated a notch at a time.

In roof deck conversations, I told visitors as we looked over city lights that Baltimore could be America's best little city if you could magically eliminate criminals. They were a depopulation wrecking ball. Despite its dazzling moments — Harbor light shows, visiting tall ships, community theater and Blue Angel flyovers — after the murders of Sowers, Pitcairn, Leto and Ponsi, Baltimore felt like a slow-motion hellscape.

During my Baltimore honeymoon, "safe" areas existed where muggings, not murders, were the risk. But from 2007 to 2015, Zach and Kim (Highlandtown), Stephen (Charles Village) and Robbie (Waverly) died in decent neighborhoods, signaling that fatal risks for the law-abiding citizenry lurked everywhere.

A rogue prosecutor

The election of soft Baltimore prosecutors worsened the city's crime crisis. Patricia Jessamy lost in 2010, partly due to the Sowers and Pitcairn murders, replaced by Gregg Bernstein.

Enter Marilyn Mosby. In 2014, Mosby ousted Bernstein, promising to jail repeat offenders. Instead, she adopted lenient policies — ignoring low-level crimes, offering soft plea deals and clashing with police — fueling a homicide surge from 211 annually (2014) to an average of 333 a year during her 2015-2023 tenure. A 2022 study by Sean Kennedy of the Maryland Public Policy Institute suggests her lenient plea-deal policies explained up to 79 percent of the city's homicides, such as when Jason Billingsley, a repeat sex offender released early in 2022, killed tech CEO Pava LaPere. By rights he should have still been in prison serving a full term.

Critics, including *The Baltimore Sun* editorial board and prominent restaurant owner Tony Foreman, as well as family members of dead Outliers, accused Mosby of neglecting victims like Robbie Ponsi and 2017 homicide victim Jim Forrester while prioritizing personal ventures, like flipping Florida homes. Her 2018 re-election, despite rising crime, relied on strong Democratic machine support.

In 2002, Mayor O'Malley had termed the firebombing of the Dawson family over drug "snitching" as Baltimore's "Alamo," and kept a photo of the children on his desk.

In contrast, Mosby never seemed to take responsibility for the more than 2,600-plus homicides under her watch. No pictures of Robbie Ponsi, Molly Macauley, Marcus Edwards or Andras Horvath, 2016's Outliers, were displayed on her desk. She wasn't even *at* her desk. Instead she was in Long Boat Key in Florida, flipping vacation homes, or on travel junkets to Africa. A Baltimore City inspector general's report on Mosby's travel and expenses showed that she was out of town for 144 days in 2018 and 2019. Seeing her mismanagement, during her tenure 55,000 residents also left town — for good.

Three and a half months after Mosby was sworn in, 2015 bought another trauma to the city.

Freddie Gray, hurt after an arrest for knife possession, died seven days later, triggering Baltimore's worst riots since 1968. The last thing Baltimore needed, as it reeled from homicides in "safe" areas, was juvenile gangs stomping on cars of Orioles fans attempting to flee downtown.

During the riots, my hairdressers' compact, not-fancy salon was broken into and the cash tray stolen. The staff shrugged off what was to me an alarming symptom of civil decay — a warning signal to pull up stakes — as just part of doing business in a rough city.

Packs of juveniles roamed my neighborhood on their way to ransack shops on Broadway, Eastern Avenue and Fleet Street. The sight was so alarming that a good friend and neighbor, who watched the excited teens race by her front door on Bank Street, left her home for a hotel in Annapolis. She moved away shortly thereafter.

"I loved the culture, the art, the focus on learning, and the people and the water and everything," she reflected, "but I'll never go back."

She was one of nearly 38,000 residents to move out in the decade from 2011-2020.

In March 2020, I wrote an Amazon review of the book *Five Days: The Fiery Reckoning of an American City*, by Wes Moore, later to become Maryland's governor. I introduced myself as a lifelong Marylander, a Baltimore resident for 33 years, and a former *Baltimore Sun* and *Washington Post* journalist. "I've been to the pivotal New Shiloh church mentioned in *Five Days* for elementary school graduations," I wrote. "I ordered this book because I and many others have witnessed a profound and tragic deterioration in the city since the 2015 riots."

My review continued as follows.

'Five Days'

This book digs into varied perspectives on the five days surrounding the riots after Freddie Gray's death — that of a police supervisor, a baseball executive, a public defender, a masked man who cut firehoses near the burning CVS, and many others. I've read numerous accounts about the riots, and this material seems new, thorough and varied.

The book overlooks two critical angles: a skeptical view of liberal narratives that have harmed Baltimore and a deeper probe into what truly caused Freddie Gray's death.

First, re: liberal narratives. Gray's mother raised him and his twin sister without the benefit of a father in the home. Given her poverty and addiction, she could not properly care for and house her children, nor did Baltimore fulfill its duty to protect its citizens with a properly functioning housing department.

So the children ended up with lead poisoning. The mother's landlord didn't abate the property's lead either, but if he had, he likely would have raised the rents outside the slight finances of this family. We have failures here at the individual and government levels that are vaguely ascribed to structural racism.

Second, this book also lacks interviews to determine **what really happened to Freddie Gray**. Did he have a fragile neck from a childhood accident? Did he fracture his neck banging on the bolts of the police van's back door, self-harming as lead poisoning victims are wont to do?

A murky tragedy

No discussions or interviews are presented with Caesar Goodson Jr., the van driver, who may be able the only person who may know what really happened. It's quite possible that this was one instance when the cops actually did not harm a person in custody.

I've watched the video of Freddie's arrest a half-dozen times or more, where he appears to be wailing in pain and dragging his feet. It looks to me that the arresting officers carry him gently to the van.

So either he was beaten very early during his apprehension before the cell-phone cameras rolled, something happened off camera during the van ride, or he had a self-inflicted injury. Or he was suffering from an acute case of "jail-itis" — loud complaining of non-existent aches and pains at the beginning of the ride down to Central Booking. By the end of the ride, police discovered him unresponsive and not breathing.

Knowing what happened to him is key to coming up with a conclusion as to whether the rioters were somewhat justified in responding to bona fide police brutality, or if Freddie was another guy with jail-itis who may have self-injured.

If the latter, the 2015 riots inflicted extraordinary and lasting damage to Charm City without any redeeming moral benefit. 2015 unraveled the city's laborious struggle to repair earlier devastation from the 1968 riots. Much as the city steadily emptied after the '68 riots, the annual loss of residents zoomed from 6,000 before the riots to 10,000 after.

There is nothing noble about rioting if the police involved, for a change, were not a factor in Freddie's death. And that has never been clarified.

Looting paper towels

The riots are recast in this book, as they are by young social justice warriors in Baltimore, as an "uprising." This framing attempts to legitimize the stealing of $1 rolls of paper towels from the Penn North CVS, as part of a justified response to long-suffered civil rights violations.

This sort of framing may seem justified to the authors, but the images of looters coming out of CVS brandishing paper towels sickened a number of my black friends and family members. They observed correctly that there is no one in Baltimore who lacks the wherewithal to either earn $1 from working an odd job, or to borrow from family or friends. Further, that burned-up CVS provided essential household items, prescriptions and most of all jobs to the underserved area of Penn North. Some "uprising."

Four miles from l'affair Freddie, down the street from my home, my hairdresser's shop was broken into, glass front door smashed, and the cash drawer taken. Are we to take this as a justified action, a call for justice?

Dozens of pharmacies across town were similarly hit and prescription drugs lifted for resale.

Right after the worst night of riots, I overheard jocular accounts from a pair of giddy, unashamed looters in the checkout line of the Harbor East Whole Foods. “Hey, did you get yourself some new sneakers Tuesday?” one asked the other with a knowing chuckle.

This after I’d seen an interview with the proprietor of Sports Mart on Exeter Street, broken hearted, having seen his regular customers breaking in and stealing on the security cameras, his business destroyed.

This is not an "uprising," this is societal rot. And it was much much worse than it was portrayed in the media or as dismissed by President Obama, on April 28, 2015, as “a handful of criminals and thugs who tore up the place.”

Protecting the rich

The bands of youths devastated many retail establishments far from Penn North, where the riots ignited. Protestors moved southeast, to Mount Vernon and then Fells Point, leveling destruction more widespread than the media at the time indicated. Harbor East was only spared due to the National Guard encircling its ritzy buildings, and Canton Crossing by private security measures.

There are no good guys here. Turning our attention away from the looters, firehose cutters and other miscreants, we find no better among the Baltimore police. They have a sordid record of beatings and violating the civil rights of residents that just about eclipses the misdeeds of the criminal element of the city population. It's barely a racial matter anymore, as depicted by a heinous 2018 video of a black officer, Arthur Williams, savagely beating a black pedestrian, DaShawn McGrier, on Monument Street.

Five Days favorably mentions Elijah Cummings, then serving in the U.S. House of Representatives for Maryland’s 7th congressional district, who is as big a part of the problem as every other leadership failure in the city, including the past three mayors with their corruption and ineptitude. Sure Cummings shows up at New Shiloh and speechifies. Meanwhile *The New York Times* reports $1 billion in aid over the decades to Sandtown-Winchester, a troubled area of the city flanking the riot-torn zone. Where might these wheelbarrows of cash be? It certainly isn't visible in that neighborhood in Cummings' district.

So, while *Five Days* doesn't dig to the bottom of that distressing chapter, we still have a good deal of material to ponder as dug up by these reporters. A compelling depiction relates how outside agitators linked to the riots in Ferguson, Missouri, hijacked a peaceful march to Camden Yards and turned it violent, to the puzzlement and mounting horror of native Baltimoreans. The damage done to this city by these outside agitators is incalculable.

No one whose car was jumped on by a stomping pack of juveniles ever returns to an Orioles game, or downtown or anywhere in the city, if they have any sense of self-preservation. It's an impossible level of anarchy to tolerate for anyone in search of a peaceful life who only wants to watch Dem O's play.

Page 225 chilled me with a quote from Cecilia Partee, the wife of a police official. Her father was a cop, and she wondered "if the police force in 2015 was different from the one she remembered growing up around." She also wondered if Baltimore had changed irrevocably. She's right, and that's a shame. The events of April 2015 choked the life out of a city that was fighting to regain its footing.

***

At the end of the review, I wrote, "Wave it goodbye and sigh as Baltimore recedes in the rearview mirror." Which I would do a couple of weeks later.

Few cities could endure two major riots in two generations. The 2015 riots triggered or coincided with a downward spiral of incompetent leadership — a trajectory that, if graphed, would resemble a treacherous ski slope.

Corruption, chaotic schools and rampant crime eroded the city's ability to produce another William Donald Schaefer, the mayor from 1971 to 1987 who fought decline with passion and some success. With only faltering attempts to turn itself around, like $1 billion in investment in the Baltimore Peninsula (a ghost town at the time of writing), the city struggles to reverse its troubled path.

An army of ghosts

Marilyn Mosby overcharged six police officers in the Freddie Gray case with serious crimes like second-degree depraved-heart murder, implying extreme indifference to life. All charges failed by mistrial, acquittals or drops.

A 2017 U.S. Department of Justice report found no evidence of excessive force or a "rough ride," though Gray wasn't seat-belted, possibly due to hostile crowds gathering. Mosby's whacky approach, over-prosecuting cops while under-prosecuting criminals, boosted her 2018 re-election but caught up with her in 2022, when she lost the Democratic primary.

In 2024, Mosby's convictions for mortgage fraud and perjury led to home detention. Her bid for a presidential pardon from Joe Biden, citing racial persecution, failed.

Her tenure saw 2,500 murders, many enabled by her leniency, as she prioritized personal ventures over justice. Baltimore's art community honored victims through exhibits such as *Stains on the Sidewalk* and *Murder Ink* readings, reflecting the toll of her policies.

Of Stephen, Kim, Freddie and Mosby, only Mosby survived 2015. Stephen and Kim were part of an army of thousands of ghosts lost to homicides. In a paradox, Mosby had ordered police to crack down on drug selling and loitering on the corners where Freddie hung out a few days before his arrest. That led to a chain of events that hurt the young man, even if a rough ride did not. It seemed that everything Mosby touched turned out badly.

Counting the Outliers

There's no rhyme or reason why criminals take a cell phone from some people and go away, and take a cell phone from others and put someone in hospital.

— Phil Lassahn, former robbery detective, Baltimore Police Department

Within Baltimore's soaring homicide tolls lurked the atypical killings of Joel Lee, Zach Sowers, Stephen Pitcairn, Kim Leto, Robbie Ponsi and others. These "Outlier" cases — law-abiding citizens with no criminal ties, usually killed by strangers — revealed a chilling subtext to the city's violence.

Unlike Baltimore's typical homicides involving criminal victims, Outliers are regular folks with no criminal record. These killings of non-criminals, often by teenagers or opportunists, destabilize entire communities. Overall, they comprised about 1 percent of victims from 1993 through 2024.

These 44 law-abiding citizens have rarely been studied as a group despite their impact. Their demise has driven countless residents to flee, spotlighting the city's danger to those who play by the rules and must live among others who don't. While high-profile cases like Pitcairn's drew national attention, most received fleeting local coverage, leaving critical questions unanswered. Each Outlier's death is a confounding tragedy, begging for deeper investigation.

Why did a stranger bypass others in a Catonsville liquor store in 2008 to slit the throat of Aysha Ring, a charismatic young educator, in a brutal attack?

In 2013, who shot Alysia "Nick" Strickland and Taewon Tuck in the head, leaving the close interracial couple in a burning car near Mondawmin Mall? Firefighters, stunned to find bodies, got no answers. The media in Roanoke, Virginia, mourned Strickland, a top student whose attorney father defended *Hustler* publisher Larry Flynt and whose mother, a judge, investigated the Virginia Tech shooting, yet Baltimore offered no solid tie-ins to Nick's high-profile parents.

How did the killers of nine Outliers — Glen Footman, Peter Marvit, Molly Macauley, Marcus Edwards, Johnny Tobash, Wadell Tate, Jesika Tetlow, Henri Jones and Mary Lou Schuman — vanish without a trace? At best, grainy gas station footage or doorbell cams captured fleeting shadows.

While local TV and online outlets like the Baltimore Banner and Baltimore Witness cover Outliers consistently, legacy print media often downplay these cases, perhaps to stem panic and population loss. Or perhaps they simply fail to see the larger picture.

In 2024, with homicides down to 201, four Outliers still died, doubling their share to 2 percent of victims. However, reductions in total homicides won't reassure residents or convince them not to leave, if law-abiding residents remain targets.

"Overkilling" — excessive, gruesome violence — further erodes confidence, as residents fear not just death but pain and desecration.

Somber turning points

Early Outlier murders marked grim milestones. Joel Lee, a Korean computer science student and the first Asian victim, was shot in Northeast Baltimore despite complying with robbers. Zach Sowers, a Johns Hopkins employee and the first white victim, was attacked on his doorstep in a "safe" neighborhood.

The killing of Pitcairn, a second Hopkins employee, sparked statewide attention due to his brutal death while on the phone with his mother and given that lenient judges freed a repeat offender. Sowers lived near Johns Hopkins' medical center and Pitcairn dwelled close to the undergraduate campus three miles to the northwest, threatening the giant employer's safe zones.

Leto was the first of four Outliers killed in a home invasion and the first of five hospitality worker victims. Aysha Ring was actually the first female Outlier, her 2008 death underreported. She died of a gruesome neck slashing, targeted by a stranger. The 2016 death of Ponsi, the 15th Outlier, who was stabbed by a group of eight teens, was frightening for its brutality and its indication that the toll of innocents was mounting.

As the total rose to at least 44 through 2024, these patterns underscored a growing threat, as Outlier killings shifted from rare tragedies to a hauntingly regular occurrence.

More and more frequent

Outlier murders revealed chilling patterns: targeted were five Morgan State University students, two Cristo Rey High School affiliates (Ring and Fabian Sánchez-González), eight professionals, two grandmothers (Cheryl McCormack and Mary Lou Schuman), and four gay men (Glen Footman, Alex Ulrich, Larry Peterson and Chesley Patterson). While often random, occurring either indoors or on the street, most victims were middle-aged, with exceptions like 97-year-old Wardell Tate, 18-year-old Jesika Tetlow, and 8-month-old Reese Bowman.

What did all the Outliers have in common? They were ordinary people doing ordinary things, watching TV in their living room (Jordan Taylor), walking to or from their car

(Peter Marvit, Manuel Luis, Chesley Patterson, Henri Jones), sleeping on the sofa (Kim Leto), working retail jobs (Jose Abreu, Carmen Rodriguez, Fabian Sánchez-González). And they were not involved in criminal activity.

Outlier killings surged, crushing hopes of safer days when robbery victims survived. From one case (Joel Lee) between 1993 and 2006, the average rose annually to one (2007–10), two (2011–14), and nearly three under Marilyn Mosby (2015–22). Under Ivan Bates (2023–24), four Outliers have perished yearly.

Outliers by state's attorney

Mosby	23
Bates	8
Bernstein	8
Jessamy	4
Simms	1
Total	44

These brutal attacks — often by sociopaths wielding knives or bricks, or using their bare hands to strangle victims — terrified residents, spurring many to flee. A 2022 study by the Maryland Public Policy Institute suggests nearly 80 percent of Baltimore's homicides, including Outlier cases, were preventable with tougher sentencing, a failure tied to lenient policies by Mosby and other prosecutors.

Decent Baltimoreans lived in fear of a gruesome death — on their front steps, at work, in their living room, at baby day care, or even on their apartment rooftop — often comforted in their last moments only by a traumatized Good Samaritan. Lenient plea deals failed to deter sociopaths like Trayvon Ramos, John Wagner and Prince Green. Outliers often were not even in the "wrong place at the wrong time." Kim Leto was killed sleeping on her sofa, and Jordan Taylor was shot through his front door.

Kim Leto's 2014 murder sparked a chilling realization: a pattern of innocent victims, many near my home or workplace, was emerging. I began tracking Outliers —

Baltimore 'Outliers,' 1993-2024

Law-abiding victims of homicides killed by strangers, indicated by Baltimore City state's attorney in office

Year Victims

State's attorney Stuart O. Simms (1)

1993 Joel Lee

... Patricia C. Jessamy (4)

2007 Zach Sowers
2008 Aysha Ring, Glen Footman
2010 Stephen Pitcairn

... Gregg L. Bernstein (8)

2011 Joseph Calo
2012 Alex Ulrich, Larry Peterson, Peter Marvit
2013 Alysia Nicole "Nick" Strickland, Taewon "Tae" Tuck
2014 Jose Abreu, Kimberly Leto

... Marilyn J. Mosby (23)

2015 Kendal Fenwick
2016 Robert "Robbie" Ponsi, Molly Macauley, Marcus Edwards, Andras Horvath
2017 Reese Bowman, Sebastian Dvorak, Wadell Tate, Alex Wroblewski III, Jim Forrester, Johnny Tobash
2018 Timothy Moriconi
2019 Kevon Dix, Manuel Luis, David Caldwell, Jordan Taylor, Carmen Rodriguez
2022 Chesley "Chesco" Patterson, Cheryl McCormack, Timothy Reynolds, Victor Malabayabas, Jesika Tetlow, Henri Jones

... Ivan Bates (8)

2023 Fabian Sánchez-González, Darrell Benner, Pava Marie LaPere, Anton Kancir
2024 Mary Lou Schuman, Carl Bodine, David Philpot, Cameran Holt

Sowers (2007), Pitcairn (2010), Leto, and later Ponsi and Macauley (2016) — in an electronic note on my computer, saving news links and later adding missed cases. When Marilyn Mosby became state's attorney in 2015, Outlier murders surged, prompting deeper research for this chapter to uncover additional victims.

The Leto murder offered a moment of insight: Something bad was afoot. Then a pattern of other victims revealed itself. These were moments of realizing the risk is real to anyone still living in Baltimore, and the post-traumatic stress of this realization persists even though I have left.

Finding the Outliers

This list of Outlier homicides comes from research on *The Baltimore Sun*'s "Baltimore Homicides" interactive website, news archives, and annual TV station memorials, covering 4,967 homicides from 2007 to 2024.

Limited information often made identifying every single Outlier difficult, as many victims lack news coverage, obituaries or photos, with local TV memorial lists using stock funeral candle images. The list is as complete as possible given these constraints. It may not list every Outlier, but it shows enough to indicate a trend and a problem.

I tracked many Outliers in real time via news reports. Seeking possible Outliers I'd missed, I examined the *Sun's* homicide database maps, focusing on low-crime areas such as the waterfront, Midtown and Northwest. Pushpin icons in the database provide victim details (name, date, race, gender, age, address, weapon), which I cross-checked with news articles to exclude cases involving petty arguments, drugs, domestic disputes or gang ties.

Outliers were victims unknown to their assailant or with professional ties (for example, at recovery houses, clinics or child-care facilities), not personal ties, with no evidence of criminal activity or late-night presence in drug-heavy areas. Some attacks, like those on Sowers, Pitcairn and Pava LaPere, were planned after stalking, while at least one, Glen Footman's 2008 murder, showed premeditation tied to bias against gays. Victims like Alex "Albo" Wroblewski and Andras Horvath were targeted impulsively after they displayed cash, and Robbie Ponsi's killer escalated a robbery to stabbing. Alex Ulrich and Larry Peterson, with nothing to give their would-be robber, were shot after a wisecrack provoked their assailant to return.

'Misdemeanor homicides'

A 2005 *New York Times* article noted that Baltimore posed little threat to residents who avoided criminal activity, even amid intense drug-related conflicts. Health Commissioner Peter Beilenson told the paper that the city was generally safe for those uninvolved in drug trafficking. That year, 90 percent of the 38 homicide victims had prior criminal records, with an average of eight arrests each, primarily linked to narcotics.

Police call these "misdemeanor homicides," reflecting detached humor about criminals killing criminals. Acting Deputy Police Commissioner Marcus Brown noted victims' records mirrored those of suspects. From 2015-22, Baltimore averaged 333 homicides annually, mostly tied to the drug trade (battles over territory, money disputes or robberies), petty conflicts escalating to ambushes, mistaken identity, domestic violence, murder-suicides, bar stabbings or gang shootings.

In Baltimore, "people kill because they're angry over a slight. Frustrated over a hard look. Pissed off because somebody talked to their girl. They kill and are killed for nothing," wrote former homicide detective Kelvin Sewell in *Why Do We Kill.*

In 1983, a Baltimore junior high schooler was killed over his Georgetown jacket, and in 1989, a 15-year-old in nearby Anne Arundel County died, targeted for having coveted Air Jordans. At the time, among my friends in Washington, D.C., there was shock and almost voyeuristic interest that such a thing was possible. Over time, as murders over trivial possessions, social media posts and relationship jealousy continued, shock lessened.

If not involved in a petty dispute, black victims were likely drug-involved, while some white victims died in domestic cases. Hispanic victims often faced gang-related shootings, such as a 1999 incident on my block of Ann Street, an execution slaying through a windshield, which didn't alarm neighbors as it seemed "intramural." Beilenson's claim of safety for non-criminal residents held until Zach Sowers' 2007 murder marked a shift.

Outlier clusters

Online link; Graphic by the author
https://beaumonde.net/fleeing-baltimore/

The map pins above mark the locations of Outlier homicides. These incidents are concentrated in middle-class, gentrified neighborhoods where Outliers are often perceived as easy targets. Key areas include Riverside, Federal Hill, the Inner Harbor and Canton, with a notable cluster in Fells Point, just south of my former residence.

This cluster, encompassing the losses of David Philpot, Chesley Patterson and Jim Forrester just blocks apart, underscores a friend's observation: "Crime doesn't stay in rough neighborhoods." The concentration in these gentrified areas highlights the city's failure to protect its middle-class residents, a pattern that felt increasingly suffocating near my former home.

Additional clusters appear east of Patterson Park and in Mount Vernon. In contrast, high-crime areas like West Baltimore, Cherry Hill and Sandtown-Winchester see fewer Outlier homicides, as murders there often involve criminal-on-criminal violence tied to score-settling or drugs.

Victim backgrounds

As time went on and bodies stacked up, patterns emerged in the backgrounds of the victims. The leading category was professionals in science, technology, engineering or finance, with eight victims. In fact, it is striking that there were only three blue-collar victims: Kendal Fenwick, a truck driver, Henri Jones, an aspiring electrician, and Cheryl McCormack, a food delivery driver.

Background	Number
Science, tech, engineering or finance *Sowers, Pitcairn, Marvit, Macauley, Moriconi, Reynolds, Malabayabas, LaPere*	8
Students *Lee, Strickland, Edwards, Tobash, Dix, Luis*	6
Restaurant, bartending, food delivery *Leto, Ponsi, Wroblewski, Dvorak, Patterson, McCormack*	6
Informal "mayor" of their community *Peterson, Wroblewski, Luis, Malabayabas, Philpot*	5
Johns Hopkins connection *Sowers, Pitcairn, LaPere, Macauley*	4
Musician, photographer, singer *Ulrich, Marvit, Ponsi, Forrester, Dix*	5
Gay *Footman, Ulrich, Peterson, Patterson*	4
Educator or coach *Ring, Footman, Taylor*	3
Slain at retail job *Abreu, Rodriguez, Sánchez-González*	3
Drug treatment, recovery center staff *Caldwell, Bodine*	2

Assailants often targeted perceived easy marks — white-collar workers, students, the elderly or homeless. Still, eight Outliers were athletic and if not ambushed, resisted: cyclist Robbie Ponsi, runner/ice skater Molly Macauley, rugby/basketball player Jonathan Tobash and soccer midfielder Alex Wroblewski III, baseball players Manuel Luis and Henri Jones (also a wrestler), fitness buff Timothy Moriconi, snowboarder Sebastian Dvorak and hiker and triathlete Pava LaPere.

A cluster of five Morgan State students (Alysia Strickland, Edwards, Tobash, Kevon Dix, Luis) and one Towson

University student (Lee) were attacked in Northeast Baltimore.

Six victims were bartenders, waiters, restaurant managers or on food deliveries, vulnerable as they moved through the city at night. Baltimore's colliding cultures of crime and cuisine put these workers at risk, though bartender Kim Leto was killed in a home invasion. Other clusters included musicians, educators, coaches and drug clinic staff.

At least five victims were community "mayors," informal leaders respected in their neighborhoods, their optimism and cheer possibly hitting their assailants the wrong way. Many of Baltimore's core economic engines — health and medical research, undergraduate and graduate education, a robust food scene — were devastated emotionally by these murders.

Outliers and assailants analysis

With at least 82 assailants for 44 victims, many attacks involved multiple perpetrators. In some cold cases, video evidence shows the number of assailants and may indicate race, while for others, such as Molly Macauley and Henri Jones, we can only say for certain there was at least one assailant.

Where the race of the assailant is known, 66 out of the 69, or 96 percent, are black. For 13 assailants, not seen in the area, apprehended nor captured on film, race is not known. Two white assailants emerged in 2024: Harley D. Frost, who stabbed his recovery house manager, and Timothy Clinedinst, who curb-stomped Fells Point resident David Philpot. One Hispanic assailant was among the three criminals charged in the 2024 murder of Cameran Holt.

Of the 44 Outlier victims, 31 (70 percent) are white — disproportionate to their 28 percent share of Baltimore's population averaged from 2007-24. The victims also include seven black, four Hispanic and two Asian individuals.

Race	Victim	Assailant
White	31	2
Black	7	66
Hispanic	4	1
Asian	2	0
Unknown	n.a.	13
Total	44	82

The prevalence of black assailants targeting white Outlier victims suggests robbers seek easy prey. An online commenter responding to a 2025 robbery in Fells Point openly stated that anyone presenting as an easy target would get what was coming to them.

"If you in fells point or fed hill and you are not ON POINT, stay yo ass in the house cuz some of you are just soft targets," the commenter stated. Similarly, the getaway driver for the murderer of Tim Moriconi in 2018 was told by her boyfriend to drive to Riverside, where they could find an easy victim.

There is some evidence that criminals view muggings as easier than even low-effort jobs. For instance, John Wagner targeted Pitcairn at Penn Station after dispassionately discussing with roommates how to spot vulnerable victims.

Street robberies, requiring less effort and risk in Baltimore's dysfunctional justice system than honest work, may reflect criminals making economic choices as rational actors. Promoting concealed carry for Baltimore residents could shift this calculus, deterring robbers by raising risks, potentially steering them toward jobs. This isn't about promoting violence but creating a negative deterrent.

This may be the only way short of martial law or sending in the National Guard to counter lenient juries, weak prosecutors and reduced policing post-Freddie Gray riots, and ultimately protecting law-abiding residents. However, two Outliers, Darrell Benner with a BB gun and Timothy Reynolds with a baseball bat, lost their lives to attackers who were armed and quick on the draw.

Resisting the assailants

In many Outlier homicides, whether victims resisted is unclear, especially in unwitnessed ambush shootings. Post-2016, some Outliers, aware that cooperation failed victims like Lee, Sowers and Pitcairn, fought back.

Robbie Ponsi, outnumbered 8-to-1 by aggressive teens, swung his bicycle to fend them off. Alex Wroblewski, days before his 2017 murder, vowed to resist after local robberies prompted conversation, as recalled by a chef colleague. Timothy Moriconi, killed in 2018 near the site of an earlier attempted robbery, had previously chased robbers to retrieve his phone.

Still, cooperation may improve survival odds: in 2023, Jeffrey Tyree of Canton followed the orders of robbers and survived, while his uncle Darrell Benner, intervening with a BB gun, was killed.

Tyree told WBAL-TV that he was moving his car when he was stopped at gunpoint. The robbers told him to empty his pockets and kick the items toward them. He instantly complied, stating, “Take my phone, my keys, my wallet, take it. I don't want it. I got babies to go home to. That's more important.”

Response to attack	Number
Resisted (2016-2023) *	13
Did not resist (1993-2014) **	5
Unknown	26

* *Ponsi, Horvath, Wroblewski, Forrester, Tobash, Moriconi, Luis, Taylor, Patterson, McCormack, Reynolds, Tetlow, Benner*
** *Lee, Sowers, Pitcairn, Abreu, Rodriguez*

Many of the vigils for victims decried gun violence, which claimed 29 of the 44 victims studied. But another 15 victims were killed by other means, with eight succumbing to knife attacks.

Weapon(s) used	Number
Firearm	29
Knife	8
Beating, stomping	2
Thrown onto street	2
Brick, beating, strangulation	1
Broken bottle	1
Suffocation with blankets	1

“Overkilling" — violence exceeding what’s needed to kill — occurred in at least eight Outlier cases: Leto, stabbed 11 times; Ponsi, 17 times; Alysa Nicole Strickland and Taewon Tuck, shot execution-style and left in a burning vehicle; Macauley, stabbed at least thrice; Jessika Tetlow, shot twice in the head; Timothy Reynolds, shot in the face, chest and three times in the back (four shots while down); and Pava LaPere, beaten with a brick and strangled.

The Good Samaritans

The lost lives reveal touching patterns. Five victims were comforted by Good Samaritans as they died, reflecting Baltimore’s better nature. Six were nearly home, and four were celebrating or nearing a birthday.

Time and space paired some of the victims and attested to the scale of the slaughter. In 2022, Cheryl McCormack and Chesley Patterson died two hours apart. Tuck and Strickland were killed together, and Alex Ulrich and Larry Peterson were shot together, but died nearly two years apart. Peterson’s 2014 vigil in Mount Vernon Square would be echoed nine years later when hundreds gathered to mourn Pava LaPere.

In 2017, Jim Forrester and Johnny Tobash were slain 3 1/2 hours apart. Six years after Sebastian Dvorak’s 2017 killing on Canton’s 2500 block of Boston Street, Fabian Sánchez-González was murdered in a T-Mobile store on the same block.

Counting the Outliers

Pattern	**Number**
Steps/minutes from home	6
Sowers, Pitcairn, Fenwick, Ponsi, Moriconi, Malabayabas	
Good Samaritan offered comfort, aid	5
Pitcairn, Ponsi, Dvorak, Dix, Marvit	
Birthday imminent or being celebrated	4
Pitcairn, Ponsi, Dvorak, McCormack	
Killed within hours of each other	4
Patterson and McCormack, Forrester and Tobash	
On the phone with loved one or friend	4
Pitcairn, Edwards, Forrester, Tobash	
Killed in the same Canton block	2
Dvorak, Sánchez-González	

One victim, Joseph Calo, was killed in the Inner Harbor after the Fourth of July fireworks, a surprisingly low total given the frequent mayhem at the event. And we know of only two homeless Outliers, Horvath and Anton Kancir, being killed. I suspect there are more.

Four Outliers — Pitcairn, Marcus Edwards, Forrester and Johnny Tobash — were on the phone with loved ones or friends when killed.

Haunted by Outliers killed while distracted on phones, I avoided making calls or listening to playlists on the street, hoping others would learn from these tragedies. One late afternoon, I saw a young woman on her Pratt Street stoop, engrossed in a call, oblivious to her surroundings — an easy mark for any thief. I waved to catch her eye and gently urged awareness, citing a recent robbery nearby. She brushed me off, annoyed, blind to the risks I'd tracked for years.

Pava LaPere and the gift of fear

Mercy to the guilty is cruelty to the innocent.

– Attributed to Adam Smith

National and international coverage in 2023 and 2024 made Pava Marie LaPere, attacked at age 26, far and away the most publicized among the Baltimore Outliers. Her grisly slaying drew coverage from not only Baltimore media but also CNN, NBC News, Forbes, AP News and *USA Today*. Print and online media in Britain and India also published articles, with the *Daily Mail* and cable station NewsNation garnering photographs and video of the scene of the crime.

CNN described the surveillance footage and manhunt for her murderer, while Forbes and tech publications highlighted LaPere's status as a Forbes "30 Under 30" honoree. NBC News covered both the murder and the suspect's criminal history, emphasizing policy failures like his early release from prison.

The Associated Press and *The Washington Post* offered in-depth accounts of the investigation, vigils and community response. NewsNation reported on an interview with a fellow resident of LaPere's building, who managed to keep her cool during a face-to-face encounter with the young woman's killer.

Originally from Tucson, Arizona, LaPere was a 2019 Johns Hopkins graduate with dual degrees in sociology and entrepreneurship. She founded EcoMap Technologies in 2018 from her dorm room, aiming to help novice entrepreneurs, small businesses and nonprofits access local resources through digital tools that map complex systems such as industries and communities.

LaPere's goal of boosting minority entrepreneurship was ambitious, but the city already had successful black-owned startups selling body cream, vegan foods and other products. And Baltimore's underground cash economy supported ubiquitous micro-businesses such as cleaning services and nail and hair salons, with no need for technical startup networking.

In 2023, LaPere earned a spot on Forbes' 30 Under 30 for social impact. She vocally supported causes such as Black Lives Matter on social media, posting, "EcoMap Technologies stand against systemic racism ... We commit to being anti-racist in all aspects." This won her a following, including Baltimore Mayor Brandon Scott and Maryland Gov. Wes Moore.

Described as visionary and compassionate, LaPere grew EcoMap into a nearly 30-person team, 50 percent women and 50 percent minorities, championing equitable tech access and community building.

Walking home alone

On Sept. 22, 2023, LaPere attended Baltimore's Artscape festival and walked home 20 minutes south with a friend. After the two parted ways, she was followed by Jason Dean Billingsley.

The 6-foot-5, 310-lb. convicted sex offender had been released early from prison in October 2022 due to a lenient plea deal from Marilyn Mosby's office and good behavior credits. The good behavior dissipated once out of prison. Three days before killing LaPere, he had raped and slit the throat of a woman, tied up her and her partner, and set them on fire in a West Baltimore rooming house. While he left them to die, they fought to free themselves and survived. The police broadcast no information on this case or the suspect.

At 10:32 p.m., LaPere entered her seven-floor apartment building at 306 W. Franklin St.

This location, slightly too far west and south of the safe heart of Mount Vernon, was just a bit close to rough West Baltimore and Lexington Market. Commenters on the Lipstick Alley website, which focuses on black social issues, agreed: "I don't consider '300 block of West Franklin St.' to still be Mount Vernon," one posted. "It's not the safe enclave that folks are trying to make it out to be."

From 2015 to 2023, six men had been killed within two blocks of her apartment. The area, with its chilly, concreted high-rises and converted hotels, felt riskier to me than East Baltimore's neighborly rowhomes, where stoop-sitting and community vigilance foster safety.

LaPere's EcoMap Technologies, located on her building's ground floor, likely drew her to live and work there for affordability and convenience. The area's risks would be camouflaged for a transplant like LaPere by the classic architecture of the structure, built in 1903.

A difficult path to the roof

LaPere entered the building's lobby, and Billingsley showed up wearing a gray hoodie. Reports differ: some claim that LaPere, seen on surveillance video sitting in the lobby, let him in after he waved, as if expecting him; others say he feigned forgetting his key at the glass doors.

They conversed briefly before entering an elevator.

Letting Billingsley in was a fatal mistake for the 5-foot-2 LaPere, a triathlete and weightlifter, but no match for the towering stranger. The elevator likely stopped at the top floor, the seventh; next they seemed to have climbed a narrow ladder to the roof, a hard-to-access spot not listed as an amenity but favored by LaPere.

Did she know Billingsley and invite him to see the view, or was she naive, suggesting it to a stranger? He may have forced her up, knowing the roof's seclusion, but that's unlikely given the obstacle course access.

With a panoramic view of downtown as a witness, 100 feet above the rest of the block, Billingsley took off some of LaPere's clothing. Billingsley beat her with a brick — knocking out three teeth — and strangled her, leaving her red shoes to be found scattered on the rooftop, as well as a broken hair clip. He exited 36 minutes later, wiping his hands, hoodie in hand. LaPere's body remained face up and undiscovered until 11:30 a.m. Monday, after she missed a work meeting. A veteran police officer on the team who discovered her called the injuries "absolutely brutal," and her father, who flew in to identify her body, told the Maryland Legislature the grief was unbearable.

Billingsley was arrested five days later in Bowie, Maryland, and later pleaded guilty to first-degree murder, receiving life in prison in August 2024.

Billingsley's mug shot reveals a heavy lidded giant, lips pursed, looking like a brawler. My initial reaction to photos and descriptions of him was there was no way I would let him into my apartment building at night: no no no no **no no no.**

Commenters on news coverage uploaded to YouTube chimed in:

> *Sometimes the fear of offending someone is greater than the fear for one's safety. Although in Pava's case it was probably just to be kind and trusting to this man.*

> *I'm a woman and I would let a 6', 5" male of any race freeze to death before I let him in my building. But then again, I'm almost 50 and I'm from the Bronx. ...*

This poor girl was nice and naive. I'm neither. But not being nice has kept me alive so far.

Stranger, no danger?

The challenging countenance of Jason Billingsley's mug shot screams danger, at least to anyone not a recent transplant. LaPere should never have let him into her secure building, a duty owed to herself and other residents.

Yet a Facebook photo with Jason's mother shows a softer side — glasses, white T-shirt, gentle expression. His sister recalled a "cuddly" child before his descent into violence. Billingsley's ability to seem harmless likely helped him gain LaPere's trust.

Additionally, LaPere's mother, Caroline, told a Tucson TV station that her daughter, raised to see her "privilege," was nonjudgmental and trusting. Not always a good thing in the urban Northeast.

LaPere's opening of the door to a probable stranger, her mother stated, "was beautiful act from her heart just to help someone else," she told the TV interviewer. "That's what she did."

Double-checking, the interviewer asked, was Caroline referring to opening the door? Yes, Caroline indicated.

"She didn't know him?" asked the interviewer. My sense was, the interviewer was stifling astonishment.

Caroline LaPere replied, "No, there were no bulletins or anything."

Why did LaPere let a stranger into her secure building, if Billingsley was indeed unknown to her?

The gesture reflects pathological altruism, a concept from a 2012 book by Barbara Oakley, where well-meaning actions harm oneself or others. Unlike rational actors who weigh costs and benefits, pathological altruists prioritize kindness over safety.

Caroline's comments hint that political correctness may have dulled the "stranger danger" warnings my generation grew up with in the 1950s and 1960s, when films like *Dangerous Stranger* and Officer Friendly visits taught elementary school kids to avoid unknown individuals offering candy.

Today's focus on "tricky people" over strangers encourages children to ignore gut instincts, as seen in a claim on the Reddit Parenting channel that "strangers pose almost no threat." This isn't precisely true. FBI data show strangers commit 10 percent of homicides and 40 percent of nonfatal violent crimes. And Baltimore's crime landscape certifies that strangers often pose a genuine hazard.

On the Lipstick Alley website, where black women and others gather to discuss social issues and celebrities, none were fooled by Billingsley. How had he made it "into a secure building looking like Wee Bey's cousin?" asked one bewildered poster, citing a menacing character from the HBO series *The Wire.*

While those in LaPere's social justice circle tiptoed around the land mine of the racial angle of the murder, given a black murderer and a white victim, Lipstick Alley was not so timid.

"Don't know why so many women on this site are so invested in the suspect not being black," wrote one commenter, receiving 71 upvotes. "Only God knows how many black women and girls he has tortured to feel so bold to do something to a rich white girl. These dusties [socially undesirable men] are NOT on our side and are our real enemy."

Indeed, Billingsley's previous assaults involved a white woman on drugs, as well as a black couple.

Another commenter with dozens of thumbs-up was equally unsparing of political niceties and aptly criticized Maryland's lax early release of Billingsley. "I was ... hoping he wouldn't be black but here we are. These pieces of sh!t just won't leave a single crime for another male group to commit. They just have to do it all, and more brutally. May she RIP and I hope the cops shoot first and ask questions later, since the state has no interest in keeping him behind bars."

"Don't tell me that white liberal women are this altruistic around black men," posted a third. "It is simply naïve, especially considering the race of men who are typically in the news for violent crimes in large, urban areas. Do y'all watch the news, ever? Women need to be smarter than this."

Many Lipstick Alley commenters, scathing toward Billingsley, were ultimately sympathetic to LaPere despite her perceived naiveté. "I can't imagine how terrifying this had to have been. A real life horror film," concluded one.

A second woman

Saturday afternoon, Sept. 23, tropical storm Ophelia bought soaking rains to the city. On Sunday afternoon, Sept. 24, as LaPere's body lay drenched and undiscovered on the roof for a second day, Jason Billingsley returned to the apartment lobby steps, per a female resident. NewsNation's Evan Lambert told show host Ashleigh Banfield how the resident sensed danger and stalled, refusing Billingsley entry as she entered her security key code as slowly as possible.

Claiming he sought a building in the 500 block, as he stood there in the 300 block, Billingsley failed to convince the resident he deserved entry. She entered alone and reported him to police. Banfield called his return "crazy."

Lambert added that the roof, accessed via a ladder, wasn't an amenity, yet LaPere favored it. Surveillance showed her and Billingsley in the elevator. Did she go to the difficult-to-access roof willingly? Again, forcing her up seemed unlikely.

At a vigil, friends described LaPere as trusting, possibly explaining her naiveté in letting him in. The second resident's appropriate caution contrasted with LaPere's openness. Without knowledge of Billingsley's prior rapes and attempted murders, the resident's gut instinct saved her; LaPere, missing or overriding red flags, died within 40 minutes. Did she know Billingsley from Artscape, or was her trust ideological, shaped by her anti-racist stance? Plea deals that averted a trial and discovery of the details of Billingsley's actions obscure such details.

Charmed by Charm City

Transplants from safe cities captivated by Baltimore's architecture, waterfront, foodie scene and animated locals often miss danger signals. As a Tucson native who loved Charm City, Pava LaPere mirrored my own affection. Like myself, she had been a headstrong child who rode her bicycle far from home, lifted weights, adored her building's roof, and embraced Baltimore for all of her eight years as a resident.

LaPere championed minority entrepreneurship, earning admiration from Baltimore's black elite, but lacked the street smarts to spot danger, such as an ex-convict waving through her lobby door.

Yale sociologist Elijah Anderson notes black parents rigorously teach children to avoid trouble, a lesson LaPere's parents and peers didn't impart. Her mother even called her trust in strangers "beautiful." So in fact, LaPere's parents withheld the vital lesson on how to scan for and avoid threats.

This gap in the "gift of fear" led me to examine Outlier hometowns for patterns.

LaPere, uniquely from a Western state, lacked experience in high-crime Northeastern urban settings.

Outliers from states like Virginia or Florida as well may lack the street smarts to survive Baltimore, where even Maryland or D.C. Metro natives fell victim to ambushes or car breakdowns that left them vulnerable, or encountered robberies in progress.

Hailing from Arizona, LaPere faced a steep learning curve: Tucson's homicide rate from 2020 to 2024 (an average of 12 per 100,000) is far lower than Baltimore's (50 per 100,000). Baltimore has nearly triple the violent crime and 50 percent more property crime per capita, despite similar total populations. Moreover, Baltimore's deeper socioeconomic issues make it far rougher than Sun Belt cities like Tucson.

Fleeing Baltimore

Hometown	Outlier victims
Baltimore	14
Other *	9
Baltimore suburbs	6
Elsewhere in Maryland	4
D.C. Metro	4
Overseas **	3
Virginia	2
Florida	2
	44

* *One each from Alabama, Arizona (LaPere), Hawaii, Maine, Massachusetts, New Jersey, Pennsylvania, South Carolina, and unknown*

** *The Philippines, South Korea, Hungary*

Notably, Outliers were twice as likely to be female than other homicide victims: while only 10 percent of Baltimore's 5,000-plus homicide victims (2007–25) were women, more than 20 percent of Outliers (nine of 44) were female. A September 2023 Baltimore Banner article called indoor female homicides rare, but it missed Outliers Kim Leto and Jesika Tetlow, as well domestic violence victims like Arnesha Bower.

A Swiss cheese model

LaPere's fatal encounter with Billingsley stemmed from multiple failures, beyond her lack of street smarts. Opening her building's door to him breached a critical defense, but other factors contributed, akin to the Swiss cheese model, where safety gaps (like holes in cheese slices) align to cause disasters.

The first failures were by Baltimore prosecutors and Maryland policymakers. Billingsley, once a happy child, turned sociopath after childhood setbacks. Despite multiple violent crimes, he secured a lenient 2015 plea deal, enabled by staff in prosecutor Marilyn Mosby's office. As a violent sex offender, he won early release in 2022 for "good behavior" after serving just seven years of a 30-year sentence. Such offenders often behave themselves in prison to obtain release and re-offend. YouTube commenters expressed outrage at Billingsley's brief sentence:

> *Of course these offenders are going to appear to be model inmates, because they have no access to their preferred victim type (women and children).*
>
> *I was imprisoned for several years for a nonviolent crime and every year that went by in there I would watch sex offenders getting released early left and right for good behavior and it made me sick. Most offenders I met in there did less than 3 years.*

Many criticized the police for not publicizing the attempted murder manhunt for Billingsley during the three days before LaPere's murder.

But detectives, surveilling him, believed a bulletin would make him flee — as he did. Billingsley had an existing relationship with the couple he attempted to murder, and his male victim's criminal record suggested a targeted attack, not a public threat. The police made what seemed to be the right call at the time, but as rarely happens in homicides, Billingsley switched from targeting victims he knew to a random attack (assuming he didn't know LaPere, which some observers question).

LaPere's choice to live and work just a bit too far from the middle of Mount Vernon put her just a 30-minute walk from Billingsley's listed West Baltimore address. Errors compounded her fate: walking home alone the last blocks, her friend not accompanying her to her building; opening the lobby door to Billingsley, and entering the elevator with him.

The gift of fear

A skilled manipulator, Billingsley likely projected charm and innocence to convince LaPere to let him into her building's lobby. His playbook had been described years earlier, in a 1997 book by Gavin de Becker.

The Gift of Fear argues humans evolved to detect threats through subconscious cues like tone or posture, but social conditioning often mutes this intuition.

At a 2013 lecture almost exactly a decade before LaPere's demise, De Becker eerily foreshadowed her fate.

"Imagine a woman in a building late at night," De Becker said. "She's on the 10th floor and she pushes the button for the elevator, and the elevator comes, and the doors open, and there's a man inside who causes her fear. It might be the look of him or what he's wearing. ... She has a feeling of fear [but] she says, 'I don't want to be the kind of person who doesn't get into an elevator ... I don't want to be the kind of person who is afraid all the time.'

"And so she gets into a steelsoundproof chamber with someone she's afraid of. And there is not another animal in nature that would even remotely consider such a thing. There's not another animal in nature that would say, 'ah danger, I'll go [in] there.'"

An antelope would never get on an elevator with a lion, De Becker continued. "But human beings do that every day. We undermine our own intuitive signals [despite] a universal code of violence that we understand ... we know when someone is likely to be a predator, we've [refined] a whole series of signals over millions of years."

Judging a situation entails split-second processing: the amygdala, the brain's region that processes emotions and fear, flags danger before we can even think through the evidence. The second resident lagged as she entered the code on the building security keypad, suggesting she heeded that flicker; LaPere rationalized it away.

LaPere's killer had been stealthy. There was a turning point in the young woman's final moments at which he revealed his violent intent. Too late, betrayed by ideology, LaPere then would have realized she was in huge peril against hopeless odds. Overwhelming panic must have ensued.

Two days later, the second female resident picked up a whiff of danger — perhaps a lingering stare or off-tone — and stalled, defying the "niceness trap" de Becker describes, where women prioritize politeness over fear.

Like seven other Outliers, Pava LaPere was overkilled – bludgeoned and strangled – though speculation about sexual assault, if true, would make her unique among the Outlier group.

In a May 2019 TEDx talk titled "Forget About Your Life Plan" – a painfully ironic title – LaPere recalled her devastation watching a 2015 Syria car bombing and touted her own putative safety as a "privileged" Hopkins freshman. Ironically, Baltimore became her "Syria," ending her ambitious life abruptly.

Commenters on the TEDx video noted the jarring contrast between her diversity advocacy and, echoing Lipstick Alley posters, her frightful demise at the hands of a black criminal.

As for the substance of the talk, one summed it up as shallow, like "a kid playing dress-up, trying to be the next Steve Jobs while parroting a [simplistic] life philosophy." She copied the cadence and hand chops of a Jobs or Bill Gates, and wore the requisite wireless headset microphone, while making prosaic observations about wanting to "change the world" and "make a difference."

LaPere made a forced attempt to connect the bombing in Syria to a personal epiphany on the need to solve all the world's problems by following the money. This led her to value entrepreneurial zeal as a way to enact change outside of Wall Street. She seems to be implying that innovative widgets made by virtuous and networked business leaders will solve major problems, like conflict in the Middle East. Grading on a curve, it's an ambitious and lofty talk for a 22-year-old, but a critic will note giant gaps in logic.

In my view, it was a 2016 Outlier, space economist Molly Macauley (to be discussed later), not LaPere, who came closest to being a Steve Jobs in her specialty.

LaPere's unpunctuated X posts reinforced a lack of depth, as did articles she uploaded on Medium heroizing minor events like skipping a triathlon or neglecting to send a get well card to an inspirational teacher who became terminally ill.

But her drive and determination, and her social justice platitudes, camouflaged any deficiencies in genuine brilliance. LaPere's death drew a 200-person vigil in Mount Vernon Square — nine years after a vigil in the same spot for the community's informal "mayor," Larry Peterson. Several other Outliers had drawn especially large memorials. Little Italy restaurant manager Chesley Patterson's vigil closed Eastern Avenue and attracted 300 mourners a year earlier, and a crab feast honoring Tim Moriconi drew more than 240 attendees.

Even saviors getting eliminated

LaPere's parents didn't impart the essential gift of fear. But they did push Maryland to junk its policy of early release for violent sex offenders. The 2024 Pava Marie LaPere Act eliminated good behavior credits.

Her death, more than any other Outlier's, spurred swift and significant change to prevent a repeat.

A Pava LaPere Legacy of Innovation Act also launched grants for student-led tech startups in Maryland. Johns Hopkins renamed its FastForward U tech incubator after LaPere. The university saw silver linings from her loss and those of other Outliers, with a scholarship memorializing Stephen Pitcairn and brain trauma research in honor of Zach Sowers.

In recent years, the university bolstered security and enhanced safety lectures, with parents on online forums noting they feel reassured. But four people — LaPere, Pitcairn, Sowers and Molly Macauley — linked to the city's most prestigious institution had been killed in heinous ways. Has this ever been seen in another American city?

While LaPere's murder was not entirely in vain, it was another blow to the city. "Baltimore is hopeless," one user wrote on X.com.

McKeever "Mac" Conwell, Pava's friend, countered, "That's not true, nor how Pava felt."

Another poster agreed with the first: “It’s how I felt. Glad to be out.”

A fourth added, “That’s not how she felt, but it’s how she died. Baltimore must clean up — even its saviors are brutally murdered.”

Paradoxically, city officials touted 2023 as a year when homicides went down to 223, from 334 in 2022. Credit went to Mayor Scott for targeted policing and social service intervention. More likely, it was the ouster of prosecutor Marilyn Mosby or uncounted bodies being hidden in vacant buildings. (“Check the boarded up rowhomes. I’ve seen this before,” quipped a Baltimore Redditor.)

Either way, the “achievement” of lower homicides overall failed to mask the worrisome total of four Outliers killed in 2023, including LaPere — and the economic fallout.

Economist Anirban Basu, a leading Baltimore consultant, weighed in on how a single highly publicized murder of a productive citizen can wreak more havoc on Baltimore than any number of criminals whacking other criminals.

“It's fine for the mayor to say every homicide matters, and he’s right about that,” Basu told WBFF-TV.

But politicians “miss the broader ... point which is that some homicides generate more economic damage than others. That’s true whether we like it or not. We need to make the entire city safer.”

Exactly. The “Baltimore is hopeless” comment on X showed 2023 as a year where Baltimore’s pit of difficulties got that much deeper.

The golden glow of Molly, Reese and Henri

If I have to read about the death of another honor student or normal, good person, I may vomit.

— Brett Stevens on Baltimore homicides

A "bad death" — marked by suffering, indignity, an unsuccessful search for the killer and unfulfilled dreams — shatters families, friends and communities. While all 44 Outlier deaths were heartbreaking, three stand out for their quiet yet profound devastation: Molly Macauley, Reese Bowman and Henri Paul Jones. Unlike Freddie Gray's death, which ignited riots, or the vigils for Pava LaPere, Timothy Moriconi and Chesley Patterson, which drew hundreds, these losses left quieter grief: international tributes, a judge's tears and a friend's anguished collapse. Each ravaged Baltimore's soul in its own way.

This trio represented heart-hurting losses of a visionary, a baby and a dearly cherished friend. They raised questions about possible hit jobs. In their final moments, these innocents encountered rage killing, over-killing and depraved heart murder marked by indifference to human life.

'She was important to humanity'

It's difficult to reconcile the life force in a profile photo of Molly Macauley with her fate. Neat dark blond hair frames a kind face, a genuine smile, and light grey eyes that shine with curiosity and intelligence. A pioneer in space economics, she spoke with authority at conferences on solar energy, satellite data valuation, orbital slots and space debris management, fields she helped shape.

Macauley lived in Roland Park, a quiet, tree-lined neighborhood of Tudor Revival houses in north central Baltimore. Described as streetwise, she took her two large dogs, Thatcher and Leo, as she jogged.

The 59-year-old was vice president for research at Resources for the Future, a Washington, D.C.-based environmental think tank, and earned respect across NASA, NOAA and academia. A Johns Hopkins graduate and adjunct professor there for decades, she was known for her love for Baltimore and for animals, and her devotion to her partner, Lee Lasky. Lasky recalled his first impression upon meeting her as being someone he could talk to about anything.

On July 8, 2016, around 10:47 p.m., Macauley was walking Thatcher and Leo after returning from an Orioles game. The 70-pound Plott hound and the senior Weimaraner did not bark, but Macauley emitted a scream heard by a neighbor who rushed out. She was found bleeding profusely, still clutching the leashes. The economist had been slashed in the neck at least twice in the 600 block of West University Parkway.

She died shortly after at a hospital.

The attack wasn't a robbery — nothing was taken — and no weapon was found. Despite extensive canvassing of the neighborhood, which hadn't seen a homicide since 1998, and a $10,000 reward, her killer remains unidentified.

Macauley's death stunned colleagues worldwide, her loss in space economics as profound as Pava LaPere's was for Baltimore's civic scene. Like Aysha Ring in 2008, she suffered a brutal throat slashing.

Originally from Falls Church, Va., she showed no inclination to depart Charm City to be closer to her office on P Street in Washington, D.C.

A clue to why she stayed in Baltimore, where neighbors enjoyed discussing gardening and pets with her, was that despite working in D.C., she was not a classic Type A personality. A colleague remembered:

> *After first getting to know Molly, I remember asking, "Is she really as nice as she seems to be?" I was already used to the aggressive, competitive, self-serving habits of so many people I'd encountered in Washington. [My colleague] laughed and said, "Yes, she really is that nice."*

We were quite alike in both being natives of the D.C. Metro area and not being Type A. We both lived in Baltimore and commuted to Washington jobs at prestigious institutions rather than moving back, so as to preserve our decompression zone.

The sentiments on the page "Remembering Molly" from Resources for the Future and a similar tribute page on the Space Policy website express profound grief, admiration and appreciation for Macauley. The tributes highlight her intellectual curiosity, kindness, professionalism, and significant contributions to environmental and space economics. The pages convey a deep sense of loss, with many noting her lasting impact on their lives and work.

She was the author of more than 80 articles, reports and books, and often testified before Congress. Her loss was a gut punch to commenters:

> *She was a profound thinker and genuinely kind person who combined a razor-sharp intellect with boundless compassion in a way that did not seem possible for one person.*

The golden glow of Molly, Reese and Henri

I used to work for her. Probably one of the finest women I ever met in my life. Tears in my eyes.

I'm absolutely heartbroken. #mollymacauley was an amazing mind, boss, and mentor; but she was an even better person.

When I was in graduate school she provided the class with a mini lecture and Q&A session. ... Despite all being trained/educated in politics, policy and or economics, she left the class in awe.

Dammit, she was important to humanity...

Macauley "had a quiet wisdom about her that you knew at a meeting when she said something and expressed a view that it was really worth paying attention to," said Michael Moloney, the director for space and aeronautics at the U.S. National Academies of Sciences, Engineering, and Medicine.

What really happened?

Friends described Molly as street-savvy, her large dogs a protective choice, yet they didn't bark during her murder. Police ruled out domestic motives, and theories ranged from a robbery in progress — unlikely in Roland Park — to a spurned student. Or even a conspiracy tied to election-rigging satellites, possibly linked to Seth Rich's killing 29 hours later in Washington, D.C.

Though the conspiracy sounds far-fetched, Macauley's integrity and expertise in space economics made her a potential threat to any fraudulent schemes. Colleagues noted her fearlessness and drive to right wrongs. Her killer left a clue: her dogs' silence. Could a state actor have neutralized them and executed a precise attack? There's no evidence, only speculation.

The case attracted the attention of three heavyweights of the Baltimore investigative journalism scene. In 2023, Taya Graham, Jayne Miller and Stephen Janis held a podcast in October, a month after the slaying of Pava LaPere, and pivoted to Macauley's cold case.

Miller gave voice to my own suspicions of the possibility of a hit job.

"There seems to be an active suppression of information. Was it a hit job?" Miller wondered. "The beautiful thing for a hitman is that suspicions will be muted and it will go down as another case of senseless violence, not a hit."

Janis recalled with admiration Macauley's proposal to handle space debris by charging a tax on satellites before they go up, and rebating it when the fallout is cleaned up. Debris from failing satellites threatens other satellites vital to telephone communication and geo-tracking.

"That's why she was revered by her colleagues as being a pioneer, but also a really excellent critical thinker," he noted.

Host Graham and her investigative team followed up with a December 2023 podcast with Pete Nelson, a colleague and friend of Macauley.

"Over time, my inclination is to believe it wasn't a random act, it was targeted. Police seem to think that now too," Nelson told Graham.

He noted the crime scene's seclusion, with dense shrubbery forming a hidden tunnel, ideal for an ambush Nelson had learned that Macauley, intensely private, had been dealing with a stalker from a class she taught. Despite her prominence in her field, she asked for no photo on her employer's website and owned a handgun, suggesting real fear.

Let that sink in for a minute. For a think-tank woman in Baltimore, where obtaining legal guns was an uphill battle, to go through the hoops to get a weapon means a very dark shadow had fallen across Molly's world.

A stalker seems plausible — a bona fide robber would typically avoid women with dogs, and her killer knew her routine and chose a secluded spot. This could mean she wasn't a random victim. Baltimore's low homicide clearance rate (under 40 percent at the time) make it an ideal site for a hit job, with odds in favor of the perpetrator not getting caught.

Jayne Miller echoed friends of Macauley in criticizing the police for minimal effort, stonewalling on reports, and barring interviews with the detective handling the case. This detective consulted FBI profilers in Quantico and searched Roland Park, but found nothing, according to initial reports, and then was blocked from media interaction.

Speculation persists of a local or federal cover-up, suggesting either a stalker with good connections to quash discovery, or in fact a state actor. Macauley's unsolved murder, a profound loss, leaves haunting questions: Her loyal dogs failed her, and her final moments were likely petrifying. She either didn't have her gun on her person or didn't have time to shoot. Her killer remains a shadowy demon.

While Macauley's unsolved murder left a void in a vast intellectual community, the death of Reese Bowman, an 8-month-old, struck at the Baltimore's heart with equal force.

A baby struggles on surveillance video

As with Molly, Reese's poignant photographs — a smiling 8-month-old with fuzzy brown hair and ruddy cheeks — evoke heartbreaking purity. Though killed by her caretaker, not a stranger, Reese qualifies as an Outlier for her utter defenselessness, a victim of a psychopathic act.

A photo of Reese shows an engaged and pleasant expression, and tiny hands playfully grasping the feet of her pink onesie with a teddy bear pattern. In another photo, flanked by toys, she is overcome with a crinkly-eyed smile, possibly at the sight of her brother, Sawyer.

Her parents left Reese with staffer Leah Walden at Rocket Tiers Learning Center, a day care not far from Shot Tower and East Baltimore Street. I frequently passed the day care on my bike route to downtown.

On May 23, 2017, frustrated that Reese wouldn't nap, Walden told a co-worker, "Girl, I'm frustrated. ... I'm sick of this little bitch. I hate this little bitch. ... She makes me want to punch her in the face."

Surveillance footage captured Walden slapping Reese, holding her by one arm and swinging her up, and smacking her with her free hand. Walden pinned the baby down and covered her face with blankets. The baby kicked wildly in a vain attempt to avoid suffocation.

Walden's brutal act – suspending Reese by one wrist and smacking her – echoed abusive behaviors I'd seen in public on Baltimore streets. Could such treatment have shaped Walden's own path to violence?

Initially claiming the incident was accidental, Walden pleaded guilty to first-degree murder in 2018, and was sentenced to 70 years in prison. During the sentencing, the judge, who broke down in tears watching the surveillance video, stated, "I'm just reflecting on everything I heard. There are tears everywhere in this courtroom."

Reese's father, Justin Bowman, told Walden, "Reese Annette Bowman accomplished more in her short life than this woman ever will."

Little Reese became the only Outlier killed by a female, and as studies have shown, the means of death (suffocation) is one consistent with female assailants.

The daycare closed permanently, and Reese's parents sold their house and left Baltimore, devastated. A large memorial service was held in their Pennsylvania home town, Mahanoy City. Baltimore's Criminal Investigations Chief Stanley Bradford called the act "just evil," noting, "Reese Bowman, in my opinion, was tortured."

Parents at the day care who knew Walden as a decent person speculated online about a psychotic episode. They said the Bowman family cut ties to Baltimore and was trying to make a new life. Some parents found it difficult to even drive by Rocket Tiers.

For myself as an observer at a distance, even just writing about Reese is a misery. God knows how the family copes. Reese, like Molly, was a fallen star.

Reese's loss was an inexplicable tragedy, while the story of Henri Paul Jones adds a layer of profound mystery, another life cut short with no answers.

Mon cousin français

The story of Jones, 23, struck a deeply personal chord. An outlier among Outliers, he blended European roots with American passions — coaching baseball, competing in wrestling and visiting family in Bretagne, not far from my ancestral home in France, the Loire Valley. With light brown hair, a charismatic smile and signature grey bowties, he reflected the influence of his mother, a French language tutor.

A 2017 Towson High School graduate, he was an aspiring electrician who had recently completed training and in 2020 bought a house with his sister, Monique. Born to William and Claudine Jones, he grew up in Anneslie, a historic area of Towson. He was engaged to be married and was a devoted godfather.

At 3 a.m. on Thanksgiving morning of 2022, in the 100 block of North Lakewood Avenue near Patterson Park, Jones had been enjoying a gathering with friends and former classmates when he left for his truck. He was fatally shot in the head at close range as he approached his vehicle. The unknown assailant exclaimed "oh shit" and fled.

Found wounded in the street, this young man without an enemy in the world died the next day at a hospital. The case remains unsolved, with a doorbell video offering the only lead — an image of headlights, too blurry to identify the killer's vehicle. Online speculation wonders about a gang initiation, mistaken identity which seems unlikely, or a robber who fled, shocked by the amount of blood.

The location, just north of Patterson Park, was deemed "safe" but felt borderline to me, given nearby rundown properties along Pulaski Highway.

A family friend named Dani noted Henri's family, friends and fiancé were shattered: "Grown men like my son, on the floor bawling their eyes out."

Henri, you should be married now, taking your kids to the family homestead in Bretagne, your mother teaching them French. You were too good for Baltimore, along with Molly, Reese and everyone else. How on Earth did your destiny get interrupted so brutally? The distance from rustic and timeless Bretagne to dangerous Baltimore was too far.

Our shared French roots made Henri's death feel personal. I used to stand on my roof deck and look at the Northwest Branch of the Patapsco, which leads to the Chesapeake Bay, and think, *This connects to France.*

And in 1981 I had in fact taken a freighter from the nearby Dundalk Marine Terminal to Le Havre, the French port on the English Channel. Coincidentally, Outlier Robbie Ponsi's grandfather took his ashes to Europe, and sprinkled a portion in Le Havre.

I wish I could have known Henri as a friend and neighbor and ancestral cousin. Instead, we are left with no clue whatsoever as to who took his life. His killer and Molly Macauley's are out there somewhere.

Attacking the beautiful

Many Outliers shone like stardust, their warmth and goodness both a magnet and a provocation to their attackers. Beauty seemed to mark some for tragedy. While this chapter honors Molly, Reese, and Henri, two other striking victims, Lauren Hayden and Aysha Ring, echo their stories.

Hayden is a case in point. She wasn't killed, so she isn't an Outlier fortunately, but in 2016, the T. Rowe Price account manager was attacked in Upper Fells Point, two blocks from my house. She and a friend were walking home after a bar get-together in Federal Hill.

The silent assailant grabbed her luminous blonde hair. He slammed the 31-year-old's head into the bumper of a parked car and then dragged her screaming across Bank Street, scraping most of her body and fracturing her skull. She lay motionless while a friend and neighbors responded to help.

Hayden had just made her first mortgage payment on a house in the neighborhood.

That same month, a close neighbor a few doors down was robbed by a male at knifepoint and her children, ages 2 and 3, were threatened if she did not cooperate. Another neighbor on Pratt Street was beaten by two women, maced in the face, and had her phone taken. Bad things were happening just steps from my front door.

The attack on Hayden particularly factored into my decision to leave. It also came up in a discussion on the Baltimore Reddit subforum.

A potential homebuyer was spooked by the attack, and her brother insisted she back out of the deal.

Upper Fells Point residents, naively in my view, downplayed the attack, insisting the area was "basically safe" and "incidents happen." One commenter wrote, "I wouldn't let a few anecdotes dissuade you," while another dismissed "once or twice a year high-profile incidents." Their remarks, unintentionally alarming, suggested a steady stream of violence.

One dissenter was more to my line of thinking: This incident was a harbinger of a new and disturbing direction, which would be born out as carjackings and violent crime soared over the subsequent decade. This dissenter wrote:

> *The Patterson Park area is in a battle between good, hard-working people and families and the criminals who recognize us as easy targets. Most everyone is ... downplaying the reality because maybe, like me, they have a vested interest in good people moving in and don't want to scare you off.*
>
> *Make no mistake about it, street robberies, unprovoked assaults, vehicular burglary and home invasions DO happen. You might get lucky, as many do, but if it does happen, you're going to be affected ... or your wife, or your kids. We have experienced more than our fair share of crime in the 4 years we have lived here and it's getting old.*
>
> *Every day I wonder if my front door [will be] kicked in when I get home. Walking to the bar last night I had pepper spray and a knife in hand in my pockets.*

You see a group of kids — no matter the time of day — and you create distance. Yes, you have to cross the street to get away from groups of 12 year olds here.

I hope this dissenting voice heeded his own advice and has gotten out to safety.

As for Hayden, her attractiveness reminded me of Outlier No. 3, Aysha Ring.

A striking 24-year-old, in an exceptional photo with her long auburn hair and shy smile, Ring looks reminiscent of a young Carly Simon. She was an administrative assistant at a Jesuit high school called Christo Rey, six blocks from my house. Friends say she could "light up a room."

The first female Outlier, Ring had her throat slashed in November 2008 while waiting to pay for her purchase at a liquor store in nearby Catonsville. Her killer bypassed other customers to target Aysha, a stranger. He spent no time in jail after being adjudged to be mentally ill.

Was it safer to be plain in Baltimore, if sociopaths so hated beauty? Why was her story, so close to my home, underreported, so I only learned of it years later?

These victims were beautiful, bright, beloved. Even many of the male victims, such as Stephen Pitcairn, Sebastian Dvorak, Johnny Tobash, Henri Jones, Manuel Luis, Chesco Patterson, Alex Wroblewski and Tim Moriconi, could readily be described as handsome and charismatic.

They shone in their communities. Their murders weren't just crimes; they were breaches of the social order, ruptures that no speech or mural could mend. It seemed that the brightest lights attracted the darkest fates.

"Zach Sowers, beaten and kicked into a coma, left to die on the street near his home," therapist Myra MacCuaig wrote to *The Baltimore Sun*. "Stephen Pitcairn, stabbed to death while talking on his cell phone to his mother. And now Peter Marvit, shot to death as he was returning home from a rehearsal. What these victims have in common is their commitment to humanity, their dedication to our city, their limitless potential, their lives cut short."

If all 44 Outliers had been killed at once, it would have been deemed the Baltimore Massacre, with profiles of the talented souls lost. Observers with exceptional empathy expressed anguish over the grim scale in essays across varied media — poet Shirley J. Brewer, therapist and letter writer MacCuaig, photographer Amy Berbert. Others simply left town.

The co-victims

Homicide grief experts estimate that each murder victim leaves behind three to 10 loved ones — family members and friends, often called homicide survivors or co-victims. This doesn't count the shaken neighbors and co-workers, or compassionate chroniclers like Brewer, MacCuaig and Berbert.

The Outliers received expressions of sorrow from classmates, ex-wives, ex-husbands, brother-in-laws, customers, neighbors, work supervisors, acquaintances, sports teammates and overseas colleagues. Judges at trials of two of the assailants were in tears. Maryland's governor and comptroller, and Baltimore's mayor and a university president, were shaken by Outliers they knew on a personal level.

Virtually the entirety of the Locust Point neighborhood, on its cozy peninsula leading to Fort McHenry, united to mourn native son Alex Wroblewski, whose parents were also lifelong residents. Little Italy similarly mourned Chesco Patterson.

Upon moving to Baltimore, and being confronted with news reports about Outlier homicides, MacCuaig noted grappling with "an inescapable reality and one which seems at times to suck the very sacredness, beauty and preciousness out of life."

From the year I arrived in Baltimore, 1987, through the end of 2025, the city has endured 10,892 homicides. This likely indicates, in close-knit "Smalltimore," more than 100,000 such co-victims, and thousands more neighbors and co-workers, scarred and grieving.

While grief from a natural death may last around three years, the intense grief from a homicide may last decades or for a lifetime. In writing this book, I encountered this with the families of survivors, who even decades later seemed to be downcast and lost, with exceptions among co-victims with hidden wellsprings of energy, fiercely determined to stand and fight for their family member's memory.

Vast sorrow rippled outward. Baltimore, the prettiest little city on the magical Patapsco River just off the Chesapeake Bay, in the "Land of Pleasant Living," was drowning in something that wasn't just lawbreaking – it was a nightmare.

Part IV.
Slipping away from ‘Charm City’

Finding Copper in the Gem State

Baltimore's relentless homicides, often just blocks from my door, cast a shadow over my daily life. Brutality against people not much different to me tainted ordinary moments, a pattern that lingered across years, even decades.

Yet, amid this urban decay, a distant promise emerged: Idaho, a place of open skies and safety, began to pull me away from Charm City's grip. A pair of 2017 visits to the Gem State offered hope and a way out of a city floundering amidst the losses of Outliers.

In 2015, while Freddie Gray's death sparked riots, the quieter loss of Kendal Fenwick, a 24-year-old single father and truck driver, went underreported. Building a fence around his Druid Hill Park home to protect his three children from drug dealers, he was gunned down in a tragic case of mistaken identity. As Outlier No. 14 on my tally of 44, he was the first black victim on my list.

In 2016, four more Outliers fell: Robbie Ponsi, a warm-hearted restaurant server; Molly Macauley, a space economics pioneer; Andras Horvath, a homeless man; and Marcus Edwards, a 21-year-old Morgan State social work student shot while on the phone with his girlfriend. They marked nos. 15-18 on my grim tally.

In March 2016, between Ponsi's and Macauley's murders, I watched my niece handle the lighting for *Hairspray* at Annapolis High School. John Waters' 1988 comedy, with Tracy Turnblad dancing through 1960s Baltimore, stirred nostalgia for the city's endearing peak. My eyes misted during the rousing opener "Good Morning Baltimore" — "I love you Baltimore ... The rats on the street / All dance round my feet." Charm City at its unpretentious best.

By 2017, the weight of urban problems continued to press on me. There were no riots, just multiple crime sprees. In January, neighbors reported an armed home invasion by teens right around the corner on Pratt Street. In March, one of my closest friends, a male nurse, was stalked and managed to scoot into a Wolfe Street bar until the juveniles gave up — same group?

My days remained routine — planting perennials, renting rooms to Johns Hopkins visitors. At a May 2017 Nationals-Orioles game, I wore an Orioles cap and a resplendent Nationals jacket, my loyalties torn between Baltimore, my home for decades, and Washington, my childhood roots. Other Marylanders, in similar mixed gear, cheered across the divide.

That same month, tragedy struck six minutes to my west by bike: Infant Reese Bowman was killed at a day care, becoming Outlier No. 19. And in June, bartender Sebastian Dvorak was shot in the stomach near the Boston Street Safeway, 10 minutes away in Canton. A stranger tried to comfort Outlier No. 20 as he died in agony. The proximity of these losses sobered me. At the trials of each of these assailants, judges wept, moved by the evidence and grieving parents.

Meanwhile, life moved along. That June, I played squash with female Chinese students from Hopkins' Carey School of Business, whom I'd met at my athletic club and taught the game. I shared my deep love for the challenging, lightning-fast sport and forged genuine friendships.

In July, I caught Tom Petty's smashing show at Baltimore's Royal Farms Arena, one of his final performances. As he performed "Learning to Fly," Petty handed some of the choruses to the crowd.

"Some say life/will beat you down," we sang lustily, lighters aloft, swaying in unison. "Break your heart/steal your crown."

The lyrics hit home and were the soundtrack for what came next. That same month, Wadell Tate's daughter discovered her 97-year-old father's battered body in a humble rowhome east of North Broadway. A South Carolina native with a gentle spirit, he became Outlier No. 21, his murder unsolved.

"Well the good old days/may not return," thousands of us had sung with Petty, a stark echo of the city's unrelenting toll.

As Baltimore's violence closed in — home invasions, stalked friends and Outlier deaths — I sought escape. A trip to Idaho offered a glimpse of a safer world.

Heading to Idaho

In August 2017, I joined a Maryland-born friend in Salt Lake City, driving north to Idaho, a state I'd never visited despite travels across six continents. My travel philosophy — "go where friends invite you" — had taken me to Brazil, Italy and Alaska, where you could uncover a place's soul while renewing ties. As well, Idaho beckoned as a refuge from Baltimore's chaos.

I was intrigued to check the Gem State off my list. My friend's hometown, Driggs, nestled in Idaho's southeastern corner near Wyoming's Grand Targhee ski resort. It drew ski bunnies and upmarket retirees, including a Nobel laureate.

Asked what I wanted to see, I tossed out Craters of the Moon National Monument, clueless about Idaho's sprawling geography. "Too far," she said.

I pivoted: "Preston. Where *Napoleon Dynamite* was filmed." She was neutral, not much interested in the cult classic that critics say, more than any other film in memory, splits viewers into 5-star raves or 1-star groans.

"This is bucket list," I insisted. It wasn't far out of our way, so she relented.

Napoleon Dynamite had hooked me years after its 2004 release, a quirky time capsule of a town lost in the 1950s with an Idaho twist. It felt like Baltimore's *Hairspray*, another offbeat teen-centered comedy tethered to a locale slathered in personality. Despite the contrast between rural Idaho and urban Baltimore, both films elevated phenomenal dancing as the key to finding high school acceptance. And each mined a deep vein of nostalgia.

My block's street sonics — profanity like "m-f-er" echoing in stereo — clashed with Napoleon's quaint "gosh," "yessss!" and "dang!" Baltimore's public profanity was off the charts, and Idaho's appeared nonexistent. This movie assumed a spot in my heart and eventually played a role in my move to Idaho.

Unlike Baltimore, Preston had no Outliers or notable homicides. The closest event to a murder was a scene in *Napoleon* where kids scream on a school bus as a farmer shoots a cow — filmed with a friendly, $10,000 show cow, unharmed but based on a real incident. Set to elevator music, reviewers call the shooting "traumatizing but hilarious."

In Preston, we cruised by the high school where Napoleon ate cafeteria tots and gyrated with a panache that astounded his entire high school. We hit Deseret Industries, the thrift store that supplied his prom suit. I snagged a Preston High School Indians T-shirt, and the staff barely blinked at my fan-girl pilgrimage.

Idahoans are split on the movie — some Mormons in this Latter-day Saint stronghold lacked the humor gene. One LDS friend from Clarkston, Washington, however, "got" the film. She gasped with mirth at Napoleon, having lived every detail: granddad shooting a cow in front of the kids (for real), gimp keyring micro-businesses and yelling at llamas to come eat.

Great potatoes

We departed Preston and rolled through Idaho's Upper Snake River Valley, where volcanic soils and a climate of warm days and chilly nights nurture perfect russet potatoes and certified seed spuds, pest-free thanks to harsh winters.

We drove through the vast, chilly acres stretching to the beautiful late-afternoon alpenglow of the Tetons, shining like a pinker version of the Emerald Palace in Oz.

Driggs was home base. My Maryland-born friend thrived here, though she grumbled about snow flurries lingering until July Fourth. At Grand Targhee, just over the state line in Alta, Wyoming, the ski resort swapped winter slopes for summer trail rides and mountain biking. Hayden Haviland would be my guide for a solo ride. I was assigned to Waverly, a stout and steady chestnut horse who responded to the lightest rein pressure.

The author aboard Waverley.
(Photograph by Hayden Haviland)

Wary of a potentially preachy East Coaster, Hayden relaxed when I proved not to be doctrinaire. We chatted easily as he led me through meadows bursting with lavender and lemon-colored asters, as he shared tales of transporting 14 to 20 horses from Arizona each June. The Tetons' peaks and pines framed a breathtaking ride.

Another day, I braved Targhee's ski lift despite my fear of heights, riding blind, hoodie over my head, until my friend signaled to hop off. Mountain bikers carried their wheels as they rode the lift, hopped off and zoomed down serpentine trails.

Later in Driggs, I marveled at a softball practice where the boys' bikes leaned unlocked against a fence, unthinkable in Baltimore.

The wide-open Teton Valley eased my soul. We savored huckleberry ice cream at an old-school soda fountain in Victor, the dry, sunny late-July weather perfection. A whitewater rafting trip in Wyoming's Snake River Canyon, 30 minutes south of Jackson, had us screaming through a steep drop, captured by a photographer's well-timed snap.

I flew home from Jackson Hole's ranch-style airport, its giant log beams and Teton views drawing celebrities and ski greats. Unlike Maryland, Idaho and Wyoming were harmless, and you could relax around people.

A chain reaction

Back home, I dove into writing *Eden Under Siege,* a mini-book updating the Madagascar chapter in my book *An Amateur's Guide to the Planet*. They are in a genre I think of as "insight travel," looking deep at what we can learn from new places. In a sense, Baltimore felt a bit like a foreign country to me, a D.C. native, and this book is a continuation of my earlier ones.

In September, I hiked the Virginia side of Assateague Island's wild beach with Zoey, my 11-year-old rescue. The sable-and-white Shetland sheepdog, raised in suburban Anne Arundel County with its Chesapeake tributaries, adored leaping into the Atlantic surf. A Labrador retriever had taught him as a pup how to leap from docks into creeks, an unheard-of avocation for a sheltie. They normally hate water.

We stumbled on a humpback whale's bleached vertebrae, washed ashore in February. The blazing sun and lack of shade tired Zoey, so we took breaks, missing the island's northern tip but catching Ocean City's distant high-rises shimmering in the haze.

Back home days later, Zoey staggered across my living room. Distracted by a bathtub leak, I initially brushed off the stumble, but his misery was clear. The vet diagnosed a ruptured spleen and a grim prognosis. After a telephone consultation with his former owner, I chose euthanasia. Zoey's Assateague fatigue now made sense, yet he'd been game despite mounting health problems, grinning as he rested. His final gift was to lead me to his successor sheltie, who would in turn lead me to Idaho.

Eager for another sheltie, I found the rescue landscape decimated. Eight years earlier, the last time I had searched for these dogs resembling small collies, breed-specific rescues offered numerous choices. Now, slim pickings and strict rules made getting approved for a dog almost as challenging as adopting a baby. Rescue organizers would reject full-time workers on the grounds they would leave dogs alone all day, and stay-at-home folks for shaky finances insufficient for vet bills. It was a Catch-22. As well, Millennials were a generation that reveled in dog ownership, snapping up rescues and shelter dogs. And breeders' litters for show dogs were booked years out.

This lack of local rescue shelties played into my move out West.

On Craigslist, I found four sheltie puppies in Idaho. "I'm coming to pick one," I told the unfazed breeder, who'd had calls from as far as Alabama. Using reward points for flights, rental car and Airbnb, the 5,000-mile round trip cost just $65. Another Idaho adventure awaited.

After landing at the airport in Spokane, Washington, I drove south through the Palouse's humpbacked hills, carved by Ice Age floods from Lake Missoula's melted ice dams. This grassy expanse, named for a local tribe and the French word for prairie, grows wheat, barley, lentils and chickpeas. At Lewiston, Idaho, U.S. 12 swept east, pacing the Clearwater River to rural Kooskia, beyond which sprawls a vast wilderness up to Montana's Lolo Pass and Missoula.

The germ of an idea to move

Greener than the sprawling Teton Valley, the narrow Clearwater Valley features a milder climate. The Rockies steered Arctic weather away to the east, so the valley enjoys being part of a "banana belt," the temperate Columbia River Basin. I took in the shift from the Palouse's rolling hills to the Clearwater's steep humpbacks flanking U.S. 12.

"*Pretty*," I thought, intrigued by how this part of Idaho was cozier than the Tetons, green with a twisting river, not intimidating jagged mountains.

Baltimore pushed me away with Outlier murders, carjackings, riots and looted shops. Idaho pulled me in with meadowlarks, magpies and chorus frogs at dusk, replacing Baltimore's clatter of basketball rims, profanity and construction. Distant gunshots here came from hunters, not drug dealers.

The Clearwater River winds past Orofino and Kamiah to Kooskia, a town of just over 600. Its name — pronounced KOOS-kee — comes from a Nez Perce word for a modest river, as the Clearwater is dwarfed by mighty Snake.

'I'll be back'

On a remote forest road southeast of Kooskia, at 3,500 feet, I found the breeder and met four junior shelties. They lived in an outdoor pen, which contributed to their fluffy coats and sturdy conformations. The little pups exploded in a multicolored riot of joy at a visitor.

The boldest jumped the highest, knocking its siblings out of the way to see me. The large male smothered me with puppy kisses, his confidence perfect for Baltimore's challenges — renters in my home, bike rides to Patterson Park. I named him Copper. We stayed overnight with the friendly breeder. As I turned to leave, I said to her, "I'll be back," for a visit or a move, and meant it.

Unused to a collar, a leash, a crate, cars or airplanes, Copper braved the journey from Spokane to Dallas-Fort Worth, his straw-and-dirt farm scent clinging to him. A flight attendant smiled, "He can sit with you on this leg, but keep him in the carrier at DFW." In Dallas, the crew chief disagreed: "Oh no, he needs to meet everybody!" Passengers flocked to our window seat, snapping photos of the star pup.

Copper in exile (Photograph by the author)

Back in Baltimore, I raised Copper true to his Idaho roots. One night, he nosed a black decorative metal eagle on a neighbor's white storm door, alerting me to a "predator." I laughed, praising my "Idaho ranch dog." In November, I enrolled Copper in obedience training. He was banished to his own training area for barking. Practicing the sit/stay command, he looked very pleased with himself. "Copper in exile," I captained the photo, sharing it with his breeder.

That same month claimed another Outlier, No. 22. Bartender and restaurant manager Alex "Albo" Wroblewski, South Baltimore's unofficial mayor, stopped for milk and cookies at a convenience store. He was shot, in the abdomen, like Sebastian Dvorak five months earlier, after flashing a large bill. The obligatory candlelight vigil, mayoral pronouncements for "accountability" and calls to action ensued. The rituals to memorialize the dead were so important for friends and family, to handle the grief of an abrupt loss. Meanwhile the politicians' faux-earnest pledges to curb the murders were futile as the bodies continued to fall. I began to interpret the word "accountability" spoken by Baltimore politicians as shorthand for a "complete lack of accountability."

On Dec. 17, I got Copper chipped at Fells Point's Petco Unleashed. Dec. 18, I paid my January mortgage early for the interest write-off. That evening, something very bad went down a few blocks away in Fells Point.

Around 7:30 p.m., body piercer Jim Forrester was shot dead outside the Baltimore Tattoo Museum, mid-call with his wife. Outlier No. 23 was a devoted family man and a bass player in doom metal bands. A suspect was caught but not convicted.

The killing wasn't over. To the northeast and just a few hours later, at 10:55 p.m., Jonathan Tobash, a Morgan State industrial engineering student, got out of his car at a convenience store. While on the phone with a friend, he stumbled into an ongoing robbery by gang members.

His mother, Mary Harry, recalled Tobash as a peacemaker, who always wanted people to get along and to avoid disagreements. Though he likely tried to smooth over the situation, the former rugby player was killed for $6. Multiple shots ended his life on a day when he should have been celebrating the Amazon job offer he'd just received.

As Outlier No. 24, the year's final loss, Tobash's murder left family and friends reeling; his father died not long after, having lost the will to live, Tobash's mother notes. A classmate at Baltimore Polytechnic, Keombré McLaughlin, recalled him in a column for *The Baltimore Sun* as handsome and kind, descriptors that applied to so many of the Outliers.

"The thug life was never a part of his world, which makes his death that much harder to comprehend," she wrote, spotlighting the common thread running through all the Outliers. "He deserves more, a legacy based on his life, not just his death."

Thus the year 2017 recorded six Outliers meeting untimely ends. The later killing of a gang member, revealed to be the one who killed Johnny, brought some closure for Tobash's family.

Sheltie dominoes falling — the loss of Zoey, the acquisition of Copper in the Intermountain West that same year — showed me a different world and a way forward.

Looking to get out

In 2018, Copper turned one, a metallic reddish-brown patch — hence his name — gleaming behind a snowy mane. A peacock of white, tan, brown, and black, he sported a white rump patch and dark face mask. His sable sire and blue merle (a silvery grey) dam gifted him vibrant colors. A clever little guy, he dazzled his Tricks class teacher, who whispered to me, "He's a Ferrari."

In July, I escaped Baltimore with a Hopkins nurse friend to Shepherdstown, West Virginia, staying in a quirky school bus Airbnb. We were on a joint scouting mission to escape Baltimore. West Virginia's forested hills were lovely but not as exotic as Idaho's dramatic vistas.

In September, I took a woodworking class at Station North Tool Library's sprawling workshop and tended caladiums thriving in my pocket garden out front, soaking up the the last of the summer heat.

That month, I read about Tim Moriconi, a 25-year-old Northrop Grumman contracts professional. Born in Baltimore and raised in Virginia's Blue Ridge foothills, he was emblematic of every athletic, fun-loving twenty-something in Federal Hill, Riverside and Canton, navigating their first career jobs, welcomed by name at his favorite pub and sharing rowhomes with roomies. I had good friends just like Tim. They were finding their way in life.

A year earlier, Moriconi had survived a gunpoint robbery in his neighborhood, posting a cautionary tale online about staying vigilant. Around 7:20 p.m. on Sept. 27, 2018, history repeated itself, in a deadly way.

Moriconi was striding home from his father's house, dodging raindrops, carrying a bag with four cans of Michelob Ultra. The young man appears to have been blindsided by an assailant with a long rap sheet for violent crime, who in a sane and competent city would have still been behind bars serving multiple sentences. After shooting Moriconi, Deandre Devon Sleet, then 23, got rattled and fled without taking any of Tim's belongings. He grimly told his getaway accomplice to just "drive." They fled, going the wrong way down a one-way street.

Neighbors ran out. One yelled, "We need help!" Another sorrowfully asked the police if Tim would be OK, hoping against hope. A third neighbor went to her basement, her family's surveillance "command central" to see if the cameras captured a suspect. Yes — her video showed a silver sedan rolling to a stop, and a bowlegged gunman stepped out, walking after Moriconi as he pulled a mask up over his face.

Tim's father got the bad news from a detective and had the awful task of informing Tim's mother, whose son so resembled her. She screamed and fell to her knees crying.

The news ran coverage of the murder. I winced at Moriconi's photo, at his young age, at the location near one of my favorite outdoor public swimming pools. *Oh no,* I thought, **no**. His vigil showed a tidy tree-lined block not much different from mine.

The bodies were stacking up, many not far from the waterfront. I entered Moriconi's name on my growing Outliers list. That Stickie note was evolving into a kind of unofficial ledger of grief and remembrance, a reckoning of urban failure and human regression. My list was mapping the patterns, as they grew closer and more personal.

Meanwhile the city government essentially forgot them, as it never had an effective response and in fact exacerbated the problem with all the soft plea deals and juvenile releases. These brushed-off lives represented a crescendo of grief. For me, this wasn't just list-making; it was a moral reckoning, and a set of events that demanded analysis.

A Reddit commenter took aim at Sleet: "Real story here is this guy should've been locked up before he had the chance to kill Tim. He had a long rap sheet. Not his first violent offense."

Moriconi, like Stephen Pitcairn before him and Pava LaPere after him, would still be alive if Baltimore would just keep its most violent criminals locked up.

The neighbor's surveillance video, featured on an episode of "Real Crime Time," captured Moriconi's final moments, a haunting echo of other victims' unseen ends. The young man is steps from home, unaware of that his life is about to cease. Moriconi's killer received life plus 25 years; the getaway driver, 25 years. Eighty heartfelt messages filled his obituary page, marking him as 2018's sole Outlier, No. 25 on my list.

A neighbor strolling home from the library heard sirens, not knowing they signaled an ambulance carrying Moriconi to the University of Maryland Shock Trauma Center. He paused to photograph Light Street's retail blocks gleaming in the rain. Posting the image on Reddit Baltimore, the neighbor thought nothing of the piercing sound until learning of Moriconi's death. "Baltimore is a fascinating juxtaposition of beauty and tragedy," the neighbor concluded.

Paternal devotion

In 2026, Tim's father, Andy Moriconi, shared an update. Tim "left two sisters behind, Becca and Bella," he wrote in an email to me. "Tim actually wrote a journal he started just a few months before he died. Not many men his age do that. His very last entry read: 'I want to spend more time with my sisters.'"

Distracted by his Xbox, Tim's high school grades suffered until he enrolled at Fishburne Military School in Waynesboro, Virginia. "Fishburne turned him around," Moriconi noted, "so we honor Tim by establishing an endowed scholarship in his name." He described the annual crab feast fundraiser.

"The endowment has accumulated $150,000 so far and has awarded a partial scholarship to one student each year. We now have enough – over $100,000 invested – to make it endure in perpetuity. As long as I have the energy, I'll keep doing this."

Moriconi stays in touch with Tim's friends in Maryland and Virginia. "In fact, one of them asked me to stand in their wedding party to represent Tim. All of them are getting married and having kids. It really hurts to wonder if Tim would be married now, with kids of his own."

At Tim's favorite haunt, the One Star bar in South Baltimore, "his prayer card is still on the wall behind the bar," Moriconi reflected. "The owners held a memorial for Tim the week after he died. Those proceeds paid for his funeral. When Tim's sisters visit me, we always stop there in his honor."

Like the enduring bond between Good Samaritan Reggie Higgins and poet Shirley J. Brewer – traumatized by the 2010 slaying of Stephen Pitcairn in Charles Village – Moriconi has found a similar anchor in shared adversity. He enjoys quiet solidarity with the parents of Alex Wroblewski, another victim killed a year earlier about a mile southeast. They hug when they see each other at their shared Roman Catholic church.

His outlook on Baltimore mirrors my own.

"I love this city – the Ravens, the Orioles, the history and culture," he wrote. But he added, "I still walk to Fed Hill bars and restaurants every time wondering if it's going to be an encounter. When I retire, I will not stay here."

Along with the parents of Pava LaPere, Wroblewski and others, Moriconi worked to enact positive change in criminal law and scholarship funding, in memory of their loss.

'A stand-in for the Clearwater'

Up the block, a Peruvian chicken joint hosted a poetry slam. Fresh from my second Idaho trip, I wrote a poem on a Friday afternoon and read it that night.

The crowd, polite but puzzled, gave a lukewarm nod to my words, which described my personal bridge between Baltimore's undeniable but tainted magnetism and Idaho's growing pull.

My Own Private Idaho

I want to head to the beautiful Gem state
And read books above the Clearwater River
But meanwhile to get that nature fix
Copper and I roll each morning to the crest of Lombard Street
Then through the granite pillars, a gate to a different dimension.

Sunrise touches the battleship grey stratus clouds with flamingo lowlights
We descend Pagoda Hill, a raptor on a branch just above the footpath.
"That's a HAWK," yells a burly uniformed man on the riding step, above the engine noise from the trash truck.
"Red-tailed hawk," I shout back in passing.
The red-tail shares his kingdom with a newly arrived peregrine falcon.

I greet the herons, "Hi Blue, hi Night,"
They stare right back, habituated to humans
Sip today's coffee on a bench on the boardwalk.
A redwing blackbird lands on a branch to my right
He makes eye contact and sings
As kinglets and warblers flit from tree to tree
Completing the dreamlike Disney movie.

The Audubon kids come screaming into view.
Unhappy joggers stream through, wearing frowns,

missing everything.
The Salvadoran kids smoke dope on the retaining wall
Skipping out from classes at Patterson High.
An angler catches a bass, a photographer
immortalizes nine rescued ducklings.

The cormorant circles above
and lands like a float plane.
A broken man tells me that
his wife murdered his two children,
Somehow it didn't make the news.
The birders keep up their hunt
Under their binoculars some are snobby and remote,
others generous with insights.

Hampstead Hill pupils, energy aflame, emerge
to stroke Copper
Delighting in his soft fur and puppy kisses
While the teachers are annoyed at the children's fascination.
I hand each child my binoculars and point out the night heron.
"Look for something on the island
that looks a bit like a penguin."

We head home, past the prisoners spearing litter
The mothers with strollers,
the German shepherd holding a perfect down-stay.
People smile at us, or scream at us,
or greet us by name.

We stop and chat about Smalltimore goings-on
We deal with it all, and for now,
It will do as a stand-in for the Clearwater River
Just blocks from my door, my own private Idaho.

Daily I found a slice of nature's solace in the urban wildness of my local routine, with its hawks, herons and community characters. Here I could process the havoc in the news, or conversely be informed of murders unreported, if the father's tale was credible. Patterson Park stood in for my dream of reading by the river.

Wildlife managed to thrive amidst city life, even lacking the Clearwater River's pristine ecosystem.

The poetry slam showcased hyper-local talent. Not academics or New York literati, but neighbors a few doors down reciting soulful lines from poems written on and read from their phones. Baltimore's affordability nurtured a bohemian haven, where artists and dreamers still flourished.

'Committed to the city'

One of the poets du jour had told me her boyfriend had been carjacked. This crime entails the violent theft of an occupied vehicle. There had been four recently on our block of just 53 rowhomes. Baltimore's online crime tracker showed an average of 437 carjackings yearly from 2012 through 2024, often conducted by juvenile rings.

Another victim, Miss Joan, a gentle 80-ish piano teacher living six doors down, was carjacked as she tried to park, returning from a lesson just after sunset.

"Miss Joan, what now?" I asked, expecting her to flee. "I'm committed to the city," she replied, stunning me.

Her resignation, shared by neighbors, normalized violent crime. In June 2025, an armed robbery victim in the 400 block of South Regester Street, lucky to be alive, told WBAL that he didn't intend to leave, as he loved his block and his neighbors. A 30-year-resident of the block agreed, saying she was frightened but staying.

Similarly, at a "safe streets" event just up the block, a self-defense "expert" urged women to carry shoulder purses for easy surrender to muggers. The passivity floored me — encouraging easy targets over resistance. Of course it likely increases the victim's chance of survival, but it also creates a happy hunting ground for criminals who find it easier to rob than to work a job.

I loved Baltimore's soul: Patterson Park's green, Fells Point's pastel waterfront like an Irish village, discount-night eateries, Artscape's world-beat concerts, and the Visionary

Art Museum's quirky but riveting exhibits. Rowhomes bloomed with pocket gardens, tiled sidewalks, Art Deco wall mosaics and three-story murals.

Miss Joan's love for our fairy-tale neighborhood was understandable, but one truth stood firm: Carjackings aren't normal. Around this time, at least six households that I know of on our block or nearby agreed, fleeing to varied destinations, from rural Maryland to as far as London.

There was no way Idahoans would stand for teen carjackers terrorizing their state's counterparts to Miss Joan. They'd arrange armed patrols every night to address the problem. Potential carjackers with any sense of self-preservation would get a real job and pay for their own transportation. Problem solved.

Heck, an Idaho counterpart to Miss Joan would probably have 17 guns of her own and be ready to use them. Annie Oakley types are not unknown.

It's impossible to ignore Baltimore's lack of negative incentives. The city's leniency invited crime, as if signs at the county line read, "Welcome! Enjoy Your Carjacking."

As French economist Frédéric Bastiat noted in 1850, "When, then, does plunder stop? It stops when it becomes more painful and more dangerous than labor."

Idaho's promise of proactive security beckoned. Despite Baltimore's charm, Idaho's promise of peace grew stronger. Copper, my Idaho-born sheltie, embodied that hope, a tangible link to a safer future.

Idaho was more than just a beautiful landscape. The rural state was opposite to urban Maryland: fewer criminals, with firearms a cultural norm among the law-abiding and viewed calmly as a practical tool for safety in the countryside. The odds of a carjacking are vanishingly small. Copper's home county has recorded precisely zero, ever. In fact, you could leave your car unlocked, and valuables would remain untouched.

Painting the cornice

In 2019, Baltimore gamboled along with its usual outsized personality, unaware of the Covid storm looming. Spring saw me at Patterson Park, clearing invasive phragmites by the Boat Lake, or visiting the dog park, where carjackings dominated chatter.

A friend brought his sheltie, Moose, a black-and-white version of my Copper. His screaming teenaged daughter had been carjacked from their garage and managed to escape from the trunk a few blocks away.

“Baltimore’s just 300 cops shy of a turnaround,” he insisted.

“Those 300 good officers don’t exist,” I countered, “and if they did, they sure aren’t signing up for this place.”

As Baltimore’s violence pushed me toward escape, I began transforming my rowhome at 203 S. Ann Street, preparing it for sale. I could scarcely believe I was leaving, but the complacent part of my psyche that hated change and was OK with inertia was letting the resolute part take charge. I was placing one reluctant foot in front of the other to depart.

Tragedy struck relentlessly. On April 24, Kevon Dix, a 26-year-old Morgan State choir star, became Outlier No. 26 on my tally. Known for singing his conversations, the music major and toll collector was gunned down after a study session, en route to celebrate his brother's Morgan State acceptance. His untouched iPhones, Apple Watch and laptop lay nearby as a Good Samaritan held his hand. Each loss fueled my resolve to leave, though part of me could not fathom that I was really going through with this plan.

Summer rolled in, blazing hot. On July 10, with Copper a few days past turning one, I taught him to "clean up" his toys, mimicking a YouTube star, a golden retriever. Pure joy. I uploaded his endearing performance.

But again the city's pulse faltered. The next day, Manuel Luis, a 19-year-old Morgan State business major, was found slumped in his car, riddled with bullets. A former high school baseball standout with a 4.0 GPA and a megawatt smile, Riverdale native Manny was the "mayor of Parkdale High School baseball," lifting teammates with boundless encouragement. His killers vanished into the night.

Four days later, David Caldwell, a 52-year-old phlebotomist, was shot at the methadone clinic where he worked. An animal lover, David had long feared for his safety, leaving a chilling note: "If something happens to me, it's probably gun-related." His death left two foster canines waiting for an owner that would never return.

While Outlier deaths darkened Baltimore, my Ann Street block carried on, its quirks pushing me further toward departure.

In July, our block hummed with kids drawing on sidewalks using giant chalk I'd left out. But at the other end of the block, a young tech worker posted an obscene poem at kid-eye level on his window, sparking no outrage from parents who chatted warmly with him. The police called it vile but took no action. To me, the parents' warmth toward him signaled Baltimore's skewed norms. I felt like an outsider in my own block, another nudge that Baltimore and I were drifting apart.

Baltimore's reputation abroad

In September, I flew to Emilia-Romagna for the wedding of friends Valentina and Davide, an escape to one of Italy's most stunning regions. In 2015, Valentina had stayed at my Baltimore rowhome during her Johns Hopkins research on cancer treatments, armed with a 10-item bucket list: to catch a play ("*Teatro*") and to explore Hampden's quirky streets from John Waters' *Pecker*. We biked to Hampden, rifled thrift shops and caught a show at the Fells Point Corner Theatre.

The night before her 2019 wedding, Valentina's *Nonna* hosted a dinner in her elegant three-story home for us foreign guests: hotshots in radio-wave research from Germany to Palo Alto. As I sat among the brain trust, Valentina's parents breezed in, making a beeline for me. Her dad spoke almost no English but managed a heartfelt "thank you," pressing a Chianti bottle into my hands, labeled "For Jeannette, Thank you, Mamma e Papa." Mom, fluent and warm, gushed gratitude for keeping their daughter safe in Baltimore's wilds.

At the wedding, nearly all of the more than 100 guests, from scientists with flawless English to elders with just a few words, thanked me for shielding Valentina from trouble. Their words, halting or eloquent, hit like a tidal wave of warmth. I'd never felt so embraced, a hero for simply sharing street-smarts honed over decades in Charm City.

The global infamy of Baltimore's violence was suddenly laid bare.

Before flying home from Bologna, I roamed Parma's safe piazzas, photographing the Palazzo Ducale's gardens and the Cathedral's soldier-and-lion carving. Chatting with a sheltie owner, I felt Parma's calm allure. Why cling to Baltimore's chaos, I wondered, when a place like this, secure and stunning, beckoned? Idaho was still my first choice, but if it didn't work out, there was always Italy.

Parma's peace lingered, but Baltimore's reality awaited. Back home, I dove into preparing my rowhome for sale.

Serious about selling

By October, I began the work needed to sell my rowhome, a surreal leap after three decades. With determination, I hauled paint samples, steel wool and sandpaper to my roof deck, starting the grind to prepare for market.

First up: the cornice — that decorative tin strip crowning the facade, mispronounced as "cornish" in true Baltimore-ese, hon. When I bought the place, its stamped diamonds, dentils and architraves were slathered too thickly in sun-damaged black paint, almost hidden. After a decade, a so-so painter had sloppily splashed on garish red and yellow, now painfully passé in 2019's era of teal, bronze and goldenrod. Time for a glow-up.

Three stories above Ann Street, my roof was a serene escape. Muted sirens and chatter drifted up, but I worked unseen, a ghost rarely noticed by passersby below.

Clad in a safety harness, carabiners clipped to orange Harbor Freight tie-downs looped around deck posts, I sprawled over the edge of the asphalt roof, upper body in mid-air, wire-brushing and scraping away decades and perhaps centuries of paint. A long dress mirror dangled on additional straps from the roof, revealing hidden nooks — dentils' upper curves, panel recesses — tricky to reach from my bird's-eye angle.

During breaks, Copper and I strolled Butchers Hill, snapping pics of its meticulously maintained, historic facades for color ideas. A local painter specialized in restoring cornices. His detail and harmonized hues came with a hefty price tag, so I had already decided to DIY. But I could tour his masterpieces, learning cornice detail lingo in the process: fillet, ogees with their gentle swoop, dentil bands, fascia, modillions anchoring the ends. Each walk sharpened my eye.

Weeks later, the cornice was stripped clean enough to prime. I tucked red rosin paper under its lower edge to shield the brick from drips, painting with surgical focus. The rowhome was transforming, and with it, my future.

Outliers No. 29 and 30

By Nov. 5, I was in the final sprint of my cornice reno, scraping and painting the tricky edges. Soon, I'd need to rent a lift for the far corners and window trim. The rowhome was shaping up, inching closer to market ready.

That night, around 9:40 p.m., tragedy struck in West Baltimore. Jordan Taylor, 31, a beloved youth sports director at the Catonsville Y for over a decade, was unwinding in his Clifton Avenue townhome with his wife, Twila. Three men pried at their front door with a crowbar. Jordan fought to barricade it, but bullets tore through, hitting him.

Twila's frantic 911 call captured the intruders demanding a safe the couple didn't own. They fled in a stolen SUV, leaving Jordan to die in the hospital hours later. Police later confirmed they'd targeted the wrong house.

Known as a "gentle soul" with a servant's heart, Jordan was mourned deeply. The two main assailants got hefty sentences.

Three days before Christmas, at the Kim Deli at Fayette and Kenwood north of Patterson Park, came the next slaying. Carmen Rodriguez complied with an armed robber who wanted cash to bail out his girlfriend. Rodriguez handed over the money while pushing one of her four children present out of the way, then put her hands up. Despite complying, she was fatally shot in front of the youngsters. Her youngest was in a child seat only feet away.

Her husband noted she was beautiful and hardworking. A mourner at her vigil sang in Spanish, "All that I ask God, is that the pain doesn't leave me indifferent."

The deli where Rodriguez perished is an area that felt sketchy to me from the first time I saw it, soon after arriving in Baltimore and boarding the wrong bus home. A Redditor described having his house near the deli broken into, and a gun pointed at him by a 15-year-old while he was in his car. A friend's security camera caught a group of 10 or more kids, the commenter continued, "swarming upon a guy walking by himself not even drunk or on the phone or anything and they all beat the snot out of him for no reason at all." This showed that even the mildest restraints on the prison code — looking for distracted pedestrians to rob — had morphed into *Clockwork Orange* ultraviolence, purposeless, engaged in just to pass the time.

In my view, every moment Carmen, God rest her soul, worked in that deli was borrowed time, given the surrounding neighborhood. There was no juncture in Carmen's lifetime, if not longer, that the area didn't appear sketchy and rough. I had first noticed its threatening vibe in the 1980s, and Patterson Park gentrification simply didn't reach that far north. The family must have blocked out this reality thinking they could make it work and create income. But the magic shield they thought might be generated by their kindness to customers who were low on funds didn't protect against everyone.

Fate marked Rodriguez as the third Hispanic Outlier involved in retail (along with Jose Abreu and Fabian Sánchez-González) and the last Outlier during my Maryland years. After I left, Baltimore's shadows only darkened, and I was able to track the Outliers from a distance.

Anchors and ship's wheels

At the dog park, a librarian from the Anne Arundel County Public Schools informed me of a valuable resource: Every school had a 3D printer. I scoured a website with 3D patterns called Thingiverse, snagging designs for anchors and ship's wheels, appropriate decorations for historic captain's house in a maritime neighborhood.

The librarian printed them, and I embedded the anchors into a sleek board, performing the work on my roof deck top rails. The completed installation, I would mount a foot below the cornice. Ironically, I would be weighing anchor.

Time to rise high. I rented a Genie scissor lift, soaring 38 feet. Add my 5'4" frame, and I could reach the cornice. My safety harness, with carabiners and an arrest lanyard for a gentle catch if I slipped, became my second skin. Local roofers working at the other end of the block tweaked it to fit like a glove — just a few fingers under each strap. They were careful in checking the fit, gently tugging on each strap, as if sending me up on a NASA mission. It was my high-altitude security blanket.

Days blurred into stripping window flashing, painting it a chic green-grey (ditching the tired maroon), and riveting ship's wheels into the metal arches above the windows. The lift's platform swayed with the wind and my movements, leaving me wobbling like a sailor on shore leave each evening, back on solid ground. I gave neighborhood kids joyrides (platform lowered). Rolling the lift down the sidewalk, I was able to re-fastened the custom Upper Fells Point metal sign I had designed for the neighborhood: a Fourth of July fireworks scene with roof-deck revelers.

By Dec. 12, the 3D accents gleamed, and the window trim popped. Up high, the cornice work was zen but laser-focused. One neighbor tried to chitchat while I was 30 feet up, scraping and painting. She must have thought I was whipping up brownies, feet on the ground, not wrestling tin and my own nerves.

Behind the left-hand modillion — a dashing, wave-crest arch at the terminus of the cornice — I found trouble. The careless rehab at 201 had knocked the scroll-shaped piece askew, loosening its brick anchor and letting drafts plague my third-floor bedroom for five years. No wonder the drywall tape puckered and winter drafts bit hard. I texted photos to my brother-in-law, who coached me on fitting a block of wood, insulation and shims to secure it.

Long-festering flaws were finally fixed, just as I prepped to leave: a paradox, patching up my nest for someone else to enjoy.

Solace as a mason in the sky

Christmas 2019 hit me with one foot already out Baltimore's door. I went big, curating unique gifts for every niece and nephew at the family bash, but kept my reasons hush-hush.

For the siblings' cutthroat gift exchange, I ordered a *Bluenose* sailing ship replica, a nod to our Nova Scotia roots.

My brother won the ship's model, but my eager attempt to share its history got drowned out by a bored sister's chatter — classic. Being talked over was getting old. The disconnect stung; I was drifting from the family orbit, soon to break free physically, emotionally and mentally as the world braced for shutdown.

Post-holiday, I dove into my rowhome's fireplaces, long just for show. I installed dampers, coated the fireboxes with refractory cement and extended the lintels to reduce and direct airflow. Both now roared to life.

Cornice and brick sidewall
(Photograph by the author)

Next, I tackled my third-floor external sidewall, extending above the neighbor's sloped roof. I stirred up historic lime mortar, mixed with sand and water, which dried slowly and to a relatively plastic consistency. It was less likely to fracture soft historic bricks than rigid cement mortars.

Painting the cornice

On a sloped work platform that I assembled, I chiseled off decades-old tarpaper and crumbling mortar, water-jetting the brick clean. Bathed in February's south-facing sun, the spot was warm and street sounds muted — even more peaceful than my roof deck. I mused: Should I have been a mason? The work was rewarding aesthetically.

The finished wall and chimney, paired with the freshly painted, teal-goldenrod-copper cornice, were so pleasing to the eye. I slapped leftover copper paint on the metal flashing: cheers to my dog and my color vibe. At street level, I admired my handiwork, an audience of just one who appreciated the improvement.

By mid-February, the house was a gem. Meanwhile, a new virus crept from Wuhan, China, hitting Singapore, Japan and the U.S. As a former NIH medical writer who'd roomed with Johns Hopkins public health experts, I tracked the news, sipping worried coffees with nurse pals. We puzzled over incubation periods and silent carriers, concerned how a pandemic would jolt my move. One silver lining: 2020 and 2021 saw no Outlier deaths. But 2022 would bring a brutal rebound.

I was sculpting my dream home only to leave it. Sick of janky bifold closet doors, I ripped them out, opened up the drywall above and to the sides, and installed open cedar shelving. My realtor scoffed; but later the buyers' husband fell for its aroma and charm, sealing the deal. The 1990s track lighting? Yanked, sold, swapped for Tiffany lamps, farmhouse chandeliers and industrial fan-light combos.

With Ray, a neighborhood handyman with a full head of red-blond hair and mustache, I replaced every electrical outlet and cover — I'd read that this was a smart move to freshen an older home's appearance. A rugged transplant from West Virginia, Ray had me play country gospel music while we worked.

I'd always wanted wall niches in the en-suite bathrooms. I carved one into the third-floor bathroom's drywall, revealing historic red bricks with mortar gaps. Time to mix more lime mortar and tool it in. For shelves I used long, thin salvaged tiles from a nearby renovation. Time ran out for copying the niche idea in the second floor bathroom. The realtor pushed for a dated grey paint throughout, a color I associated with 1990s office decor; I vetoed it for a Benjamin Moore cream, a warm accompaniment to the reds of the exposed brick and fireplaces.

My rowhome shone, a stunner in my realtor's appealing video. The video's beauty underscored the polarity of Baltimore: showpiece interiors, perilous exteriors.

Part of me yearned to hoist my rowhome on skids and trailer it to a safer place, an impossible notion. I didn't ache to stay, yet I regretted not refreshing my home base sooner. As spring 2020 neared, I sold three decades of belongings amid Covid's chaos, often leaving items for sale out on the sidewalk in sunshine to "disinfect," and taking cash payments at arms' length.

I was determined to leave yet in awe of my own resolve. I was truly going.

A dying and reviving supernova

Soon enough, I'll leave this place and give it nary a thought. So count me as a minus-one.

Nostalgia for what's been lost will be overwritten by what's in my nightmares.

— Online commenter on the city's population loss, September 2024

Fifty years ago, Baltimore and Idaho each held about 850,000 people, though Idaho's residents sprawled across 1,000 times the land area. In the summer of 1975, the trendiness crossed, with Baltimore collapsing and Idaho booming. By 2025, Baltimore had lost almost 300,000 residents to riots, crime, failing schools and high taxes, while Idaho's population zoomed to 2 million, a haven of safety.

Neighborhood voices chronicled the city's decline. Waverly blogger Ryan McElroy, writing as "The Chop," documented endless violence, including attempted murders and assaults, that wore him thin until he finally decamped for Nashville after Robbie Ponsi's slaying. My neighbor in Upper Fells Point, Mark Adams, an ex-bail bondsman, called our area "under siege" in 2017. I concurred and set my sights on the Gem State.

Crime without boundaries

A friend asked why I didn't leave earlier; I replied, "Because you can't see around the corner to know whether the crime is continuing or not." The reality that crime would continue was captured by a former roommate. "Safety is always a concern," he observed. "Crime doesn't stay only in rough neighborhoods."

Staying would have felt like a brusque dismissal of the Outliers' brutal lessons, scornful of the sacrilege of their murders. Baltimore's livable, affordable rowhomes kept me tethered for decades, but not forever.

By 2020, many finally accepted reality. Black professionals like my friends Helen and Sylvia had bolted a long time before to safer Columbia and Ellicott City. The Baltimore Banner reported 57,000 black residents left between 2010 and 2020. Ethnic whites — Irish, Italian, Polish — had already ebbed away in the '60s and '70s. Yuppies took their place, only to join the exodus later. Everyone craved safety.

In 2020, Baltimore burned out like a collapsing star, Covid's chaos scattered the city's fragile population, shrinking it from 585,000 to 576,000: 1.42 percent lost, the nation's steepest decline per the *San Francisco Chronicle*. Only Detroit lost more from 2010 to 2020. I was among the 9,000 who left in 2020, which works out to 25 residents a day fleeing. Actually, let's be precise: a net 20 moved away daily, plus four dying of overdoses and one murdered.

Yes, each year, 200 to 300 were murdered, and 700 to 1,000 overdosed. Residents didn't just pack up, they vanished. In 2023 alone, 1,043 fell to drug or alcohol deaths, 261 to homicide, a staggering 1,304 souls erased.

Events spurring departures

Baltimore's population leached away despite flashes of strong leadership. Mayors like William Donald Schaefer and Martin O'Malley slowed the slide, but subsequent weak governance, riots over Freddie Gray and savage murders – Sowers, Pitcairn, Leto, LaPere, Patterson – lit the fuse for mass exits. Marilyn Mosby's 2015-23 tenure as state's attorney, marred by soaring homicides and carjackings, made the city feel like a war zone. Fleeting population gains flatlined under waves of unrest and crime.

Baltimore population loss by year, 1970-2024

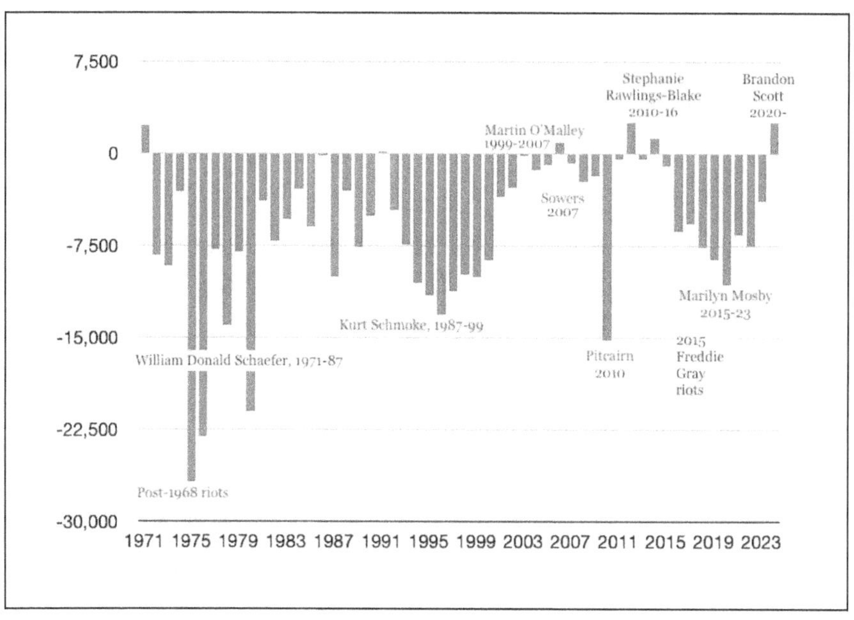

Graphic by the author

A sharper prosecutor might have caged Stephen Pitcairn's killer, John Wagner, who had a 20-year rap sheet: assault, armed robbery, auto theft, domestic violence, drugs. Instead, "second chances" and smooth courtroom apologies freed him to murder Pitcairn in 2010, helping to spur 15,000 to bolt the next year. Wagner was a one-man wrecking ball. State's attorney Patricia Jessamy had a role in the collapse.

Baltimore's voters, backing soft-on-crime prosecutors, and lenient juries fueled a Rust Belt-style exodus, unlike growing Northeastern peers. The outflow could be seen both in Census data after Pitcairn's murder and in anecdotal reports. Following the murders of the Dawson family, Sowers, Patterson and Robbie Ponsi, horrified friends, neighbors and complete strangers told news outlets they would be leaving the city.

Outliers and depopulation

Economist Henry Canaday, in a report summarized on Governing.com, has hypothesized that urban depopulation is explicitly tied to high homicide rates. This isn't surprising, of course.

Sustained rates above 2 homicides per 10,000 residents, seen in cities like Detroit, St. Louis, and Baltimore, lead to strong population outflows, he concluded. Below that threshold, safer cities like Boston see growth.

"Murder rates around 1 per 10,000, reminiscent of the 1950s, are apparently comfortable for city dwellers," Canaday wrote, as reported by Governing.com. "But once that rate gets much above and stays above 2 per 10,000 people, start to leave."

When I crunched the numbers myself, I couldn't precisely replicate Canaday's conclusion that 2 per 10,000 is the clear depopulation trigger. To me, the relationship between the homicide rate and depopulation appeared even more stark: Most U.S. cities *anywhere* above the national average of around 0.5 to 0.7 per 10,000 were losing population.

In Baltimore's case, depopulation since the 1950s has closely tracked homicide rates that are double, triple, or even 10 times higher (in 2015) than the national average.

Baltimore, of course, carries the added burden of a concentration of innocent, law-abiding Outliers killed by remorseless assailants. More than the general homicide rate, these Outlier homicides seem to correlate with spikes in depopulation – particularly after the attacks on Zach Sowers in 2007 and Stephen Pitcairn in 2010, and during prosecutor Marilyn Mosby's tenure from 2015 to 2023. Outlier deaths signal extreme discomfort for city dwellers, who begin sensing that the benefits of Baltimore residency have to be compared to the risk of serious harm.

Baltimore, U.S. homicide rates per 100,000 by year, 1951-2024

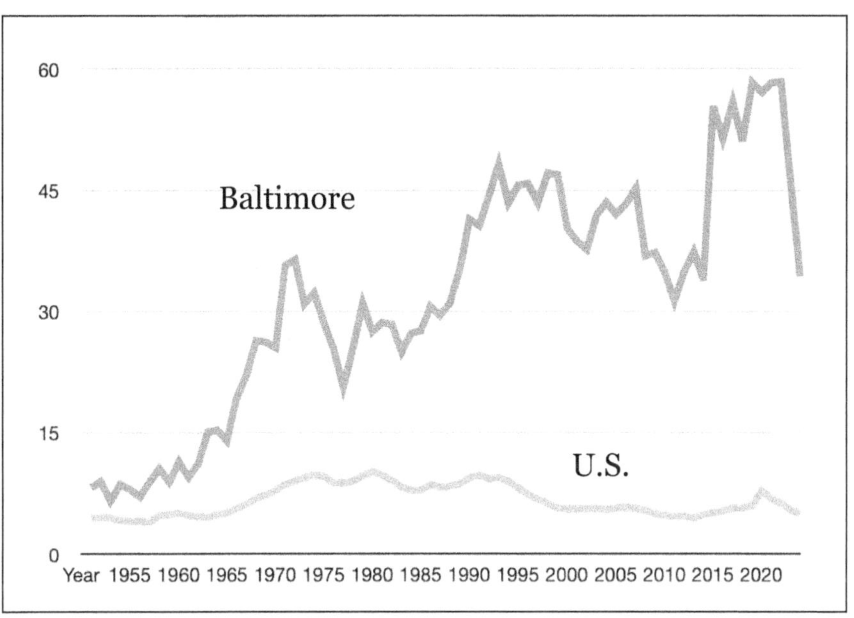

Graphic by the author

This is why Anna Sowers, widow of Zach, noted that crime rates in Baltimore may go down, but people still don't feel safe. It's why economist Anirban Basu observed correctly after Pava LaPere's killing that some homicides generate more economic damage than others. In other words, there is no comfort to be found when innocents are slain, especially in "safe" areas.

It isn't just crime. "People are paying double the taxes, getting half the services," Towson University economist Daraius Irani observed.

By 2023, nearly half of U.S. cities shrank, and urban sustainability expert Sybil Derrible warned that holdouts face crushing taxes for crumbling relics like Baltimore's Inner Harbor, "impossible to maintain."

A much-loved restaurateur

Also impossible to maintain was the Covid-fueled respite from Outlier murders. After none in 2020 and 2021, 2022 set a record with seven. Two occurred hours apart, prompting victims' friends to vow to leave.

A Little Italy restaurant manager was one of the closest victims to my former home on Ann Street, meeting his end outside a liquor store on Broadway that I occasionally patronized. Chesley "Chesco" Patterson received the largest vigil of any Outlier: 300 people gathered on Eastern Avenue.

Many at the vigil said they were done with Baltimore. They had toughed out the grim roll call of other murders nearby — Zach Sowers, Aysha Ring, Kim Leto, Sebastian Dvorak and Jim Forrester, as well as Albo Wroblewski and Tim Moriconi just across the harbor. But Chesco's death erased all hope. "This is the straw that broke the camel's back," one mourner told reporters.

Patterson, 44, ran La Scala Ristorante Italiano for 17 years. He was known for his signature espresso martini and generosity — he once raised nearly $30,000 for a colleague's family after a tragic accident.

The evening of Jan. 23, Patterson closed the restaurant and visited Bristol's Wine Store in the 500 block of Broadway, three blocks from my former home.

Just after 11 p.m., Patterson placed a purchase in his car trunk. As he backed out, a gold Honda Odyssey minivan blocked him in. A passenger exited the van, opened Patterson's driver-side door, and, after a brief struggle, shot him once in the chest with a small handgun. Patterson stumbled from his car, clutching his chest, and collapsed in the street. He died at Johns Hopkins Hospital.

His assailant pleaded guilty in 2023 to first-degree murder and related charges, receiving a life sentence with all but 50 years suspended. As with the dozens of other attackers of Baltimore Outliers, the plea deal averted a trial that would have shed light on why Patterson was targeted.

Attendees among the 300 at his vigil noted "this city isn't safe at all," and "I have no belief this is going to get better." Chesco's death was "a gut punch, gut punch, gut punch," a mourner chanted. A Redditor recalled how he been sitting with Chesco a few months earlier as "people told me Baltimore 'isn't that bad.' Now he's gone."

… and a heart-of-gold grandmother

Three hours after Chesco, Cheryl McCormack, 51, became Outlier No. 32.

A married mother of three children with a grandchild, she delivered DoorDash orders to make ends meet. Known for her heart of gold, she died days before her 52nd birthday. Her brother-in-law urged people to honor her by showing kindness.

Around 2:18 a.m. on Jan. 24, McCormack and a friend ran out of gas on White Avenue. While the friend walked to a gas station, two skinny, masked teens approached him with a gun and forced him back to the car. They demanded McCormack's phone and purse. When she refused, they shot her. She died at the scene. The suspects, 16 years old, were charged with murder but the case was dropped in 2023 when the only witness died.

Reddit commenters, shaken by McCormack's death, swore off Baltimore deliveries: "It's not worth it," one wrote, robbed while wearing an Amazon vest, adding that juvenile murderers are just released to do it again. "Eventually nobody will want to work in the city. It's not only drug dealers and people in the game getting hurt. That woman was a mom just trying to do her job."

The voice of another Redditor cut through the noise: "I was raised poor as shit by a single mom and I was at home at 10 p.m. and amazingly managed to not murder a poor woman doing a [tough] job just to survive."

A stealth sanctuary

Both black and white Baltimoreans were leaving, as were friends who found the deaths of Patterson and McCormack the last straw. Meanwhile, for decades, officials had turned to immigrants, especially Hispanics, to prop up a fading city. Their arrival partly offset the overall exodus, and raised the Hispanic population share from 1 percent in 1990 to 8 percent in 2020.

Baltimore might yet find a future in reclaiming its 19th-century role as an immigrant magnet. Newcomers appeared not to share long-term residents' dissatisfaction with public safety and schools, grateful, perhaps, to be in the U.S. at all. But they weren't immune to danger: Six of 44 Outlier victims were Hispanic or Asian.

Sitting in my home office in Upper Fells Point, I witnessed this transformation first hand. By 1998, overheard conversations in Spanish had replaced English floating in on warm days when I left the window open.

Forty-five minutes away, D.C. was becoming the nation's richest metro, driven by government expansion and thriving businesses. Meanwhile, Baltimore quietly became a stealth sanctuary city: officially just "welcoming" but tacitly recruiting any newcomer. Mayors saw opportunity in the federal money flowing to their sanctuary city: $9,000 per resident, legal or otherwise, in 2019. More residents meant more money, more clout. Warm bodies also fluffed congressional apportionment, creating "rotten boroughs" packed with non-voting immigrants who padded political power without an ability to vote out unresponsive leaders.

Since the '80s, Mexicans and other Latin Americans flocked to Highlandtown, Upper Fells Point and Greektown, lured by cheap rents. Under Mayor O'Malley, sneaky ads (in Spanish) in *El Tiempo Latino* pitched Baltimore to Spanish speakers, a quiet pivot that favored immigrants, likely not to report crime given the illegal status of many, ahead of protecting legacy residents.

For mayors of decaying cities, it was a no-brainer: More bodies meant more cash and clout, and a quiet, compliant demographic to boot.

By 2024, Hispanic and Asian newcomers nudged Baltimore's population up, barely offsetting the white and black exodus and the losses to homicides and drug overdoses. Some appeared on the Outliers list: In 2014, Jose Abreu, a 49-year-old Dominican, was gunned down at his Southwest Baltimore deli, nothing stolen. In 2019, Morgan State baseball star Manuel Luis fell to bullets, as did a deli operator, Carmen Rodriguez. In 2023, Filipino Victor Malabayabas was killed in Canton, the second Asian after Joel Lee, 30 years earlier. In 2024, Fabian Sánchez-González, a son of Mexican immigrants, died clerking at a Canton T-Mobile.

Baltimore's new arrivals were dynamic entrepreneurs but unable to escape the city's bloody landscape.

Noticing the trend

In the late '90s, an Upper Fells Point neighbor griped about undocumented immigrants moving next door, only to be told at a community meeting: no enforcement unless they broke other laws. Soon, the community association's newsletters went bilingual, Spanish alongside English.

In 2015, the Baltimore Hispanic Chamber of Commerce president dubbed the city "a paradise for people that do not have legal status yet," touting loose enforcement of immigration law, solid transit and job prospects.

There were perks, like Tortilleria Sinaloa, where the scent of toasted corn and lime tortillas lured Hispanic patrons from miles away. The proprietor imported a gigantic tortilla machine from Mexico that took four hours to clean daily. I built their website in exchange for free meals for life.

Challenges emerged too. Undocumented families tapped Maryland's Independence card for food aid, even as they flashed thick wads of cash at Highlandtown grocery checkouts. This double-dipping magnet drew more immigrants.

In 2016, Mayor Rawlings-Blake codified a decades-old unwritten rule — cops wouldn't check immigration status — echoed in community and police meetings since the '80s. Mayors O'Malley, Catherine Pugh and Brandon Scott leaned on the "welcoming" buzzword to sidestep the sanctuary city tag and negative federal attention. Pugh's 2018 move to funnel $200,000 into deportation legal defense sparked backlash, with crime fighting and school funding crying for cash. Black residents, bristling at job competition with immigrants, packed up for Columbia, Towson, Owings Mills, White Marsh and Ellicott City, feeding the city's relentless exodus.

Martin hits the job running

A painter from Puebla, Mexico, Martin was a standout in Upper Fells Point's shifting tapestry. Middle-aged, 5'6", with grey-flecked hair and a paint-splattered backpack, he wielded a well-maintained brush and roller like a maestro. Unlike a prior Baltimore contractor I hired — chatty, sloppy and overweight, making ladder work look dangerous — Martin (pronounced Mar-TEEN) was a pro. Plucked from a convenience store lot to tackle my basement ceiling's joists, he jumped in, yanking historic nails with my hammer before I could even brief him. His "lunch"? Just a soda. I shared my homemade tostadas.

Working atop a step stool, stretching over a furnace and shelves, he nailed the job with precision. Our joint words of Spanglish kept planning and scheduling smooth. The primer covered smoke smudges from wood burning in bygone centuries.

Unless they were foolhardy enough to run a deli in a rough area, Hispanic immigrants like Martin had a knack for dodging Baltimore's dangers. Armed with tight-knit networks, street smarts and a dose of gang muscle, they sidestepped crime's worst traps. They steered clear of West

Baltimore's shadows, drilled "stranger danger" into their kids, and sniffed out trouble before it could snag them. These newcomers brought a survival instinct honed by generations of navigating tough odds.

A 'liberal' outlook

In Upper Fells Point, my mostly Democrat neighbors — including some unreformed '60s hippies said to be former Weather Underground radicals — floored me one night at a Greek restaurant gathering. A social worker hailed Hispanic immigration for displacing black residents, claiming Latinos brought less crime and harder hustle. I pushed back: "But blacks helped build our waterfront," their legacy as ship caulkers and stevedores undeniable, a historic debt unpaid. Baltimore had been the crucible for Frederick Douglass and Thurgood Marshall. My words fell flat, met with shrugs.

Early migrants, a good number from Puebla in Mexico, fumbled trash day, sweeping garbage into Regester, Durham, Castle and Chapel alleys, fattening the rats. Single men fueled chaos: drunken knife fights outside a cantina, a 1999 execution-style shooting near my rowhome. Suspected Marielito Cubans loitered across from my door, tossing liquor bottles and yelling; I'd slip them cash to scram when showing rooms to potential housemates. Over time, the Puebla folks got the memo on trash schedules and settled into family life, nudged by community norms.

Back at the restaurant, neighbors floored me again, cheering slumlords. Their view was that slumlords housed the poor — better than homelessness, they argued. They had a point, but the slumlords overcharged for inadequate shelter.

One noontime, I ran across a Mexican mom and her daughter with a sprained ankle heading home from Wolfe Street Academy. I helped carry the daughter home. There I glimpsed their Regester Street reality: a single second-floor room, owned by an African landlord, with no clear kitchen or bathroom, hemmed in by closets stuffed with cardboard boxes, like the back room of a warehouse. I'd seen more functional thatch huts in Guatemala. Yet, neighbors weren't entirely wrong about slumlords. Pre-1960s Baltimore had near-zero homelessness, thanks to dollar-a-night flophouses by the wharves. Urban Institute and Habitat for Humanity studies back this: Bloated housing codes jack up costs, locking out the poorest.

Following the Puebla arrivals, a second immigrant wave arrived: hulking, heavily tattooed Hondurans, looking like newly released ex-cons who'd pumped iron behind bars. No one asked Baltimoreans about this shift, but politicians, landlords and merchants cashed in.

Crossing paths with one of these bruisers on Durham Street, no refuge in sight, unease hit me hard. Now in my mid-50s, the situation screamed: "This sanctuary city game's gone too far. At some point, I'll have to go." Unchecked policies ignored ripple effects and the fears of heritage Americans, especially older women. The city's leaders had picked a side. Policymakers were safe in ivory towers; I was not.

For undocumented Americans, Baltimore was a de facto sanctuary. Idaho was a sanctuary of a different kind, for those fleeing uproar and unrest in the wake of left-wing policies, particularly in California, Oregon and Washington state. And then there's me from Maryland sticking out like a sore thumb. So the U.S. has split into two radically different types of sanctuaries: sanctuary cities (blue) and sanctuary states (red).

After I departed Maryland, yet another stream of migrants began to show up.

A transgender safe haven

By May 2025, Baltimore had become a magnet for transgender migrants fleeing red states like Florida and Texas, chasing acceptance in a liberal city in a blue state. A Reddit user summed it up: "Our displaced queer Floridian population is HUGE," crediting Maryland's Southern proximity and cultural vibe. Baltimore Safe Haven's 2025 waitlist for transitional housing swelled to 300, mostly red-state escapees.

John Waters' camp legacy and Divine's cross-dressing flamboyance cemented Baltimore, alongside Chicago and New York City, as a trans destination, in Charm City's case boosted by cheap rents. Cross-dressing had deep roots. In the '80s and '90s, I'd spot males dressed as female streetwalkers on Guilford Avenue after my night shift at the Sun. They rocked spandex, puffy jackets and towering beehive hairdos.

For modern transgenders, Hampden and Charles Village offer a congenial atmosphere. Baltimore Safe Haven, founded in 2018, provided housing and HIV testing, bolstered by Maryland's 2014 anti-discrimination laws and Baltimore's 2019 trans-inclusive policies.

Yet, danger lurked. Anti-gay sentiments, rooted in religious and hypermasculine norms in parts of the black community, fueled violence. Transgender Day of Remembrance logged eight homicides of Baltimore trans in eight years, including Mia Henderson and Kandy Hall in 2014. A 2021 Reddit thread captured the paradox: "Maryland is LGBT-friendly as a whole, but Baltimore's crime rate makes it risky to be there, period — especially as a trans person."

Sometimes, the city's trans welcome felt like it tipped into hostility toward "cisgenders." My final Baltimore summer, I popped into a Patterson Park coffee shop to post a flier for a Boat Lake cleanup.

A blue-haired, tattooed barista shot me a death glare, likely pegging me as "cis" for my collarbone-length natural hair, normal BMI, and lack of piercings and tattoos. She judged me by my cover, casting me as the enemy. Ironic, since as a 1970s arts critic for the University of Maryland's *Diamondback*, the student paper, I'd championed D.C.'s Pier 9, a trailblazing drag club off South Capitol Street. Its blond, Redford-esque publicist gushed over my reviews, humble and grateful for coverage as Pier 9 rose from obscurity.

From high school on, my gay and lesbian friends — artsy, articulate, my kind of people — were genuine. Back then, there were no elaborate ideological litmus tests, no freezing you out for not being gay or trans yourself, no snotty baristas oozing hostility.

'Murders shock the conscience'

If you have white flight then black flight, then who is left?

— Commenter on the Baltimore City-Data forum

Could a blend of immigrants, trans folks and liberal red-state refugees revive Baltimore's fading supernova? This combustible demographic cocktail — Hispanic immigrants and the trans gang are not on the same cultural page — pumped in new blood.

But the city's heartbeat stayed erratic. Criminals had no interest in respecting Baltimore's hopeful reinvention. The loss of Chesco Patterson and Cheryl McCormack two hours apart was a huge blow.

Economist Anirban Basu didn't mince words: "Some of these murders have shocked the conscience — when a grandmother or a restaurant manager in Little Italy is murdered."

Talent fled, as hospitals, universities and firms struggled to recruit. "People prefer to be in Boston or New York" for safety, Basu said, urging leaders to "take really bad people off the streets and keep them off."

From 2010 to 2020, Baltimore shed 35,000 residents — "almost the size of Annapolis" — gutting economic vigor. "The cost is massive," Basu noted.

Carjackings accelerated the flight. "When people have their car stolen, they move," Basu observed.

A collapsing Eastside

The 2021 demolition of Perkins Homes near Upper Fells Point promised renewal but it only shifted crime. With almost military tactics and speed, after Perkins fell, teens deployed from rough areas further afield, and began to target

Fells and Upper Fells instead of downtown. This was an unnerving step backward.

> *This is why my friends and I never go to Fells Point or the Harbor anymore. Too much crime and nothing being done about it. Baltimore is a dying city.*
>
> *Protect us or watch us leave.*
>
> *— Two commenters respond to a Fells Point robbery, April 2025*

Carjackings spiked in 2023–24. Teen mobs turned Broadway Pier, once a tranquil gem featured in the movie *Sleepless in Seattle,* into a battleground, with shootings and fights. Juveniles flaunted curfew and drank tequila openly, snatched carryout food from passersby and narrowly missed pedestrians with their dirt bikes. Police took no action. Outnumbered, they surrendered control.

In 2023, a Butchers Hill woman was robbed by a 12-year-old serial car thief with more than a dozen uncharged heists. In 2024, a 66-year-old on South Madeira barely survived a head-stomping by at least three teens.

By early 2025, Teporah Bilezikian, a hit-and-run witness at Bank and Broadway, voiced the city's dread: "It's actually pretty terrifying living in Baltimore City right now," slamming unchecked juvenile crime and soft judges. Jillian Langley of Highlandtown added, "Yeah, we're done," after an ax-wielding thug smashed car windows along her block.

I'd been gone five years by this time. My hope was that things back East were improving or at least the same. These witnesses to my old stomping ground expressed raw fear; everything was worse. One wonders how some of my favorite former neighborhoods can survive a deteriorating reality from one I found intolerable.

The cavalry is not coming

In response to an online Reddit thread in 2022 asking for honest thoughts about living in Baltimore, one responder noted, "[This] place has really worn me down mentally, every time I come home from vacation I have to ask myself, "Will this be another vacation where I come home to find my window smashed, my car tires stolen, my catalytic converter stolen."

Baltimore's revolving-door leadership plays a huge role in its problems. Sheila Dixon (effective but corrupt, 2007), Stephanie Rawlings-Blake (clueless, 2010), and Catherine Pugh (very corrupt and clueless, 2016) ran the city into the ground. Brandon Scott arrived in 2020, boasting by 2025 about homicides dropping. "That's what vacant houses are for," a cynic cracked, hinting at a grim fix to lower the numbers.

At the state level, things weren't better. In 2023, Gov. Larry Hogan was replaced by Wes Moore, who told the National Press Club to "depoliticize" crime talk. Translation: Let's not talk about murders, it makes Baltimore's leadership look bad. Moore's framing disrespected the 10,000 homicide victims in Baltimore from 1990 to 2023, as if to say that concern over this de facto genocide was a cheap political stunt. It erased events endured by the loved ones of Johnny Tobash, Sebastian Dvorak, Peter Marvit, Alex Wroblewski, Molly Macauley and so many others — each death rattling colleagues and spurring departures from Charm City.

Moore should be censured for deliberately misleading his audience. He touted an irrelevant national violent crime dip since the '90s, a deeply cynical statement attempting to deflect away from Baltimore's bloodshed, where homicides have run 10 to 15 times above the national average since 2015. Violent crime in Baltimore had not dipped, at all.

Three months after Moore's speech, tech CEO Pava LaPere's rooftop murder shredded his "don't politicize" plea, showing Baltimore's reality to the world.

Juvenile justice advocates had their own excuse — that human brains don't mature until 25 — to argue for parole leniency. Vincent Schiraldi, Moore's 2023 juvenile services chief pick, took this view to an extreme, suggesting abolishing juvenile supervision altogether. Heritage Americans — black and white — bolted for the suburbs, leaving immigrants, progressives, yuppies and trans folks to grapple with lawless kids.

I'd seen a drug operation recruit youngsters like Baby Boy, who skated through the system untouched until he hit 18. By 2024, juveniles weren't just slinging drugs — they were carjacking, robbing, head-stomping and shooting dead Outliers like DoorDash driver Cheryl McCormack while escaping punishment.

In October 2024, Patterson Park residents and businesses demanded Schiraldi's head after a brutal Butchers Hill attack on South Madeira Street. "Juvenile offenders are repeatedly committing violent crimes, often within hours of being released to their guardians," petitioners told *The Baltimore Sun*. In June 2025, Governor Moore removed Schiraldi from his position.

Reddit Baltimore commenters discussing the murder of McCormack by a 16-year-old dissected the savvy posturing of juvenile criminals. If police show up, they hand the gun to the youngest; the oldest holds the cash. The youths know juvenile sentences are a slap on the wrist — home detention, not even court. They're back out in days.

It seemed as though every juvenile offender committed the same crimes again, one commenter posted, either sitting on their porch with their ankle monitor dealing drugs, or popping the monitor off and looking for more trouble on the streets, with no fear of repercussions.

Outlier killers by age range

Age	Number
14-15	4
16-19	16
In their 20s	18
30s and older	10

The threat of juveniles is demonstrated by the ages of the killers of Outliers; three (Kim Leto, Timothy Reynolds and

Fabian Sanchez-Gonzales) were killed by assailants who were only 14 years old. Still, two of the most savage murders, of Stephen Pitcairn and Pava LaPere, involved assailants in their 30s.

Baltimore "is a war zone," an online commenter noted, "with civilians who are not allowed to defend themselves." Unexpectedly, a truce in the war arrived with Covid-19. No Outliers died in 2020 and 2021. Baltimore's overall homicide stayed high, but it seemed that the criminals couldn't connect with their law-abiding targets while the latter stayed indoors during lockdowns. As a corollary, homicides involving domestic abuse soared.

In sum, Baltimore had a surge in homicides during prosecutor Marilyn Mosby's 2015-23 tenure. The killings slowed during a Covid lull, then rebounded.

Safety in Baltimore was ever fleeting and erratic. Supernovas are bright but indicate the end of a star's life cycle. Their energy output fluctuates as they decay, a pattern seen in Charm City.

My great escape

This city scares me to death. If I could, I would move away tomorrow. I truly don't feel safe anywhere.

— Anna Sowers

In March 2020, Covid-19 upended American life. Beyond Baltimore's ceaseless carjackings and crime, I feared a pandemic-triggered collapse of the food supply chain. The 2013 National Geographic docudrama *American Blackout* still haunted me with its vision of a cyberattack taking down the grid and, with it, the fragile system that keeps us fed.

In a city like Baltimore, already teetering on the edge, such a collapse would be catastrophic. On a good day, the city felt two steps from anarchy. With 2,000 former inmates reentering civilian life annually — many returning to high-crime east and west side neighborhoods riddled with drug networks — the city was a powder keg.

In 2020, a third of Baltimore's residents relied on food stamps, and an equal proportion lived in "food deserts," where corner stores stocked only junk and processed foods. These were not people likely to have pantries stocked for disaster, unlike Mormons in the Intermountain West, where prepping is a way of life.

I'd seen this fragility firsthand in 2007 when a grocery store on South Regester Street was set to be demolished.

One day, while walking my sheltie back from Betty Hyatt Park, I stumbled on a mob that had broken the store's door, looting the last canned goods on the shelves. "Don't do that!" I said, my voice falling on deaf ears. "It's not right." The looters, caught in a frenzy, ignored me, grabbing what little was left. The chaotic, out-of-control vibe unnerved me, and I moved on quickly.

In 2020, with Baltimore ranked the nation's 14th poorest city and memories of the 2015 riots — when mobs burned and looted — still fresh, I could easily imagine hungry crowds torching everything in a crisis. If a cyberattack, pandemic or even lockdowns crippled the food supply, the city's thin veneer of order would shatter.

Dangerous but familiar

Like anyone else, I'm a creature of habit. You grow attached to a place, even if it's rough and tumble. Familiarity is a powerful anchor, not to be underestimated. But crime in Baltimore pushed me to a breaking point, forcing a firm decision to leave, despite the wrenching upheaval of relocating at age 65, 2,445 miles away.

Yet even as I packed my bags, I wanted to understand why others were choosing to stay, despite the city's dangers.

In a 2023 interview, filmmaker John Waters celebrated the city's "poverty and funkiness," saying, "It's still affordable to live here. There's still a Bohemia, kids can be poor and creative." When in 2019 President Trump called Baltimore a "shithole with all the rats and roaches," Waters quipped, "Every news team in the world called me for a comment. I said we like our rats and roaches! You can't really harm Baltimore."

His defiance captures a certain Baltimore spirit, one echoed in a May 2025 Reddit post where an online commenter, moving from rural Maryland to Baltimore, wrote, "Baltimore has a soul, but my hometown doesn't even have a personality."

Others on the subreddit described gleeful visits or plans to relocate from red states like Texas. Time will tell how that pans out.

Yet I couldn't stay. The Baltimore I left was a city I could still imagine as magnificent — without the criminals. With them, it was unbearable. I'd miss my roof deck garden and the Tahitian beauty of its sunsets, but the reality was grim: 14 more Outliers were killed after I drove away in 2020.

Lee Habeeb, in a *Newsweek* opinion piece titled "Trump May Be Crude, but Baltimore Really Is Spiraling — That's Why I Left," nailed the reasons for leaving that made sense for so many. Citing crime, corruption, failing schools and taxes, he noted Baltimore's loss of 350,000 residents since 1950, calling it "not a population loss. That's an exodus."

Some, like former *Baltimore Sun* reporter Rafael Alvarez, refuse to leave. In his essay "Leaving Baltimore? Not an Option," my old colleague described his Italian and Polish relatives fleeing to the suburbs while he and a few diehards stayed loyal.

For Alvarez, personal ties outweigh the city's flaws. But it's worth noting he splits time between Baltimore and Washington, D.C., while Waters juggles homes in San Francisco, Greenwich Village and Baltimore's Guilford neighborhood. They have ways to take a break from Charm City's chaos. I didn't.

'It's time'

Departure loomed, and I was ready to return to Idaho, where my sheltie's roots lay. A crack-of-dawn call to his breeder — my mistake, thinking they were on Mountain Time when they were on Pacific — signaled my decision. "It's time," I told them, honoring a pledge to return made three years earlier. We brainstormed temporary housing, and they sent near-daily updates on whether snow had cleared from Lolo Pass, the route linking Idaho and Montana.

Leaving meant dismantling 30 years of my life in Baltimore. I parted with Modpodged file cabinets adorned with maps of my world travels, shelves of travel books, a giant world map hung on bamboo supports (inspired by Bloody Mary's, a Bora Bora restaurant), and batik paintings by Balinese artists. Even my self-designed Upper Fells Point metal sign, crafted by Maryland Correctional Enterprises at Jessup prison — ironically, a home for some of the Outliers' killers — found a new owner.

My neighbor Ray lent a hand, hauling away pieces of my past. Tragically, he'd be gone within months, felled by Covid after refusing hospital care. As I packed, the weight of leaving mixed with the pull of Idaho's open spaces, where I could finally breathe again.

A bank run

The final push came on March 23, 2020. At 9 a.m., I biked 10 minutes to the Wells Fargo in Harbor East to transfer my savings to a small credit union out West, my heart already pounding as Covid hysteria gripped the city.

A note on the door said the branch was closed. No warning, no call to reschedule my appointment — just a locked door. Panic surged as I stood there with two others, our shared dread palpable, the specter of a bank run chilling us.

Unnerved, I biked home, booked a Zipcar and drove to Highlandtown. Traffic was a nightmare, worse than rush hour. Two blocks from the bank, my worst fears materialized. A chaotic line of cars snaked through the streets, clogging the drive-thru lanes as people scrambled to withdraw cash, terrified the state was shutting down.

I pleaded my way into the branch, citing my appointment to avoid being turned away. As a staffer struggled to start my fund transfer, a clerk burst behind us, voice electric with urgency: "Governor Hogan is closing the state at 5 p.m."

My fear was that my life's savings would vanish into a financial abyss. I left without completing the transfer, consumed by dread. For weeks, that anxiety gnawed at me, until I finally succeeded in moving my savings West. Just six months earlier, I'd been toasting friends at a wedding in a quaint Emilia-Romagna castle, the world bright and open. Now, it was shrouded in darkness.

Downsizing was chaos, my 30 years of "stuff" a testament to my failure at minimalism. Furnishings to sell, and upgrades to install — new lighting, outlets, closets, fireplace dampers — cluttered my home. I went down the checklist to get everything upgraded.

Most poignant were the ashes of my three shelties, stored in ornate wooden boxes in a hallway niche. Beau's ashes found their place at Betty Hyatt Park, where he'd played hide-and-seek behind a tree as a pup. Pierre's went to a grassy patch at Lighthouse Point, where he'd once fallen off rotten piers into the Patapsco's murky waters, only to swim strongly to me, even though I'd rescued him only days before.

The ashes of Zoey — the sheltie who started a chain reaction of events to have me leave Baltimore — were scattered at Patterson Park, on a dandelion-strewn slope by the senior center. There I'd posed him to echo Wyeth's *Christina's World*. That field was Zoey's world. Now I'd head for Copper's, 2,500 miles west.

Packing up

In March 2020, as Baltimore teetered, I scrambled to hire a realtor and a painting crew to ready my home for sale. Despite a brutal to-do list, I clung to routine, meeting friends at 6 a.m. in Patterson Park's dog park, where one of Moose the sheltie's owners stumbled in from the night shift, or grabbing coffee with Hopkins nurses on the same daybreak timeframe.

The move was a whirlwind of preparation. A friend drove me to Home Depot to rent a 12-foot moving truck. Ray, my neighbor, helped me cram what we could inside — two bikes, travel slides, clothes, pet gear, tools, ladders and camping equipment — hastily chosen in a haze of urgency. Anything that didn't fit was Ray's to own.

Fleeing Baltimore

With Copper crated on the passenger seat and my grey tabbies, Olivia and Olive, in smaller crates on the console, I took one last look at the pansies I'd planted out front for curb appeal. I hoped my house would sell in this upside-down world; I'd done what I could.

Driving down Ann Street, a pang of guilt hit me — I wanted to personally bid farewell to every neighbor who'd made this place home, but the sun was dipping toward the horizon, the open road called, and I knew farewells would be awkward. People who moved away usually just up and left. Fear of falling behind a full day on my schedule instead of hitting the road outweighed sentiment. Driving away, I didn't have the time or courage for drawn-out farewells.

On that Friday evening, I drove the loaded truck to say goodbye to my friend who I'll call Leiah, three blocks away. "You came with the whole truck," she said, touched by the gesture. We are good friends; I had recently driven at 3 a.m. to Central Booking when a family member falsely reported her for a domestic matter and she spent the night in a holding cell. I checked on her status with the warden and reported where things stood to her grateful father.

"My work here is done," I had thought as I drove up the Fallsway on that quiet early morning to the city jail. So many encounters and stories had come my way in Baltimore, and this event was a capper for a suburban emigre from quiet Rockville.

We've stayed in touch as she builds her post-Baltimore life in Montgomery Village, her son growing up far from the city's turmoil.

With that goodbye, I steered my little pack of animals west on I-70, the weight of Baltimore's dangers fading in the rearview, replaced by the uncertain promise of a new start.

Memories from a distance

Neighborhoods and cities pulse like sine curves, long series of hills and valleys, a roller coaster defying linear progress. A friend noted that what seems like a neighborhood's permanent collapse can self-correct. He described drug dealers invading his neighborhood, Forest Park in Northwest Baltimore. They rented a house as headquarters, and chaos reigned — until they imploded, arrested or scattered. Slowly, the neighborhood stabilized.

For another example, Perkins Homes, near Upper Fells Point, was demolished in 2021, lifting a visual blight from the Pratt Street corridor. Yet a ripple effect brought teen gangs from further away, who began to frequent Broadway Pier instead of the Inner Harbor — a net downgrade. It's a reminder: When one arc descends, another rises.

Baltimore's overall trajectory wavers too. After years of rising homicides and relentless outward migration, 2024 and 2025 brought modest signs of recovery. But does a slight improvement count as progress, or just a temporary plateau?

Maybe the city's epidemics — of violence, of drugs — are simply burning themselves out. At a certain point, Darwinian forces take hold. Overdose deaths, criminal-on-criminal killings: They slow when there are no more susceptible victims.

These arcs — of places, of people — obscure what lies ahead. But the arc of transition looms largest.

The squeegee crossroad

Baltimore's initial charm, vivid and individualistic, can erode over time. For many, that erosion is accelerated by nuisance behaviors, especially those involving teens with no apparent supervision. Dirt bikers, weaving through city streets, have become a decades-old tradition of illegal thrill. In 1999, a police chase ended in a fatal crash. Since then, police won't pursue them.

Then came the squeegee kids. Once romanticized as scrappy entrepreneurs, they began demanding payment, sometimes extorting drivers with windshield cleanings no one asked for. Some ran Cash App scams. In 2022, tensions boiled over: Zhamiel Dixon, 26, shot two squeegee workers after they allegedly scammed his mother. Charges were later dropped.

The breaking point came on July 7, 2022. A series of events unfolded at Light and Conway streets, right across from Harborplace. A state senator was hit with a bottle. An 18-year-old aimed a BB gun at a driver.

Then a 14-year-old among the squeegee kids masked up and pulled a gun from his backpack. He shot 48-year-old Hampden resident Timothy Reynolds five times, killing him, after Reynolds confronted the group with a baseball bat.

The teen, who may have taunted Reynolds to rile him up, was later convicted of manslaughter and sentenced to 15 years. Reynolds had a bat; the kid had a homemade gun. Why was a 14-year-old cleaning windshields carrying a gun? To intimidate Reynolds so as to taunt him with impunity? To feel untouchable? The court and the public wrestled with questions, but for many residents, the violence confirmed what they already felt: a loss of safety, order and limits, also seen in carjackings and head-stomping assaults by juveniles.

Long before Reynolds' death, the tide had turned against squeegee kids. What had once been a grudgingly tolerated gray area — teens hustling at intersections — became a red line. The city debated a ban. Other cities had acted decades ago. In Baltimore, hesitation lingered until blood was spilled. Reynolds, a law-abiding citizen irritated beyond his limits, became a symbol — not perfect, but potent.

If you've heard of the old expression "bought a knife to a gunfight," that applies to Reynolds, who bought a baseball bat to an armed foe. Reynold's weapon of choice reminds me of the Baltimore tradition of keeping a baseball bat at hand behind front and bedroom doors for self-defense.

I had one behind each of my three doors. They wouldn't have won a gun fight.

Outliers everywhere

Reynolds' story, and those like it, point to something darker: What happens when everyday people — Outliers — die because their city never gets around to controlling nuisance behaviors creating enormous friction? Nuisance behaviors are more serious than they may appear on the surface, and fatalities are a predictable outcome.

Originally, I hadn't planned to write a book about violence in Baltimore. This was going to be a memoir about building cabins out West, with a short preface explaining why I left. I planned to mention a few chilling incidents: the murders of Zach Sowers and Kim Leto, the assault on Lauren Hayden. Events that rattled me, and got closer and closer, layering the losses deeper and deeper.

But that preface grew. It became this: a standalone book, on leaving Charm City. I had to dissect Baltimore's homicide landscape, and the distinct category of Outlier murders.

Baltimore may lead the nation in these losses. It's a grim distinction, matching its crown for fatal overdoses. These types of homicides do occur in other cities as well, apparently in a more limited fashion — a few here or there, rather than dozens as in Baltimore.

In 2019, Barnard freshman Tessa Majors was killed in Manhattan, stabbed in a park by teens. And fatal carjackings, a rough proxy for Outlier murders, are surging across the U.S.: Mohammad Anwar and Mike Gill in D.C., Gerard Grandzol in Philadelphia, of course Chesco Patterson in Baltimore. Then there's the brutal slashing of Iryna Zarutska on public transpiration in Charlotte, N.C. These victims weren't gang members. They were fathers, students, professionals, emigres going home after work: people who played by the rules.

In Baltimore, Outliers account for an average of 1 percent of the city's annual murders. To the reader this may seem a small number; to me, it's awfully high, given that a healthy social fabric and justice system would have vanishingly small numbers. And their impact is outsized. Each one ripples outward, convincing dozens, hundreds or thousands of people that the city's social contract has collapsed. That it's no longer safe to stay. That it's time to fold 'em.

The arc of attachment

There was a time when I loved Baltimore without question. When Baby Boy was still young and uncorrupted, when my neighbor Bernie played piano through our shared wall, when Lee yelled from the alley that the crab soup was ready. Before Miss Joan got carjacked and even worse, shrugged it off.

Even under Mayor Sheila Dixon — who stole gift cards meant for the homeless — the city functioned. She rallied department heads, fixed potholes, sent rat patrols. You learned to shrug off minor corruption, knowing worse was possible. And worse did come: Rawlings-Blake, Pugh, Mosby, Scott, the parade of dysfunction.

Still, the small things sustained us. Councilmen Nick D'Adamo would coax your cat out of a tree, and his successor, Jim Kraft, hosted cookouts at Captain James Landing, where the Patapsco glinted under the spring sun and burgers were served on paper plates. Kraft passed out bookmarks listing what he could help you with. First bullet point: "Potholes." These "pothole politicians" skipped grandstanding. They got things done.

Baltimore felt intimate then. "Smalltimore," we called it. At Kraft's cookouts on the water, you knew people at every table. You could believe your city might turn a corner. The top politicos including mayoral candidates were present, shaking hands and chatting. They at least pretended to listen. For a moment, your roller coaster car was at the top of the arc. The onshore breeze was in your face. The view was beautiful. Oblivious to the future, you could cherish the moment. This would be perfect if it could last.

But roller coasters come down. And sometimes, you don't want to ride again.

Every city has its arcs. So do the people who live in them. There's a moment when a place feels full of promise, and a moment when you realize it no longer loves you back.

For me, the carjackings on my block were a turning point, but not the only one. It was the cumulative toll — of Outlier murders, of civic neglect, 2017's flurry of attacks on women only steps away from my domicile, one victim's skull fractured, the other's face soaked in mace. Of feeling like I had to coach out-of-town friends on matters as ordinary as how to survive a stop at a traffic light if threats and potential violence developed.

The arc bent downward. And I knew, finally, it was time to let go.

Solace and solutions

The year 2017 was brutal for Baltimore's Outliers, claiming six lives, including two deeply beloved community figures: bartender Alex Wroblewski III and Morgan State student Johnny Tobash. Each was an anchor in his neighborhood.

In February 2026, I contacted family members and friends to learn how they had coped in the intervening years.

For Alex Wroblewski's parents, Alex Jr. and Mary Kay — lifelong residents of Locust Point, the historic, tight-knit peninsular neighborhood in South Baltimore — the loss remained evident, though transformed. A 2018 Catholic Review photograph captured their quiet heartache as they held a large portrait of their son. Eight years later, during our conversation, they appeared more at peace.

"We love our community; we're real city folks," Mary Kay told me by phone. Several factors — a massive outpouring of neighborly support, their volunteer work helping others through loss and their Roman Catholic faith — had built resilience and resolve.

The Locust Point neighborhood, one of Baltimore's safest, found ways to protect and steady Alex Jr. and Mary Kay from the first moments of loss. Alex Jr. recalled one small mercy.

"The one thing I feel lucky about, when Alex [III] got shot, we were spared the knock on the door," he said. Instead, he received a call from one of his son's friends, who often walked the waitresses home. The friend had gone looking for Alex III at the Royal Farms on Key Highway, where a clerk told him that two robbers had followed and shot the 41-year-old. This friend called the parents.

Like Kim Leto in Patterson Park, Alex III was a bartender, and like Chesco Patterson in Little Italy, he doubled as a restaurant manager. Along with Larry Peterson of Mount Vernon, David Philpot of Fells Point and Victor Malabayabas of Canton, he was outgoing and a community leader.

As did bicyclist Robbie Ponsi, Alex, a strong 6-foot-2 former athlete, tried to fight off his attackers. They were later caught and sentenced.

Flowers, balloons and Alex's photograph soon appeared on a light pole near the Royal Farms. His funeral Mass overflowed into the choir loft. A plaque bearing his image now stands in a local park, and every year on the anniversary of his death, neighbors gather to release paper lanterns into the night sky.

'Mayor of South Baltimore'

At the first memorial, the crowd roared as a friend's message was read aloud. "He was the true mayor of South Baltimore," the speaker observed. "He had no enemies, he was the best human being I've ever known."

"We have great faith, which has gotten us through," Mary Kay said. "We have a wonderful community, with all the support and love we have received. I don't feel I could have healed otherwise. I see God through the love of other people."

Notably absent was any focus on Alex III's assailants. Instead, we spoke of hope that the violence might someday abate. I wondered aloud whether the era of the Outliers might one day be viewed as akin to China's Cultural Revolution: lost years of chaos, trauma and death-by-mob that eventually ended with the arrests of its instigators.

In their daily prayers, the couple hopes "that somehow people are reached. To make Baltimore City, Charm City once again," Mary Kay said.

"Alex was our only child, our son," she said. "This is something that you never ever get over, it was an evil act, his life was taken. ... The real disregard people have now for the value of a life. It's just unreal to me. It's horrible, it should not be."

Networking with other survivors

Alex and Mary Kay have connected with others who have endured similar losses. These include Andy Moriconi, father of Tim Moriconi, who was killed a year later about a mile to the northwest in Riverside — coincidentally, a parishioner at the same church.

As well, they've met relatives of Timothy Reynolds, shot and killed downtown in 2022 by a squeegee kid. They also grieve for those they have never met — "people who lose children, grandchildren, husbands, wives," Mary Kay said. "I don't know how they get through it. Our faith is the biggest thing, and the support of other people."

Alex III graduated from Mount Saint Joseph High School, where his parents established an endowment fund. A series of golf tournaments sponsored by City Limits Bar and Restaurant, as well as other fundraisers and donations, has raised $90,000 for a scholarship.

"You never ever think you will outlive your child. It changes you, you are never the same," Mary Kay noted. The family lacks the energy for leisure travel, which they once enjoyed, and has given up their Ravens season ticket licenses.

Even so, "as God helps you, and the years go on, there are things you can do," Mary Kay added.

One such step came after the Wroblewskis heard an announcement at their parish, the Catholic Community of South Baltimore, about a grief ministry program started by the Archdiocese of Baltimore. "I said to our pastor, I've got to help other people go through this," Mary Kay recalled. She now helps fill care packages with perishable and non-perishable food.

Dreams of their son

I asked if the spirit of Alex III ever visits them.

"I've had several dreams where I'm seeing him and we're somewhere, and he says something to me," Alex Jr. replied.

"This one dream, he was in an outfit that he wore," Mary Kay recalled. "I was in our house, with other people, I specifically remember saying, looking at my back door, 'Oh my goodness, Alex is here!' It was the best dream I ever had."

Mary Kay added that Alex's spirit has also visited a sister-in-law and a good friend, assuring them he's OK.

A year after Alex's death, another victim was laid to rest.

"When that happened to Tim [Moriconi], it wasn't long after Alex," Mary Kay recalled. She believes their church pastor was the one to introduced the two families, both mourning sons whose deaths were close in time and place.

The news about Moriconi stirred difficult memories. "It's something you accept. There will always be triggers, but you know what you have to do, to deal with it," Mary Kay said.

A small detail speaks to Alex's goodness. "Some of the women that worked with him, they said to me, 'I just want to let you know, he'd come up on his day off and he would walk us home,'" Alex Jr. said.

Listening to Mary Kay and Alex Jr., a thought occurred. Had I bought a house in 1990 in Locust Point, sheltered by the surrounding Patapsco, rather than more exposed Upper Fells Point across the water ...

... perhaps I could have remained after 2020 in a Baltimore that felt, if not perfect, at least safer and more sustaining.

"We talk about this at the memorial service every year, we have bonded so much. We've become one big family now. I believe with all my heart, that is God working through us," Mary Kay said.

Bad guys killing each other

Alex Jr. turned his attention to juvenile prosecution policy. In 2022, State Senator Jill P. Carter (D-Baltimore City) won passage of a Juvenile Justice Reform Act, since modified, that limited prosecution of children under 13 in many cases. He noted that previous state's attorneys and juvenile services officials often pushed to make it harder to prosecute juveniles.

Wroblewski praised the tougher enforcement efforts of Ivan Bates, sworn in as Baltimore state's attorney in 2023. Andy Moriconi, father of homicide victim Tim, agrees. "Thinking about the recent (post-2025) celebrated reduction in murders, I'm convinced it's due to Ivan Bates," he wrote in an email.

"I also believe the bad guys have killed most of the other bad guys — so there's fewer people to target," he added.

Moriconi reflected on how he followed the news of Alex III's murder with unease.

"When this happened to other people, there was no question that there was concern and fear," he wrote in an email. "Alex Wroblewski was just about a year before Tim. I followed that story. It made me think like how in a herd of wildebeest, someone is going to die — I just hope it's not me."

The work of economist Henry Canaday on the tipping point for residents in terms of leaving when murder rates arise above 1 or 2 per 10,000, discussed in the "A dying and reviving supernova" chapter, hit close to home. "It reminds me of an old adage, 'When my neighbor gets laid off, it's a recession ... If I get laid off, it's a depression,'" Moriconi stated. "What is it when my son is murdered? What will it take to make me move? Is what happened to Tim enough? If I move, do criminals win?"

Gratitude for the empathetic engineer

A 25-minute drive north from Locust Point leads to the mid-century modern campus of Baltimore Polytechnic Institute, one of the state's premier STEM magnet programs.

Just as Alex Wroblewski III looked out for his Locust Point neighbors, walking waitresses home safely, an upperclassman at Poly named Johnny Tobash watched over newcomers. The tall young man with expressive eyebrows, a kind expression and an aura of responsibility spotted an unsure freshman: Keombré McLaughlin.

Her first thought? That Johnny was handsome.

"And he was, but he was also much more than a pretty face," McLaughlin wrote in a 2018 *Baltimore Sun* tribute.

Thirty-four days after Wroblewski's death, on Dec. 18, 2017, Tobash, aged 19, was fatally shot during a robbery outside a convenience store in Northeast Baltimore. The two perpetrators were captured on video surveillance, and one, a gang member, was identified posthumously. Fear of retribution prevented earlier identification, according to Mary Harry, Tobash's mother.

Family members recalled a devoted uncle who coached his nephews in spelling and a thoughtful grandson who happily shared birthday celebrations with his grandmother. Johnny's friendly smiles, hugs and genuine caring lifted those around him — helping McLaughlin feel far less isolated at school.

In the aftermath, Johnny's father, Michael Tobash, told WMAR in a trembling voice, "He really was my best friend." Johnny had mentioned to his father that he loved living on campus at Morgan State, where he majored in engineering, "surrounded by so many beautiful minds." Michael felt life wasn't worth living without his son; a chronic illness worsened, and he passed away. "His heart was forever wounded," Harry told me in a 2026 telephone interview.

His mother had to remain strong for the family. She had some comfort in feeling Johnny's presence and hearing this presence tell her, "Be happy." In 2022, a magical event came along. "I have a grandson who looks like him, acts like him.

... God brought me a Johnny," Harry said. "We have so many blessings." Both baby photos are together in a frame.

Also in 2026, McLaughlin replied by email to my question about her healing process.

"In comparison to the early days of Johnny's tragic passing, my grief has not gone anywhere, but my capacity for this grief has grown," she wrote. "Over the years, I have lost more friends in tragic ways, so I have had to learn how to practice gratitude."

She makes time to celebrate those good memories. A key healing moment came at the Baltimore Polytechnic Institute Alumni Association's scholarship ceremony, where she honored Johnny by creating and raising funds for a scholarship in his name. At least seven co-victims of Outliers have initiated scholarships, research programs, safety legislation or outreach programs.

As with the Wroblewskis, McLaughlin found tremendous love and support from those who knew the young man who she describes as now "forever 19." His relatives "embraced me with love and care, and treated me like family. Being surrounded by all of the love that Johnny had (and will always have) gave me a deeper connection to him."

Seeking solutions

I asked McLaughlin if she had reflections on violence in the city. She noted that since Johnny's death, she has lost loved ones to violence, and has witnessed and experienced robberies, carjackings and break-ins.

"It hurts me deeply to continue to watch senseless violence play out everyday. I do not blame Baltimoreans for the conditions that drive them toward these actions. Instead, I look at the unmanageable poverty and circumstances that we are faced with every day. I believe that is the highest form of implicit violence.

"The city itself seems to shrink under the pressure of meeting the needs of its residents," she wrote. "Baltimore lacks community investment, job access, resources, recreational activities and more. This bleak reality contributes to the violence that we experience in this city.

"I hope to see this implicit violence (e.g. poverty and segregation) addressed in the future, so that Baltimore can finally shine," she concluded.

McLaughlin's perspective emphasizes poverty and inadequate investment as root drivers of violence. While these may help explain opportunistic crimes like theft, they seem less sufficient for the gratuitous brutality seen in the Outliers murders, where victims were often killed without provocation during home invasions and street robberies.

Criminologists Matt DeLisi and John Paul Wright offer a compelling counter-theory: that severe criminality often stems from deeply dysfunctional family environments. These manifest as patterns of antisocial behavior across generations, compounded by other mental disorders, poor self-control and problem clusters such as alcoholism, drug abuse and criminality passed from parent to child.

Their research on "antisocial family trees" and biosocial criminology indicates that atrocious conditions in the family home and adverse childhood events transmit risk more directly than neighborhood disadvantage alone, producing career criminals across varied socioeconomic levels.

About eight in every 1,000 children experience substantiated maltreatment each year in the United States, with Maryland's rate aligning closely to this national figure. Specific city-level abuse data for Baltimore is limited, but rates are likely elevated compared to the state overall, given the well-established link between poverty and higher rates of child maltreatment.

The Baltimore Child Abuse Center has reported that child maltreatment occurs at the highest levels in the city's most crime-impacted ZIP codes. Tragically, an average of about 17 Baltimore children die from abuse or neglect each year — yet another grim statistic compounding the city's high rates of homicides and fatal overdoses.

Breaking generational abuse

Earlier in "The Baltimore Safety Handbook" chapter, I pondered why, unlike Europe's pickpockets, did Baltimore's street robbers so often see fit to kill their targets? The framework provided by DeLisi and Wright, which explains how intra-family violence projects across generations and produces career criminals, seemed on point. It aligned with how one of Zach Sowers' assailants had a convict father, and one of Kim Leto's killers had fathered a child at age 14, that he would not be able to raise from detention.

Evidence of killers emerging from dysfunctional backgrounds could also be seen at hearings and trials for the vicious murderers of Sebastian Dvorak, Stephen Pitcairn and Pava LaPere. As well as in the overkilling of Robbie Ponsi and Leto, who both suffered extensive stab wounds.

A particularly stark example was the shooter of Dvorak, like Wroblewski a bartender killed in 2017. His shooter had an abusive upbringing from the age of 18 months, if not earlier, followed by childhood mental health crises. At age 16, at the time of his offense, the shooter had already fathered 1-year-old, placing another child at risk of repeating the same cycle.

There were also elements of sadism indicated in Lauren Hayden's fractured skull during an Upper Fells Point robbery, in the suffocation of Reese Bowman, and the gratuitous punch of Pitcairn in the head as he lay dying of a stab wound to the heart — violence that seemed to arise from a place of childhood abuse.

The over-the-top violence inflicted on the victims yielded the assailants no meaningful gain, again indicating that their actions came from a place of darkness. Johnny Tobash's attackers netted just $6. Tim Moriconi's killers fled without taking the $30 still in the wallet his father keeps to this day.

"When I read about most of the Outliers – the prize for the those robbed was so insignificant," Andy Moriconi observed.

"For many assailants, the reason they were caught was due to using the credit cards on camera," he added. "Phones can be traced. I do not know what the prize is that makes it worth it to rob and kill someone."

At the time of this writing, Mayor Brandon Scott's administration has pursued a blended path forward, including a comprehensive public health approach to violence prevention. This includes community violence intervention programs, youth engagement strategies, school-based supports, and investments in recreation. This aligns somewhat with McLaughlin's call for investment while aiming to interrupt cycles before they escalate.

Taken together — McLaughlin's personal empathy, DeLisi and Wright's criminological analysis and pragmatic city-level interventions — these varied approaches illustrate the facets and generational challenges of reducing Baltimore's homicides.

No single explanation suffices, but together they point toward layered solutions. DeLisi's work underscores family dysfunction as the core driver, one difficult to break, but one that demands examination.

The prayers of the Wroblewskis, the tender and enveloping embrace of their neighborhood, and McLaughlin's scholarship push can't hurt, either.

Outliers afterword

A number of the 44 Outliers were tricky for me to fit into the main narrative. But their stories matter.

So they are not overlooked, I've included them here. But first, let's consider two couples who perished six years apart in high-crime areas of West Baltimore, and whether they truly fit the "Outlier" definition: law-abiding innocents, regular folks who became homicide victims.

Nick Strickland and Taewan Tuck

In 2013, Alysia Nicole "Nick" Strickland, a 33-year-old Morgan State graduate student studying architecture, and her boyfriend, Taewan Tuck, 34, were killed under mysterious circumstances. Nick's rowhome was in Ridgely's Delight, near the baseball stadium. Yet somehow, the couple ended up three miles northwest, in the 1800 block of Clifton Avenue, where residents reported a vehicle aflame behind their patios. Firefighters discovered the couple's burned bodies, each shot execution-style in the head.

Nick's background doesn't raise obvious questions. A Morgan State grad with a degree in religious studies, she had helped rebuild New Orleans after Hurricane Katrina and was a devoted pet parent. Her father, Art Strickland, is a prominent Roanoke attorney known for defending Larry Flynt in a landmark libel case. Her mother, Diane, is a retired judge. Despite minor traffic infractions, Nick's record was squeaky clean. Tuck, however, was less known — Maryland records show he was paying child support to another woman, but he was described as kind and genuine by friends.

What drew them to Clifton Avenue that night? Some speculate a professional hit. Podcast host Tia L. Lincoln summed up the mystery: "This sounds like a professional hit, but c'mon people, I know somebody knows something about this double homicide."

Britt Foster and Julien Rosaly

Six years later, in 2019, another couple met a grim end in West Baltimore, about a mile and a half from where Nick and Tae died. Brittany "Britt" Foster, 26, was from Bel Air, Maryland. She was with Julien "Rico" Rosaly, 27, a city boy who had prior convictions for robbery and drugs.

At 2:15 a.m. on Bloomingdale Road, a 17-year-old gunman and an 18-year-old accomplice stalked and shot them. Rico died from a chest wound; Britt, kneeling and begging, was shot in the head. An awful video of Britt's final moments circulated online before vanishing.

Commenters on an Unz.com article entitled "Her Name Is Brittany Foster" said they knew the victims and mentioned Britt's flashy red Michael Kors purse flaunted that night and Rico's criminal past. Commenters stated that the couple robbed drug dealers and fanned stacks of cash on social media. One poster said the couple knew enough about the Baltimore streets to know what they were getting into.

Britt's family insisted she was an innocent victim, but it was hard to ignore the weight of her choices, her visit to West Baltimore — and the ominous 2:15 a.m. hour.

Online commenters familiar with West Baltimore were agog at their defiantly unconcerned jaunt there in the wee hours: “I don't wish to blame the victims but they might as well have gone for a stroll in the lion's den at the zoo,” posted one.

Both cases highlight a troubling pattern: the fine line between Outlier innocence and the pull of riskier, hidden lives. The Strickland-Tuck murders remain especially enigmatic – Nick’s background suggests she was an Outlier, but her death in a burning car at dawn raises red flags. Britt and Rico, on the other hand, seem to have strayed further into Baltimore’s street economy, a world where retaliation for stepping over unwritten lines was swift and merciless.

These stories share threads of mystery, risk and denial. The vast majority of Outliers clearly had no part in criminal life. Others, such as Britt and Rico, lived in that precarious borderland where a bad decision or decisions could be fatal.

Beyond these couples was the case of clinical trials researcher Peter Marvit.

Peter Marvit, renaissance man

In September 2012, Peter Marvit was shot while parking his car in the Herring Run neighborhood, where he had just moved after living in Mount Washington. The 51-year-old was returning from choir practice, wearing one of his trademark loud ties. Holding a psychology Ph.D., he had worked tirelessly to bring music education to city schools.

Marvit’s case remains a cold one, with no assailant charged to date. As with victims Jonathan Tobash and Jim Forrester, however, there is video evidence of two attackers.

His ex-wife described his myriad interests: “his cat Pumpkin Seed, his collection of hundreds and hundreds of neckties, exceptional food, interesting artwork, puns, odd words, hiking in the Sierras, traveling, being super-smart.”

This exuberant personality shared a love of music with fellow Outlier Kevon Dix (a Morgan State student). Similar to cancer researcher Stephen Pitcairn, he had a scientific focus on improving hearing aids. His deep love for Baltimore rivaling that of Pava LaPere. That his ex-wife, who called him her “best friend,” wrote a loving encomium in his memory returns us to the ripples of grief among "co-victims," often dozens of family members and friends scattered across the nation and world.

A decade later, 2022 claimed six more Outliers – four discussed earlier, and two more whose deaths underline the city's random violence.

Outliers in 2022

A Filipino Navy veteran, **Victorino "Victor" Malabayabas** Jr. moved to the U.S. in 1996, worked his way up to a finance job at Morgan Stanley, and gave back as a volunteer at Patterson Park – where I myself spent time clearing invasive reeds. In August 2022, Victor was ambushed outside his Canton rowhome, thrown down his steps during a robbery, and died of head injuries. His killer was convicted in December 2024.

At Patterson Park, Malabayabas tended gardens, clearing brush and planting trees. It is more than likely that we met doing volunteer work for the Friends of Patterson Park, or that we crossed paths when he sold plants at the Butcher's Hill Flea Market.

He seems to have picked up exactly where I left off, as a photo of him smiling, standing with a shovel on the edge of the Patterson Park Boat Lake, indicates he was there pulling out the phragmites reeds.

At 18, **Jesika Tetlow** was a bright, headstrong Baltimore County teen who loved animals and dreamed of a career in medicine. She often stayed at a North Baltimore house where she and friends played board games. In August 2022, five masked intruders burst in and demanded phones. Jesika, refusing to give hers up, was shot twice in the head. She died instantly. The case remains unsolved. Tetlow was one of four outliers to suffer a home invasion, the others being Kim Leto, Wadell Tate and Jordan Taylor.

Outliers in 2023-24

In addition to Pava LaPere and Darrell Benner, previously discussed, 2023 claimed two additional Outliers.

At 23, **Fabian Alberto Sánchez-González** was a warm, devoted son working at a T-Mobile store in Canton. A Highlandtown resident and former high school wrestler, he aimed to lift his immigrant family through hard work. On April 30, 2023, two masked teens robbed the store and shot Fabian. Rushed to Bayview Medical Center, he died the next day. Both suspects were quickly caught and charged with first-degree murder.

Homeless and 69, **Anton Kancir** was waiting at a West Baltimore bus top on Dec. 2, 2023, when he was shot in the face — an unprovoked murder with no disclosed motive. A suspect was arrested and charged with first-degree murder.

And 2024 saw the loss of four Outliers.

A grandmother of five, **Mary Lou Schuman** was collateral damage in a street shooting. On Jan. 19, 2024, as she left Sooner's Tavern in South Baltimore, she was shot and killed along with the likely intended target, a man with a criminal record. No arrests have been made.

Nine months later, a stray bullet took another life. At 19, **Cameran Holt** was a caring big sister and dog lover, balancing jobs and family life in suburban Pasadena. On Oct. 27, 2024, after attending her sister's gender reveal party, Cameran was in a car near West Hamburg Street when caught in a crossfire. A bullet paralyzed her, and she died 11 days later. Her organ donations saved four lives. A trio of gunmen were arrested in November 2024, charged with first-degree murder.

David Philpot, 74, was a beloved Fells Point neighbor and retired veteran. Walking his dog Chip on Aug. 17, 2024, he was shoved and beaten during an argument. His injuries combined with a weak heart proved fatal. The assailant, arrested two days later, pleaded guilty to involuntary manslaughter in 2025. The incident on Eastern Avenue was the closest assault to my former residence.

Carl "Buzzy" Bodine Jr., 59, managed a recovery house in West Baltimore. On June 25, 2024, he was stabbed to death by a resident, Harley Frost, during a confrontation over a mandatory drug test. Frost fled but was arrested that evening and charged with murder.

Many of these chapters are an elegy to the Outliers. Framing them as a collective story gives weight to what's often lost in fragmented coverage: the human potential, the systemic patterns, the haunting what-ifs. Let them be remembered.

Bibliography

The bibliography with more than 800 references for Fleeing Baltimore can be consulted at https://beaumonde.net/fleeing-baltimore/.

It is also available in the EPUB edition of this book.

About the author

Jeannette Belliveau, who lived in Fells Point in Baltimore from 1987 to 1990, and in Upper Fells Point from 1990 to 2020, is a sharp-eyed urban observer who isn't afraid of complexity or contradiction. In *Fleeing Baltimore*, she moves through neighborhoods and memories like a documentarian with soul, charting sine waves of collapse and renewal. Her style is incisive, reflective and elegant, always reaching for the deeper rhythm beneath surface noise.

Her blend of storytelling and analysis pieced together the collective tales of a group she calls the Outliers — 44 regular folks without criminal records murdered from 1993 through 2024. Belliveau noted the personal and social tragedy in the loss of these innocents: they were some of the city's most promising people.

Her powerful and original approach turned data into elegy. Framing those "Outliers" as a collective story gives weight to what's often lost in fragmented coverage: the human potential, the systemic patterns, the haunting what-ifs. This work feels like both an act of remembrance and a challenge to the city's conscience.

From a Mac Stickie note to a story-rich manuscript, her lens is precise but never cold. She sees the deeper ruptures in neighborhoods beneath surface headlines, and is not afraid to ask: What really made me leave? What did we try not to see?

Baltimore's overlooked tragedies, the Outliers, are woven into a human tapestry, tugging threads that others have left untouched. She honors lives, names the unspoken and confronts the quiet toll that shaped her own journey westward.

Born in Washington, D.C., in 1954, Belliveau has worked at the *Washington Post*, the *Baltimore Sun*, Alaska Newspapers, and other newspapers in Maryland and England. She now makes her home in the Intermountain West.

Her previous books include *An Amateur's Guide to the Planet*, *Romance on the Road* and *Eden Under Siege*. Her publishing company, Beau Monde Press ("beautiful world" in French) can be visited at www.beaumonde.net.

www.ingramcontent.com/pod-product-compliance
Lightning Source LLC
Chambersburg PA
CBHW070343040526
44377CB00041B/523

* 9 7 8 0 9 6 5 2 3 4 4 3 6 *